John Pea ... ls and
biograph ... thor's
Club Aw ... *The Life*
of Ian Fleming, The Life of James Bond, The ... dness of
Dr Avicenna, Stags and Serpents: The History of the Dukes of Devonshire, and *The Ultimate Family* (a collective biography of the British royal family).

The *Profession of Violence* was awarded the Edgar Allan Poe Special Award by the Mystery Writers of America.

'This book is extrememly well written and is fittingly deadpan. Its great virtue is that, far from any gloating over its subject, it is by implication a highly moral book. That one talks about the subject matter of the book rather than the book itself is a tribute to Mr Pearson who has followed an intricate and often disgusting story unselfishly and without intrusion.'

New Statesman

BY THE SAME AUTHOR

Gone to Timbuctoo
The Life of Ian Fleming
The Life of James Bond
The Kindness of Dr Avicenna
Edward Rake
Facades
Stags and Serpents: The History of the Dukes of Devonshire
The Ultimate Family
Citadel of the Heart
The Sitwells
Painfully Rich: The Outrageous Fortune and Misfortunes of the Heirs of J. Paul Getty

JOHN PEARSON

THE PROFESSION OF VIOLENCE

The Rise and Fall of the Kray Twins

FOURTH EDITION

HarperCollins*Publishers*

HarperCollins*Publishers*
77–85 Fulham Palace Road,
Hammersmith, London W6 8JB

This paperback edition 1995
14

Previously published in paperback by Grafton 1985
Reprinted fifteen times

First published in Great Britain by
Weidenfeld & Nicolson 1972
Second edition published by
Panther Books 1973
Third edition published by
Granada Publishing 1984

ISBN 978-0-00-638371-0

Set in Meridien

Printed in Great Britain by
Clays Ltd, St Ives plc

Contents

Introduction to the Fourth Edition 7

1 Violet's Twins 15
2 Battle Training 48
3 The Billiard Hall 75
4 The Colonel 85
5 Gun Time 93
6 Twins Apart 113
7 Flight from Long Grove 126
8 Comeback for the Colonel 144
9 Barn of Gold 156
10 Organized Crime 169
11 Twins Victorious 193
12 A Marriage in the Family 206
13 Axe Man 221
14 The Murder Machine 240
15 Nipper's Secret War 266
16 Arrest 292
17 Retribution 302

Postscript 317
Index 327

TO FRANK TAYLOR

Introduction to the Fourth Edition

'You can't come to terms with criminals and there's no real excuse for doing so except total ignorance of the real nature of their crimes.'

H.H. Kirst, *The 20th of July*

It seems an age since I first met the Kray twins and was able to observe them at close quarters in their last extraordinary phase of freedom before their arrest in May 1968; and in retrospect I am slightly shocked by the naïvety with which I agreed to write the story of their lives. Had they not been arrested when they were it would never have been possible, and had my 'research' continued, it would certainly have become dangerous.

But in early autumn 1967 I was bored and missing England after a spell in Italy. The name 'Kray' was only vaguely familiar from my days as a *Sunday Times* reporter, and when Frank Taylor – who as Editor-in-Chief at McGraw Hill had published my *Life of Ian Fleming* – arrived in Rome and suggested I write a book about 'the top criminals controlling London', with their full co-operation, it seemed an intriguing proposition. I was curious. After writing about Ian, I was probably hankering for a touch of action, *à la Bond*, and thought I'd get it. What I didn't know was that the suggestion had originally reached McGraw in a roundabout way from a lawyer representing various Mafia interests in New York, that he in turn was doing a favour for the twins, who were hoping to extract a large sum of money from McGraw for 'world rights' in the story of their life, and that the twins had not the faintest intention of allowing anything except the most flattering picture of themselves to appear in print.

Certainly the next step in this whole bizarre adventure was extremely Bond. Tickets to London were waiting in my name at Rome International Airport. At Heathrow I was met by a very silent ex-heavyweight boxer who drove me in a silver-grey Mercedes to the Ritz Hotel where a suite had been booked for me, and at ten o'clock next morning the world of Bond continued. The silent man in the Mercedes was waiting to drive me to an undisclosed destination in the country, and half an hour or so beyond Newmarket we went through a pair of elaborate park gates and drove towards a large Elizabethan mansion. Apart from horses grazing in the paddock there was no sign of life, and the car drove round the back of the enormous house. We stopped. The driver hooted and finally a door did open. Three men emerged to welcome me. They stood with some formality and my driver announced them like some old-school boxing referee; 'Mr Charles Kray, Mr Ronald Kray, Mr Reginald Kray.' Luncheon was waiting and my book had started.

It was one of the more memorable meals of my life. There was a large panelled dining-room with a baronial fireplace and a number of bogus-looking 'ancestors' round the walls. There was cold tongue and coleslaw salad and a choice of Yugoslav Riesling and brown ale. On the moat beneath the windows swam three black swans.

There was quite a gathering of heavy-looking characters, clearly on very best behaviour but, Krays apart, the only one I really remember was the man I soon discovered was my host. This was a portly, personable 'businessman' friend of the Krays with a pale blue Rolls, a large cigar, and two extremely pretty wives (one ex, one current, both cheerfully in residence) who had lent the twins the house for the weekend. He told me he 'dabbled a bit in property' – which was more or less the truth: he was something of a specialist in high-grade arson and some years later went to prison after collecting a quite extraordinary amount of money from a number of insurance companies on a series of large country houses which went up in smoke – the one that we were in included.

As for the Krays, Charlie, the elder brother, seemed distinctly ill-at-ease and rather jumpy. He had a habit of agreeing with everything one said, and the twins were obviously in charge. Ian would have relished Ronnie, who would have made a most convincing Mr Big. Like his twin he wore a dark blue suit, white shirt, very tightly knotted tie, and solid gold bracelet watch – and managed to look permanently nasty. He had a slow, faintly sneering way of speaking that sounded threatening even when it wasn't, and his eyes bulged too much for comfort.

Although they were obviously identical twins, Reggie was very different – thinner, quicker, with a certain shifty charm. He made most of the conversation – which to tell the truth was slightly heavy going – speaking in a rapid, almost inaudible monotone. I noticed his right hand was bandaged. (He had cut his thumb rather badly murdering Jack 'the Hat' McVitie a few weeks earlier.)

'How did you hurt yourself, Mr Kray?' I inquired brightly.

'Gardenin',' he answered.

But small-talk and a great deal of brown ale apart, we did manage a fairly businesslike discussion. Reggie explained that he and his brothers were planning to retire: he made this sound quite normal, as if he and Ronnie were selling up a profitable haulage business and settling in Surrey. And like many businessmen tired of making money after the rough and tumble of an interesting career in industry, they wanted someone to record the range of their achievement.

'So much rubbish gets written about our sort of people that me an' Ron both think it's time the truth was told for once.'

'An' with no messin' about,' said Ronnie.

'Quite,' I said.

I raised the all-important question of how much they imagined they could tell me. Reggie answered airily that there were 'just a few things we must hold back so's not to get other people into trouble. You'd not want to make trouble for our friends, now, would you?'

'Perish the thought,' I said.

Reggie nodded and explained that as he and Ronnie planned to disappear from circulation now for good, they felt at liberty to tell the truth about themselves.

'We've not been angels, but we've done some interesting things and met a lot of interesting people. This book could be something quite out of the ordinary.'

Upon this modest note of hope and mutual trust, collaboration started.

The twins and their world were fascinating, and during the following few months I saw them fairly regularly. They found me a basement flat off Vallance Road in Bethnal Green where they had grown up. Part of a late Victorian tenement improbably entitled 'The Albert Family Dwellings', it was nicknamed by the twins 'the Dungeon', and they said I could stay there whenever I was in London. The curtains were permanently pulled, the windows screwed up, and after the twins' arrest, the police took up the floorboards, searching unsuccessfully for corpses.

But I rather enjoyed my periods in residence at 'the Dwellings': the Krays took a lot of trouble over me and were conscientious hosts. Their power and influence in this part of the East End was extraordinary. They had the use of innumerable pubs and houses, and there was one pub in particular, a discreet, low-ceilinged Victorian alehouse with a piano and a personable landlord, which was something of an exclusive club for the Krays and their 'Firm' when they felt like entertaining. Whenever the Krays were there, the locals got the message to keep clear, and the twins held court with considerable style and lavish hospitality to much of the criminal fraternity in London.

It was at these sessions that they often talked about the past. Both were good *raconteurs* with extraordinary memories. Ronnie could be moody, but here he would relax, and he was often genuinely funny as he talked about his childhood and his apprenticeship to crime. They had considerable nostalgia for the old East End, and enjoyed discussing the methods and morality of what they would refer to as 'our way of life'. They were highly sociable and certainly knew everyone worth knowing in the London underworld. Through them I met quite a gallery of assorted criminals of the sixties: Billy Hill, back briefly from his house in southern Spain and reminiscing about the twins in their early twenties – 'always a little wild, but willing to be educated' – and along with him a whole range of burglars, bruisers, former boxing champions, conmen, pickpockets, ponces, fences, professional gamblers, crooked club-owners, shady financiers and visiting Americans in dark glasses.

Before long it was clear the twins' hopes of a great bonanza from the world rights of their story had misfired, but I think it rather flattered them to be able to introduce me as 'our biographer'; and as well as their criminal acquaintances I got to know their family and many non-criminal friends and relations who were part of this vanishing world of the Dickensian East End.

What is extraordinary is that throughout this period the Krays were facing the final crisis of their criminal careers, but almost until the end they gave no hint of what was going on. Those who did know were under very strict instructions over what they said to me, and it was not until a month or so before their arrest in the spring of 1968 that I began to get a glimmering of the truth behind the secrets they kept so carefully to themselves – that people had been murdered, that former members of the gang had 'grassed', and that the twins were everywhere surrounded by their enemy – 'the Law'. Then for the first time too one heard references to a mysterious character called 'Read' – 'the flash bastard copper who is out to get us'.

By the time of their arrest both twins had become dangerously suspicious of almost everyone around them – me included – and a friend I had made within the Firm gave me a warning to stay clear as the twins had come to think I was working for MI5 or some other undercover group planning their downfall. I took the hint, and the last I saw of the twins at liberty was in early April when I visited them at their mother's flat at the top of a modern high-rise block on the edge of the City. It was an uncomfortable meeting. Ronnie was ominously silent and the few words he did speak were to 'Nipper Read', the young boa constrictor he had purchased from Harrods' pets' department, and named after his greatest enemy. While 'Read' coiled and uncoiled himself round Ronnie's brawny arms, Reggie talked mysteriously about their 'master-plan' to foil the police. They had their spies at work, their sources of information, and there were things that they could do that no one had dreamed of.

I knew better than ask what they were and, as I left, my last sight of the twins was of the pair of them stretched out in their mother's comfortable armchairs, playing with their boa constrictor. Behind them, through the big window of the flat, I could see the whole of London. They had 'ruled' it long enough, and suddenly I felt the city closing in on them, leaving them beleaguered, waiting for their end, with nothing but a snake for company. A few weeks later on my radio I heard of their arrest.

Then, finally, I did begin to learn the truth about them. People I had already met began to talk more freely. So did the police. Almost overnight the famous 'wall of silence' crumbled. It was as if everyone around them suddenly awoke from a collective nightmare. But even then there were certain areas I could not penetrate. Several influential criminals and businessmen closely associated with the Krays took care to protect themselves. So did certain members of the 'Establishment' who performed an extraordinarily smooth cover-up over their relations with the twins.

Most of these hardly mattered, but one relationship that clearly did was that between Ronnie and the former Conservative minister and TV celebrity, Lord Boothby. Here was a scandal that had been carefully suppressed. Boothby had lied in public over the extent of his friendship with the Krays. As the result, he had earned himself £40,000, and if I was right, the resulting cover-up helped explain the twins' immunity from arrest through much of the period when they started killing people.

But at the time strenuous efforts were made to stop me publishing the truth. To this day I have no idea who raided my agent's office and my home to steal some letters I possessed from Lord Boothby to the Krays. At the same time lawyers acting for Boothby made it all too clear that I proceeded at my peril if I tried to publish all I knew.

As a result of this, only since Boothby's death in 1986 has it been possible to give the details of one of the most extraordinary episodes in the Kray twins' whole extraordinary career.

JP, 1995

ONE

Violet's Twins

In 1929 a doctor called Lange from the Kaiser Wilhelm Institute in Munich created a stir among psychologists and criminologists by reviving the unfashionable theory of biological inheritance as a factor in the making of a criminal.

For several years Lange had been studying the character and history of criminal twins. He had started from the point established by Sir Francis Galton in England in the 1870s that there are two sorts of twins and that the differences between them are fundamental. The commonest twins are what are known as binovular or double-egg twins, formed when two female eggs are fertilized by separate male germ cells. The result is two babies who, although twins, have no greater chance of inherited similarities than ordinary brothers and sisters of the same parents. In rarer cases, something like three to four per thousand live births, a single fertilized egg splits within the womb to produce twins that are biological carbon-copies of each other. They have a uniform heredity and sex, look alike and are known as 'identical' or uni-ovular twins.

By studying the records of the Bavarian Ministry of Justice, Lange discovered thirty convicted criminals with twin brothers or sisters: of these pairs thirteen were identical twins, seventeen non-identical. When Lange compared the two groups he discovered that in only two cases did a non-identical twin of a criminal have a criminal record; among the identical twins, ten out of thirteen did.

When he investigated each pair of identical twins the parallels between their lives became still more apparent.

Almost invariably Lange found that the brother of a convicted identical twin showed signs of a similar criminal tendency himself. Although out of touch for years, the twin of a professional burglar of quarrelsome disposition turned out himself to be a professional burglar with a reputation for violence. The identical twin of a man imprisoned for company fraud was discovered to have specialized in fraud and confidence tricks himself. A homosexual in trouble for exploiting older men had an identical twin doing the same thing in another part of Germany. Lange concluded in his book, which he entitled *Crime as Destiny*, that these identical twins acted as they did, not primarily because of their environment, but because of 'inner laws' of heredity determining their tendency to crime.

Five years after Lange's book appeared in Leipzig, Charles Kray, a twenty-six-year-old second-hand clothes-dealer from Hoxton, was preparing to leave on a buying trip to the West Country. Most of the cockney dealers liked to stick to the Home Counties, but Charles Kray was a wanderer: by going farther afield he hoped to have Dorset and Somerset to himself. He had his wad of ready money, his old-clothes bag, his gold scales and was planning to catch the Monday morning express to Bristol with his partner, an Irishman named Sonny Kenny.

Charles was small and dapper, and everything about him gleamed; his greased-back hair, his sharp black shoes and his quick smile. People in Hoxton said the Krays were gipsy folk, descended from horse-dealers who had settled here in the poorest part of London. Charles had the mistrustful dark eyes of a gipsy. So had his father, Jimmy Kray. The old man had kept a barrow in Petticoat Lane, and was a wanderer too. Otherwise, father and son were very different.

Jimmy was an East End character: according to Charles, he was 'A good-looking old boy. Bigger than me with thick grey hair. He always wore a white silk stock tied around his neck and was proud of his appearance. In those days the men of the East End were very vain. He was a fighter and a drinker and was scared of no man living. He must have drunk with every villain who came out of Hoxton and Bethnal Green and he'd fight them too. When he fought he never cared what happened. He was called "Mad Jimmy Kray".'

Charles was cleverer than his wild old father. His mother had been in service with a well-off family in Highgate, a careful woman who spent her time worrying about her husband and keeping the family together. In many ways Charles resembled her: he was deferential, always careful to keep out of trouble and had a taste for money. He was no fighter but a talker with an instinct for buying and selling; in his teens he had started working on his own account. By twenty he was making a good living and generally considered one of the finest 'pesterers' around: for the door-to-door dealer, 'pestering' is the basis of success.

His younger brother says of him, 'He'd always be polite and never bullied but he knew what people would do for money. As soon as he found anyone with something to sell he'd keep on pestering until he got it. By rights Charles should be a stone-rich man today.' Gold buying went with old clothes buying. 'Once I had asked the lady of the house if she had any clothes to sell, I'd say, "Excuse me, madam, but I wondered if you'd any gold or silver you've no use for." The first time they'd say no they hadn't, and I'd say, "It doesn't matter at all, madam, but it so happens I'll be passing back this way in half an hour and call to see if you've found anything. It'll be no trouble." A bloody lie, of course. But then you gotta tell a few lies. That's business. And when you came back you'd usually find they'd got you something.'

In the mid thirties, silver was fetching two shillings and sixpence per ounce; eighteen-carat gold seven pounds an ounce. 'I always sold to Abe Sokolok in Black Lion Yard, off Whitechapel Road, every Sunday morning, him being

Yiddish. Most weeks I'd be making twenty or thirty pounds from the gold alone.'

This was wealth in the East End, where family income averaged seventeen shillings a week; and Charles had a life he thoroughly enjoyed. 'I've been a free man. That's how I like it. I don't believe in working for a Guv'nor. That's a mug's game.' But at twenty-four the time had come to marry. With his looks, and his money, he had the pick of the local girls and chose a seventeen-year-old blonde with blue eyes called Violet Lee. They met in a dance-hall in Mare Street, Hackney. After the marriage they moved in with his parents over a shop in Stene Street, Hoxton. She was soon pregnant and the doctors told her to expect twins. Instead she gave birth to a single son, Charles David. She had been eighteen then. Now at twenty-one she was once again expecting.

Charles Kray was not a family man. But when the midwife told him Violet would soon be giving birth, he decided to postpone his trip to Bristol. That Monday morning he went to King's Cross to explain things to Sonny Kenny before seeing him off. The old Irishman laughed at the idea of Charles of all people sacrificing a good trip for his family; as the train steamed off, he leaned from the carriage window and shouted, 'My love to Violet. Hope she has those twins this time. Then you'll have something to worry about, me boy.' That night, 17 October 1934, at 64 Stene Street, Hoxton, Violet Kray surprised the midwife by giving birth to two male children within an hour of one another. The first she called Reginald, the second Ronald.

Charles remembered Kenny's warning and did find the twins' arrival a financial problem. But his wife was thrilled with her two babies and that was what mattered. For Violet the arrival of the twins was the greatest event in her life. The last few years had been a struggle.

She had been one of three good-looking sisters living on the corner of Vallance Road in Bethnal Green; she was headstrong and had eloped romantically with Charles. 'I was just young and silly and my head was full of all the nonsense of young girls of seventeen.' When she found out more about her new life there was no point complaining. Her husband would not change. He had to have his beer and gambling and male company. Some men were like that.

So she made the best of things. She was a good wife. According to her sister May, 'She always kept herself nice, Violet did. Never let herself go, like most women once they're married. She was a quiet one.' With the quietness went great strength of purpose; with twins she finally had something to be purposeful about. 'I never seen no babies like the twins,' she said proudly. 'They was so lovely when they was born, the two of them, so small and dark, just like two little black-haired dolls.'

Their brother, nearly four, was a placid, easy child, with his mother's personality and looks. The twins were different: they were demanding and brought out all their mother's deep protectiveness. They did something more: for the first time they gave Violet's life a touch of the glamour she had dreamt of when she eloped. Nobody else had twins; they were something special, and when she pushed them out in the big double pram they conferred on her the final accolade of cockney motherhood. It was a pretty sight; blonde young mother, gleaming pram and these two beautifully dressed little dolls, making their way past the pubs and stalls of the Bethnal Green Road. People would stop and look, neighbours inquired about them; her two sisters begged for a chance to take them out on their own.

'In those days everybody loved the twins and wanted a go with them,' says Violet.

Hoxton, where the twins were born, lies just outside the City up the Hackney Road. A depressing hinterland of dead grey streets and tenements, it was famous in its day for pubs and pickpockets. One of their father's favourite

Hoxton pubs was The Eagle; for years children have been singing about it in the old nursery rhyme:

Up and down the City Road
In and out The Eagle
That's the way the money goes
Pop goes the weasel.

Hoxton's tailors often 'popped' or pawned their 'weasels' or flat-irons at the countless pawnbrokers along City Road to pay for beer when the money ran out, and The Eagle was one of the places where the Hoxton 'Whizz Mob' came to drink. This was the biggest gang of pickpockets in London; from Hoxton they would work the race-tracks and the Cup Final crowds, operating as a team and often picking up hundreds of pounds at a time. But Hoxton was a lifeless place; even its pickpockets were despised by the rest of the criminal East End.

As the East End had grown from the ancient villages along the river, so much of the village atmosphere remained. Each quarter kept its name and its identity, and Bethnal Green, where Violet Kray had lived, looked down its nose at Hoxton, barely half a mile away. Certainly Bethnal Green was livelier. It ran eastwards from the old boundaries of the City at Bishopsgate, with Whitechapel and Whitechapel High Street to the south and Hackney and the Bethnal Green Road to the north. Unlike most parts of the East End, the green of Bethnal Green remained a narrow patch of grass fringed with eighteenth-century houses and although Bethnal Green had some of the worst poverty and vilest slums in the country its people kept a certain local pride.

The main employment for the men was casual labour in the London markets or the docks and in the thirties after the Depression, Bethnal Green saw brutal poverty again. In 1932 a government report estimated 60 per cent of the children of Bethnal Green suffered from malnutrition and 85 per cent of the housing was unsatisfactory. But this part of the East End was used to poverty. This was where the 'Rookeries' of Dickens's time had been. In Bethnal Green before the war, the most lavish events were still the funerals, day-long wakes with black, plumed horses pulling the hearse and more spent burying a man than he could earn in a year alive.

Death was a commonplace affair in Bethnal Green; most men survived by toughness or drunkenness or both, and the family was the one firm unit of defence. This was the basis of the famous East End matriarchy, with the woman of the family keeping life going against all the odds. Without the woman and the family no one in Bethnal Green had much of a chance. Violet had learned this from experience.

'Before I ran away to marry Mr Kray we was devoted as a family. Us three sisters, Rosie, May and me, and my brother who kept a caff across the road. My dad worked in the market, but everybody used to know us. They called our bit of Vallance Road "Lee Street". Though times was hard I'd say that we was well looked after. My mum would see to that. We always lived close as a family and helped each other every way we could.

'The only trouble was my dad was terrible strict. Us girls had to be indoors by nine of a night. I used to like life. Always have, and I was the one who never could get home on time. That must be why I married at seventeen. That's what I put it down to, me bein' young and silly and him being so strict, I thought I'd do anything to get away. Then when I married Mr Kray, my dad disowned me. No proper wedding and he wouldn't even come to the register office in the Kingsland Road.'

Violet's father, John 'Cannonball' Lee, stuck by what he said, and Violet remained outlawed from her family during the earliest years of marriage. But gradually she was accepted back. 'My mum had kept an eye on me to see I was all right. Often be poppin' round with half a pound of cheese or a bit of meat for us.' The birth of Charles David brought something of a reconciliation with her family. Her father started speaking to her again. But it was the twins who really brought the wayward daughter home to the family in Vallance Road. And she returned in style, double pram and all. 'My dad adored the twins, thought they was wonderful. Everyone who saw 'em seemed to love 'em.' And everybody spoiled them. 'Somehow with the twins you couldn't help it.' 'I always dressed the twins the same. They was such pretty babies. I made 'em both white angora woolly hats and coats and they was real lovely, the two of them. Just like two little bunny rabbits.'

Some of the old East Enders like Charles Kray lived on their wits. Others, like Violet's father, old John Lee 'the Southpaw Cannonball', lived by sheer force of personality. Boxer, juggler, street performer, impromptu poet, market man, he was a famous local character. His mother's family was Irish and his father's Jewish. His father had been a butcher.

'He weren't a bad man, except that he took to alcohol, and it ruined him as it's ruined many a good man. It made him epileptic. I can remember as a boy him having five and six attacks a day. And all the time he'd still be drinking.

' "Helen," he'd shout to my mother, soon as he was over an attack, "bring me my rum and coffee."

'There was one night when he come over all peculiar and tried to kill us in our beds. Mother called the police and he was taken to the epileptics' colony at Epsom. He was there seventeen years. I saw him twice myself. He died there.'

John Lee became a passionate teetotaller; he was also a great fighter in his time. 'I had a good left hand. That's how I got the name, "the Southpaw Cannonball". I was just nine stone, so I fought as featherweight, but when I boxed professional, I'd take on any weight at five pounds a fight.'

He saved his money, started a haulage business and ran twenty-two horses before going bankrupt. Then he became a showman, working the streets of the East End.

'First thing, I made a bit of money from was licking the white-hot poker. I'd seen a big black fellow doing it before a crowd on Mile End Waste, so I took a chance with it myself. You're safe enough, long as you see the poker's white-hot. If it's just red you lose your tongue.'

Another turn that earned him money was walking the streets with his young son on a five-gallon bottle balanced on his head; but it was his barrel trick that brought Cannonball real fame. It took him four years to perfect. He used to walk down a line of twenty-four lemonade bottles which were balanced nose down on the floor. Then he would climb a pair of steps with a bottle on each rung. From the top of the steps he would jump into the mouth of a barrel, all this without upsetting a single bottle. He toured the music-halls offering fifty pounds to anyone who could do the same and never had to pay. His last appearance on the stage was at the Portsmouth Empire, when he was nearly fifty; afterwards he worked as a market porter. But however eccentric Cannonball's working life appeared, life in the home was always strict; he ruled his family with Victorian severity.

'True, we lived hard, but I could always find a bit of greengrocery from the market. Kippers was two a penny in them days, pennyworth of faggots, ha'porth of pease pudden. All things that put the vitamins inside you and help you to uphold yourself.'

He had a famous temper in the home, and his daughters went in fear of him. At table none would eat until he finished carving. No one contradicted him, and not a drop of liquor was allowed inside the house. By the time Violet had made her peace with him, Cannonball had mellowed, but he still lived within the old-style world of Bethnal

Green with all its rectitude, self-reliance and loyalties. This was the family to which Violet brought the twins. It soon became their real home. Their father was invariably away and Violet provided most of what discipline they got. Charles was regular with the housekeeping, but he seemed less and less involved in his family. The little black-haired dolls in the angora coats were emerging from babyhood, loved and adored by everyone around them. Their mother was still the only one who could be sure of telling them apart; they were inseparable and seemed to need no one but themselves, certainly no other children nor their brother. They were late talking, but showed signs of being telepathic. As they got older they shared dreams and thoughts quite naturally. If one decided he was hungry or wanted to go to the lavatory, so would the other. If one got hurt, the other one would cry although he might be in another room. They had a private language, liked the same food, laughed at the same things and lived in a self-contained world of their own. They never argued. Neither seemed dominant. Their mother still dressed them the same, but she was beginning to wonder if it was right to treat them so alike.

The twins were unusually healthy babies. At three neither had caught anything much worse than a cold. But when Violet Kray found Reggie feverish and sick one day she took it for granted that Ronnie was going to be ill as well. By evening both the twins had temperatures and the following day the doctor diagnosed measles. At first Violet refused to worry. The twins were sturdy, but they got worse and by next evening Ronnie had difficulty breathing.

'He was in a dreadful state, poor little thing, gasping away for breath, and none of us able to help him. None of us knew what it was until I saw his nose-holes moving in and out. I knew it was the diphtheria then and called the doctor again.'

Diphtheria it was: both twins were infected, but Ronnie worse than Reggie and the doctor decided to isolate them in separate hospitals; Ronnie in the isolation ward of the General Hospital, Homerton, and Reggie in St Anne's Hospital, Tottenham. There they stayed for the next few days; isolated, and extremely ill.

It was the first time they had been parted more than half an hour; the first time they had been without their mother. She was permitted to peep in at them through a small window at the end of the ward. After a fortnight, Reggie was recovering and within a month was ready for home; his brother remained critically ill. And although Ronnie finally began to mend he was apathetic. Three months after the twins were taken ill, Reggie had recovered and was back playing happily with other children in Vallance Road. Ronnie remained in the Homerton isolation ward.

Violet decided to assert herself. 'I understood my Ronnie better than all them doctors. They couldn't see what was really troubling him. He was just fretting for his Reggie an' for me. So I told the hospital I was taking him home. They warned it could be dangerous, but it wasn't no good leaving him there. When he was home I nursed him night an' day, had him in my room with me of nights. He picked up in no time.'

'His mother saved his life,' said Charles. 'No question of it. If it hadn't been for Violet an' what she did then, he'd 'ave been a goner.'

The twins were three now, but the balance between them was disturbed. Violet tried to treat them as before and be scrupulously fair. She still dressed them identically and gave them identical presents on their birthday. If one had an ice-cream, she would make sure the other had one too. They even started sharing the same name now: when anyone wanted them he would not call 'Ronnie' or

'Reggie' but always 'Twins'. It was as if they were a single person.

But Violet knew that there were differences between them now: she could not forget that Ronnie had needed her most, that he had fretted for her in hospital and that she had nursed him back to health. She saw things other people missed. Physically the twins remained the same, but Reggie was brighter. He talked more than Ronnie, was easier to handle and got on better with people and with other children. Ronnie seemed slower, shyer, more dependent on his mother than before. His moods were always changing. Children of this age can be permanently impaired by a severe attack of measles and diphtheria. Suddenly Ronnie began to sulk and to have difficulty talking. As he grew he seemed slightly bigger and clumsier than Reggie. Despite this he always needed to outdo him.

At first this competition took the form of vying for their mother's attention. Violet saw nothing wrong with this. 'It was as if he had to make up for all the love he'd missed in the hospital.' But soon Ronnie would do anything to get his mother's affection; scream, sulk and think up ways of putting Reggie in the wrong. Then once she noticed him Ronnie would smother Violet with love. As he grew, this never stopped, and soon both twins became affected.

'When Ronnie was just a toddler he would be watching all the time to see Reggie never did better than he did. And Reggie was soon watching him as well. They watched each other like young hawks.'

There is a photograph of them taken the summer war broke out, on Southend Pier: a wistful picture of two solemn bright-eyed little boys staring into the camera. All Violet's doting care is obvious in the neat suits and the carefully brushed-back hair but there is something else, something about their eyes, a look they never lost. It is as if one face is watching itself mistrustfully in a mirror. A former pimp who grew up with them says, 'Even when they was very young the twins never seemed like other children. Didn't laugh nor lark around for the fun of it. They seemed to have something more serious on their minds.'

Violet knew this too. She knew her twins were 'different' from other children. In some ways she was proud of this. They always had been special; they were twins. That made them extra precious; they needed more love than ordinary small boys.

'They seemed to gather trouble; fighting with other boys already, breaking things, getting in mischief for the hell of it. They had a devilish streak in them. But Violet knew she must be patient.'

'Twins always stand out. Bein' twins they're naturally conspicuous. Other kids pick on 'em.' And there always seemed to be older children ready to lead the twins into trouble. So it was their fault, not the twins'. For Violet knew how vulnerable they were behind their toughness – Ronnie particularly. And she could never bring herself to be hard on them. Ronnie always longed to be the favoured twin. But this was difficult with Violet determined to be fair to both, and it was clear that with his greater quickness and his charm Reggie had the advantage. So gradually Ronnie learned to manipulate things so that if he couldn't always win the love he wanted he could make sure Reggie never had it either.

One of their cousins says, 'When we was kids together, I have seen Ronnie sit down and count out the peas on their two plates, then throw a scene because Reggie had a couple more.'

Whenever Reggie was in favour, Ronnie could usually redress things. Sometimes he did it with a sneer.

'Look at Reggie, Mummy's darling. Sweet little angel, ain't 'e?'

At other times it was necessary to get him into trouble. This wasn't difficult either. Reggie was no angel, whatever Ronnie said, and Ronnie knew exactly how to handle things. He knew quite well that in a fight Reggie would always back him up and always rise to a taunt of cowardice.

Gradually the twins worked out a private code of behaviour. Good was what brought them praise and love, chiefly from their mother but also from anyone they happened jointly to admire. Evil was the opposite. And just as their lives had always been ruled by what was absolutely fair, so they began to balance up any excess of praise with an excess of trouble. The pattern is simple to identify, repeating constantly throughout their lives. What was not so easy for the twins was to come to agreement over precisely what was fair between them. There could be no cheating. Each knew the other, watched the other far too well for that. Each motive, every move they made was under mutual scrutiny. There was no escape. Everything one did was known and judged by the other. Often this became too much: one would revolt and they would fight like demons.

One of the family says, 'No one could ever stop them once they started, and none of us ever understood what the twins fought about. In the end we got used to it and let 'em fight it out. But I never seen ordinary brothers fight like those two did. They would hurl themselves at each other and scream every obscenity they knew. Ten minutes later it was over and forgotten, the twins content and quite inseparable again. I think they had to have these rucks to let off steam. They loved each other really, but sometimes I thought they'd kill themselves.'

Violet had always longed to move from Hoxton back to Bethnal Green. Now on the eve of war one of the houses on the corner of Vallance Road fell vacant. Charles agreed to move. Violet and the twins went home at last and Lee Street reunited.

178 Vallance Road was tiny, the second in a row of four Victorian terraced cottages. There was no bathroom, the lavatory was in the yard and day and night the house shook as the Liverpool Street trains roared past the bedroom windows. For Violet none of this mattered. Her

parents were just around the corner; so was her sister, Rose, the wild one with the gipsy looks. Her other sister, May, was next door but one, and her brother, John Lee, kept the caff across the street.

When war came it was in this stretch of Vallance Road, under the shadow of the soot-stained viaducts, that Violet Kray and her family built a protective colony of three generations; it became known as 'Deserters' Corner'.

This would remain the centre of the children's world, the hideout of their cockney clan: those front doors always open, letting them scuttle through the warren of small houses, the hot little kitchens at the back, thick with the smell of stew and washing, where Aunt May or Grandmother Lee would always find them cake and a cup of tea; special treats from wild Aunt Rose who never let a week go by without buying them a toy or a bag of sweets from the housekeeping; and old Grandfather Lee, who was to cycle to Southend and back to celebrate his seventieth birthday, and who still kept his famous left hook in trim, punching a mattress hung up in the yard. He would sit with the twins for hours in his armchair by the fire, talking about the perils of drink and the East End of the past and how he broke Mike Thompson's nose when he had set on him with a brick one night in an alleyway in Wapping, half a century before. Sometimes he would recite his poems. Sometimes he told them of the great boxers he had known: Jimmy Wilde of Stepney, 'who had his strength in both hands where I had it only in my left'; Kid Lewis who grew up just around the corner to become champion of the world at three separate weights, 'a good clean-living man and one of the gamest fighters ever to enter a ring'. And sometimes the old man would talk about the other heroes of the old East End – its criminals: Spud Murphy of Hoxton who killed two men in a spieler in Whitechapel and shouted to the police that he'd bring a machine-gun and finish everyone off before he was caught; Martin and Baker, from Bethnal Green, who took the nine o'clock walk after shooting three policemen at Carlisle. And for the old man, Jack the Ripper's murders were almost local happenings; the house in Hanbury Street where he had killed Annie Chapman was just round the corner.

As the twins were growing up, their father had a strange place in their lives. The 'Gold Rush' had started as the price of gold was rising and he was doing well, touring the country in a beaten-up old Chrysler, and leaving Violet back at Vallance Road. 'Mr Kray used to be off for weeks at a time, gold buying and wardrobe dealing. So we was never short of money, but everything to do with the twins fell on to me. If they was ill or in trouble I was the one who had to deal with it.' Most of the control they got came from Violet too. This soon became a source of friction between their parents. When he materialized at the weekends, Charles found the twins lacking in respect. The answer was clearly a good belting, but Violet would not hear of it. Her own life taught her what happened when parents were too strict with their children: she was not losing her twins like that. And so the arguments would start, and the twins would listen, bright-eyed and missing nothing.

Had Charles got his way, their life might have been different. Later he blamed himself for not asserting himself more and moving the whole family out of the East End. 'I should have bought a house in Gidea Park and been firmer with the lot of them.' As it was he never stayed long enough in Vallance Road to enforce his authority; he merely taught the twins to hate it. And even in those days they were usually a match for him. They could always dodge to someone's house and hide. And Monday morning he would be off again in the old Chrysler leaving his family in peace.

The twins were nearly six when war began. Charles was ordered to the Tower of London for military service but he had never been a fighting man. So he changed his name and returned to the wardrobe business on his own. For the next twelve years the twins' father remained 'on the trot' as a deserter. They had their home and their mother to themselves at last. From time to time Charles would appear but never for long, slipping into the house at dusk looking out for the police, and clambering over the yard wall next morning. He never complained about this fugitive life. He made a living and enough to pay for his drink and Violet's housekeeping. They caught him once, near Croydon, and took him to Woolwich Barracks under escort, but he soon escaped and rented a room in Southwark from an Australian pickpocket called Bob Rolfe. Occasionally the twins were sent there with messages from Violet.

This was how the twins first glimpsed the East End underworld their father knew. Since the eighteenth century the East End had been famous for its boxers and its criminals, both of them bred on poverty. Most East End crime was thieving, violence and gang fights, ghetto crime to which men turn when they have little to lose. In the poorer parts of London crime was regarded as a fairly normal way of life and the police recognized certain 'criminal areas': King's Cross for thieves, Hackney for cat burglars, Stepney for small-time con-men, and Bethnal Green and Whitechapel for their villains.

The 'villain' is a fighter who lives on his reputation for not caring what he does or what happens to him. He makes a living any way he can, chiefly from lesser criminals. His weapon is intimidation. His virtues, such as they are, are 'gameness' and an unconcern for money once he has it. The East End villain, according to one elderly ex-thief from Bethnal Green, 'generally died young and never made any money. He lived like an animal and died like one.' Bill Sykes was his prototype. Despite this, the old villains of the East End did possess a sort of glamour. Their lives were generally 'nasty, brutish and short', but they stood out from the grey world around them. Everybody talked about them and Charles knew them all – Jimmy Spinks, Timmy Hayes, old Dodger Mullins: none of them admirable men, but they were recognized for what they were and did what many better men would like to have done. They never worked. They'd scare money out of bookmakers, publicans and successful shopkeepers. 'Dodger would work his own protection racket round all the small-time bookmakers, calling each Monday morning for his "pension". Shopkeepers paid him something too; sort of insurance to keep the lesser tappers away.' Even their brutality was memorable. 'Jimmy Spinks ordered some fish and chips, and when they cut up rough because he wouldn't pay, he threw the fish-shop cat in the frier.' 'Old Wassle Newman used to throw bricks up in the air and punch 'em as they came down to toughen his hands.'

They were resolutely male. Drunken and idle, they were against home life and treated their women appallingly. 'Dodger got fed up with one bird he lived with an' threw her out of the window. The police issued a warrant for his arrest an' caught him at Epsom Races. To teach him a lesson, one of the coppers, a big fellow, took out a knuckle-duster in Epsom Downs Station an' sploshed Dodger straight on the nose. It made no difference.'

Originally the villains came from the very poorest parts of the East End. There were the Bethnal Greeners proper, who were considered 'flash', arrogant men. Then there were Watney Streeters from Whitechapel, and the local gangs from Brady Street and Dossert Street, which has still the highest number of murders of any street in London. 'In the old days you'd see the worst of the poverty here and the worst ignorance. You'd see the old women sitting in the streets, smoking their pipes. Often the woman'd keep the family alive by making brushes or matches. And this was where the poorest Irish married the poorest of the Jews. Watney Street produced the most uncaring villains of them all.'

Most of the fights were pub fights or full-scale gang fights between the Bethnal Green villains and the men of Watney Street. For the true Bethnal Green criminal, Watney Street was the traditional enemy, even more than the police. This was a part of London where policemen still went warily, and generally in twos.

'The police just didn't want to be involved. I've seen a villain stab another in front of a policeman in the old days and the copper walk away. As long as straight folk weren't molested, all the Law really bothered with was where the gear was hid if there'd been a robbery. Otherwise they left us to get on with it.' The old-time villain was a law unto himself where other criminals were concerned. Then in the mid thirties East London violence was boosted by the rise of fascism: many top East End villains were employed by Mosley; anti-Semitic rioting occurred in Whitechapel and Bethnal Green was briefly known as 'the fascist manor'.

The one thing East End violence failed to produce was large-scale organized crime. The rackets were petty ones, and up until the war the racketeers kept clear of the East End. 'Derby' Sabini, the grey-bowler-hatted 'king of the racecourses' was the nearest Britain got to an organizing gangster. But he organized his famous 'racecourse gang' at Saffron Hill, and the attempt by Watney Street to oust him one year at Brighton races was so inept that no one tried again.

The German bombs of 1940 seemed to have finished off the villains' world of the old East End. During the massed raids on the docks, whole districts died. In Bethnal Green alone, ten thousand dwellings were destroyed; the heart of the East End became a wilderness.

When the bombing began, Violet moved into the country with her three children: first to Hampshire, where the twins proved too much for the doctor's family with whom they were billeted, then to a more resilient family at Hadleigh in Suffolk. The twins enjoyed the country, ran wild, stole apples from the Rothschild estate near Tring and picked up a Suffolk burr over their native cockney: for some time, Aunt Rose became 'Aunt Rawse'. They also both developed a taste for the country, Suffolk in particular.

But no real cockney buries himself in the countryside for long, and the Krays missed the talk, the cups of tea, the smells of the streets and the constant activities of Vallance Road. So Violet gathered up young Charlie and the twins. She had their fare to Liverpool Street. They wore their best clothes; the rest of their possessions went into a suitcase and two carrier bags. Someone gave them a lift to the station in a van. And back they came to Vallance Road and the bombing.

Violet and the Lees survived, drawing together ever closer as a family. Charles appeared from time to time, but most of his energy was spent dodging the police and keeping on the run. Persistent, neat, respectful as ever to his customers, he was making a good living as he went flitting like some old cockney starling round the suburbs and back to the East End and the City. Because of the blitz, the schools had closed and the twins enjoyed total freedom. Nights were spent in the cockney fug of the air-raid shelters under the Vallance Road viaduct. Grandfather Lee had taken on a new lease of life organizing the neighbours in competitions and sing-songs there every night. He built a stage himself, and his *pièce de résistance* was a poem he had entitled 'Hitler, we'll have none of you'.

During the day the twins played on the rubble. 'Our mother saw that we never went hungry, though times was very hard. But there'd always be potatoes and stew for dinner. Reg an' me were both of us lousy and a lot of us kids had scabies. Caught 'em off the bomb dumps where we played. The medical officer came and painted us several times.' Not that the twins worried. Life was exciting. 'We started gang wars. We had our own gang early as I can remember. Reg an' me organized stone raids on the kids in the next street. Outside the house we always seemed to be fighting. Fought all the kids around. In the end we picked up such a name that if anyone was hurt or something broken, we'd be blamed. People called us the "Terrible Twins".'

The twins often played with their cousin Billy. He was five years older, but for a time they were inseparable. He showed them how to build a box-cart with a sharp front as a battering ram. To test their nerve, he rolled them over the cobbles in a barrel. And when Billy was in a fight, the twins would usually join in, taking on much older boys and learning to take care of themselves. They became vicious early. Fighting was their way of life, as with most boys of Bethnal Green, but the twins' ability to fight together gave them a great advantage over other boys.

A neighbour says, 'I can't remember the twins ever being like little boys. They never seemed to have a proper childhood at all. There was no innocence in them.'

They still observed the rules of their own private world: goodness centred on their mother but was extended to the life and the people she admired. The twins admired them as well. Violet had a strange sense of cockney decency.

Saint James's Church in the Bethnal Green Road with its High Church ritual and high red spire was an important part of the respectable world the twins aspired to. Father Hetherington, for many years its vicar, remembers them well. 'They were extremely kind boys and would do anything for me except actually come to church. But they were both exceptionally polite, to old folk in particular, and they took trouble over people. If we were holding a bazaar or a church affair of any sort, they'd always come along and help in some way or other. Few boys of their age did.'

School began again when they were eight. Neither was much of a scholar, although Reggie was certainly the brighter of the two and showed a gift for words. Outside school they were constantly involved in fights but in the classroom they were the reverse of rebels. Their principal teacher was a Mr William Evans, a genial Rugby-playing Welshman from Monmouthshire who taught at Daneford Street School for more than thirty years, certainly too long to be over-sentimental about small boys. 'Salt of the earth, the twins; never the slightest trouble to anyone who knew how to handle them. Course they were tough and they were fighters, but they weren't the sort that rolled around the playground or spat in each other's faces or used knives as some of them do today. If they had to be punished they'd take it like gents. And if there was anything to be done in school, they'd be utterly co-operative. A sporting gala or something of the sort; they'd always be the first to help. Nothing was ever too much trouble.'

But even as young boys they were already entering a different world. It was opposed to the world they respected and was exciting for that very reason. It was brutal and secret, and they first discovered it as they fought and planned their wars across the wastes of Bethnal Green. There was always someone threatening them, someone to be 'done'. The only rules here were the rules of war, and just as the twins were so much kinder and more considerate than most boys in the respectable world, so they were wickeder here.

Again, this was partly because they were twins. Each one watched the other and neither could relax. 'Even as a kid, if I was challenged to a fight and I backed down, Ronnie would know. He'd be a sort of conscience, and I'd find it hard to face him afterwards.'

But there was more to their violent world than this. In their imagination they were re-creating their father's world with their fights and secret wars and passionate vendettas, the old criminal fraternity of the East End, of Dodger Mullins, Jimmy Spinks and Wassle Newman – the world their mother hated. The reality had been bombed out of existence. When it arose the new East End would be a very different place, and the free-drinking, free-spending, dead-end cockney villain would be a figure of the past.

But for the twins the villains' world was very real. They lived it in their fights. They entered it whenever they crossed London Bridge and listened to Bob Rolfe the pickpocket reminiscing with their father. They soon met Dodger, introduced by Charles as 'the old guvnor of the East End'.

Toughness at all costs, 'gameness', pride in one's fighting name, contempt for women and the family virtues and, above all, willingness to 'go the limit' in a fight – this was the code old Dodger taught the twins, and they learned something else: that this dark villains' world had no connection with respectable society.

Just as the old-time cockney villains slashed at each other practically unmolested by the Law, so the twins felt much the same about their fights. Here they made their rules to suit themselves and anything was allowed against an enemy. As soon as Ronnie landed in a fight, he knew Reggie would be there, scrapping just as viciously beside him. 'If Ronnie was in a spot of trouble I'd know and had to be there with him, if only out of self-respect.'

By nature Reggie was quite easy-going, but Ronnie never missed the opportunity of a fight. He was immensely touchy. No possible slight, no 'liberty' from another boy went by unnoticed; whenever a chance cropped up to involve Reggie, Ronnie would take it – partly from jealousy. Since Reggie was the general favourite, there was satisfaction in proving that the 'little pet' could behave as viciously as he. It evened things up; it also kept Reggie under his domination and stopped him growing away into the respectable world and leaving him alone.

The twins used to sleep together in a double bed in the back bedroom at Vallance Road. One night at two in the morning the light went on and the twins woke to face a police sergeant from Bethnal Green Station waiting to ask some questions. Someone had tipped the Law that Charles was at home. The twins had the sense to keep the policeman talking until their father could escape over the yard wall. But the policeman was not satisfied and pulled them out of bed to question them. Parrot-like and sleepy the two nine-year-olds gave the reply they had been taught: 'Our mum and dad's divorced. We never see 'im now.'

For the twins this was another important lesson for the future. 'We were both scared of that old copper the first time we saw him in our room, but we soon grew wise to him. We never had been frightened of no copper since.'

One night the police arrived when Charles was eating supper in the kitchen. He had time to dive beneath the table which had a long white tablecloth all round it and the twins continued eating while the police searched the house. Another time when they came unexpectedly, Charles jumped into the coal cupboard beneath the stairs. Just as the police were opening the cupboard door, Ronnie piped up, 'D'you think my old man's barmy enough to 'ide in there?' The policeman missed the easiest capture of his life.

As this corner of Vallance Road became known as a place of refuge, more men began hiding there from the police. Aunt Rose's husband was on the run. So was their parents' best man, a dealer called Harry Hopwood, and there were many others. This was when the houses got the name 'Deserters' Corner'.

Nobody cared much for the Law in this part of the East End; as Mr Evans says, 'In Bethnal Green they used to have an eleventh commandment, "Thou shalt not grass." And no one did.'

The neighbours all observed the East End's code of silence and nobody was caught at Vallance Road. As for the twins, dodging the Law became a way of life. They had to keep a lookout for the police, and soon became cunning. They were often questioned, and learned to guard their tongues. The police became just one more enemy.

Ronnie's favourite memory of his Aunt Rose is how she used to shake her mats from the window when a policeman walked below, and there was a friend of his father's who had a saying which stuck in his mind. 'Coppers is like Germans. The only good one's a dead one.'

Apart from their father, the only member of the family who really understood the twins was their Aunt Rose. Their mother didn't. The twins were always careful to keep their fights and outside life from her. Even as small boys they would tidy up after a fight: whenever anyone complained about the twins, Violet would invariably defend them. 'Someone had to. Their father wasn't there. I'd say to the twins, "Well, what 'appened?" And they'd say, "Well it wasn't our fault." If a mother has to choose between her own and someone else's kids, what choice is there?' But wild Aunt Rose was not a homemaker like Violet. She had her father's toughness and his temper. 'Our Rosie was a tearaway herself.' She loved the twins and they loved her, Ronnie especially. 'She would fight anyone our Rosie would. She might see a couple of girls in the street an' think they was lookin' at her. "Oo's she lookin' at?" she'd say out loud. "Oo she think she is?" An' she'd be picking a quarrel with them in no time. Same with her husband. She'd go out to find 'im in a pub and punch him if he'd had too much. One night in Vallance Road, I see 'er fight *two* women on her own. They'd said something rude about her mum. Kept the fight going more'n an hour, and beat 'em both. Genuine punching too.

'She couldn't cook, our Rosie. Wasn't bothered. But she loved the twins. Soon as 'er 'usband gave her fifty bob on Friday night she'd say, "What'd the twins like?" And she'd get it for them straight away. So there was never much of her fifty bob left by Saturday night.'

The marriage didn't last, but Aunt Rose and her children stayed at Vallance Road, where she became Ronnie's heroine. According to his mother, 'Rosie hated the police. When Mr Kray was on the run, they was always bursting into the house at Vallance Road, and they'd ball up Rosie something dreadful. The things she'd call them really shocked me sometimes.'

When the twins were in trouble, Rosie always knew. 'You're a born devil, Ronnie,' she would say. 'You know what those eyebrows of yours mean, meeting in the middle of your forehead?'

'No, Aunt Rose.'

'They mean you're born to hang.'

When the twins were young, cockneys could still enjoy their own big annual fair in Victoria Park. Today the fair is one more part of the vanished East End, but it remains one of the twins' few childish memories: to begin with they always went with Grandfather Lee, but at ten they started going on their own.

There was always one moment the twins waited for – the opening of the boxing-booth, with five pounds to anyone to go the distance with one of the booth boxers at their own weight. Up they came, brawny dockers, rash young tearaways, anyone tough or silly enough to risk a beating from a professional for a fiver and a night's notoriety.

The first night the twins came on their own, the tent was crammed. Two of the best local boxers, 'Slasher' Warner and 'Buster' Osbourne, were on the bill and the booth boxers knew how to please the crowd. There was hard punching, several knock-outs, just the right amount of blood. One of the challengers lasted the distance to collect his five pounds.

'And who's the next gentleman tonight to take five pounds off me?' shouted the booth proprietor. 'We're giving it away.'

'I will,' said Ronnie Kray.

Some of the audience laughed, but Ronnie looked so serious that the man in charge explained it would be hard to find someone to fight him at his own weight. Reggie stood up.

'I'll fight him,' he said.

A minute later the twins were in the ring, stripped to the waist, waiting to begin the first boxing match of their lives.

They were perfectly matched and fought with the same cold fury as they did at home. The crowd was soon cheering them for their gameness, and after three rounds Ronnie had the makings of a black eye and Reggie's nose was bleeding. Everyone cheered as the owner of the booth declared the fight a draw and gave each of them seven and six. The twins' careers as boxers had begun.

It was inevitable they would start boxing sooner or later. Both their grandfathers had been fighters, and in the navy their brother Charlie was a successful inter-services welterweight. The East End had produced many great fighters. Mendoza, the greatest prize-fighter of all time, came from Whitechapel, and Charles sold second-hand clothing to one of his great-grandsons. In Bethnal Green boxing still seemed to offer a tough, determined boy the quickest way to fame and fortune.

But boxing was something more than this for the twins. That night in the Victoria Park boxing-booth, they had their first taste of notoriety; from then on, boxing was a passion, absorbing their lonely energies and setting their hopes for the future. If they were ever to find fame legitimately, this would be the way.

The East End is still full of retired boxers on the lookout for the treasure trove of 'a likely young'un' they can discover and coach to success. The twins began lessons with a wizened ex-flyweight who ran a 'Midgets' Club' for schoolboys in a cellar in Whitechapel. Charles encouraged them and they began training at the Browning Club, south of the river. At eleven they were in the ring again, fighting each other in the Hackney Schoolboys Final.

This time some of the audience were shocked by the

violence with which these twins attacked each other. Reggie won the decision on points. When the trophy was presented there was a muddle over who was who. People were saying it was wrong to allow twins to fight each other, and Violet made them promise never to again.

Charles was in the hall to see the fight. He was still wanted by the Law, but now the war was over, life was more relaxed. He thought boxing would be the making of the twins, give them the discipline they needed, take them off the streets and give them something other than mischief to occupy their minds. It could also help the family finances: champion boxers made big money. So he was more philosophical than Violet over the twins fighting one another. 'If they'd not, they'd have both needed to stand down and some outsider would have won the trophy. We couldn't have that.'

'Ronnie was a fighter,' says one of the men who trained him, 'the hardest boy I've ever seen. To stop him you'd have had to kill him. Reggie was different. It was as if he had all the experience of an old boxer before he started. Just once in a lifetime you find a boy with everything to be a champion. Reggie had it.'

In the East End a promising boxer was treated like a hopeful racehorse, and Charles's friend and one-time great professional, Ted 'Kid' Berg, became their trainer-manager. Cannonball coached them; their brother Charlie sparred with them and they suddenly became the great white hopes of Vallance Road.

The front bedroom was turned into a gymnasium for them, complete with a punch-bag anchored to the floor with a meat-hook (on which Charles gashed his foot one night when making an unobserved entry to the family home in stockinged feet). Violet gave them a high-protein diet. Every penny they could save went on boxing books, and they began training with total dedication. Some people found this worrying. They could allow themselves no slacking off. If one felt inclined to miss a training session, the other would notice. Having each other to live up to, they soon appeared fanatics. 'I've never known boxers take it more serious than the twins. Never late. Whatever the weather they were out each morning at six for road work. They was in bed by ten each night, and absolutely no smoking or drinking. I never saw either of them out with a girl.'

Soon they were in perfect condition with the punch of a pile-driver. Until sixteen, when they turned professional, they won every bout they fought. Father Hetherington blames boxing for much of the trouble of their middle teens. 'Everything went wrong once the local papers published the twins' photographs and wrote about them as super boxers when they were really two ordinary East End boys.' But with their strange shared life of identical twins, they were far from ordinary, and their career as boxers started to disrupt their private lives. Ronnie had toughness and determination, but Reggie was patently the star, with the real career ahead of him. Soon after the twins turned professional, the street violence they were involved in mysteriously increased as well.

The boy's name was Harvey; he was sixteen, smartly dressed, worked as a clerk in the East End and lived with his family in Hackney. When the ambulance men picked him out of the alley off Mare Street where the gang had left him he was still conscious. He collapsed on the way to hospital and a doctor later testified in court that he had been hit hard in both eyes and on the nose, 'had suffered multiple contusions about the neck and chin consistent with his being beaten with a length of bicycle chain', and kicked thoroughly all over. It seemed a common enough case. In 1950 the wars between the local teenage gangs in Hackney were increasing. No one knew why, but the actual woundings had been growing more serious. There were rumours of guns, and the police were half expecting someone to be killed. But this new outbreak of violence was puzzling. Nobody knew the leaders of the gangs, and nobody would talk.

But this time there were witnesses: a nineteen-year-old girl and an insurance salesman who had seen the fight and could recognize the boys. They named the twins, and Harvey confirmed this to the police. It seemed as if the twins had finally slipped up.

For years now they had kept their gang fights secret and nobody in the respectable world around them knew what was going on. Certainly few can have suspected their hidden need for violence – except possibly Aunt Rose. The only hint had come at the age of twelve when they were put on probation for firing an air rifle from a train. But this was something any boy might do and their discreet routine of violence left no evidence. Already the twins showed skill as leaders with a certain prestige for those who went with them. They were accepted as the wildest ones around, who used coshes, chains and broken bottles for their fights, and by sixteen Ronnie had already perfected the technique of cutting an enemy in the face, preferring a large sheath knife to the old-style cut-throat razor. At sixteen the twins also bought their first revolver and hid it under the bedroom floor. In all their fights one thing distinguished them once they began; the way they would 'go the limit', carried away by an orgy of violence as if blood and brutality satisfied a need they shared in secret. Even their allies could be frightened by their fury and the pleasure they obviously derived from giving pain.

At the preliminary hearing the North London Magistrate, Mr Herbert Malone, KC, examined the bicycle chains the police found near Harvey, 'in pools of clotted blood', and declared that the 'beasts' who used them evidently thought themselves above the Law, and would be taught a lesson. Both twins remained in custody and were brought for trial at the Old Bailey.

Meanwhile things were happening behind the scenes. The girl witness had been discreetly told that she would have a razor 'put across her face' if she gave evidence. The insurance salesman received a similar threat. Harvey, still in hospital, had various visitors pointing out the need to be sensible. He was an East End boy and ought to know it could be most unwise to talk. At the Old Bailey trial the twins' case was speedily dismissed for lack of evidence, and Herbert Malone was right. Their trial did teach the twins a lesson.

In the summer of 1951, the twins fought several bouts as professionals and won them all – Reggie with the precision of the natural boxer, Ronnie by slogging. In September they were at Wembley Town Hall on the same bill, and both were on form. Reggie had his man, Goodsell of Cambridge, down for a count of eight in the second round. He finished him off in the third after a display of fancy footwork and neatly placed hooks to the heart and the head.

Ronnie Kray's fight was with Bernie Long of Romford, and Ronnie steamrollered him. By the start of the third round, Long was badly cut around the eyes and bleeding from the mouth. The referee stopped the fight. People who saw the fights said they confirmed what everybody knew about the twins. Ronnie was game and vicious, but Reggie had a real future.

Within a week the twins were once again in trouble. It was an odd case. In the past they had always avoided a confrontation with the police, and it seemed out of character for Ronnie to insult a young policeman who told him to move on in Bethnal Green Road on a Saturday afternoon. It was even more unlike him to punch him on the jaw before a dozen witnesses outside Pellici's Café. Had he wanted to land in trouble, and ensure the twins a public name for violence, he could hardly have done it better. Within an hour he had been picked up and charged with assaulting a policeman.

The incident could not end there. Reggie was with his brother when the trouble started, but it was over too quickly for him to join in. His immediate reaction was that he had failed him, with Ronnie in the cells, and the policeman already back on duty. 'If I'd not done something, then I'd never have been able to look Ron in the eye again.' He spent the rest of that afternoon searching for the policeman. When he found him he attacked him just as Ronnie had. He made no attempt to escape, but went off, happy now, to join his brother in the cells. When they came for trial a few days later, the twins would certainly have gone to prison but for the efforts of the respectable world which they had courted. It was Father Hetherington who went into the witness box for them to say that 'apart from their disgusting behaviour on this occasion', he felt there were still possibilities of the Krays making good.

The magistrate was feeling generous. The policeman was commended for his courage: the twins put on probation. All that had really suffered was Reggie's future as a boxer. Managers dislike boxers with reputations for violence outside the ring, since a serious conviction usually costs a fighter his licence and ends his career.

On 11 December 1951 all three Kray brothers fought at the Albert Hall in a contest headed by Tommy McGovern, lightweight champion of Britain. It was their biggest chance so far. Charlie Kray lost. Ronnie was disqualified. Reggie defeated his man in three perfectly fought rounds.

Now that his attempt to discipline the twins through boxing had failed, Charles had given up hope, and usually kept away from home when he knew the twins were there. Ronnie had been fourteen when he first hit him during an argument with Violet. Now they invariably picked on him when he had had a drink or two. Sometimes they hit him hard. 'Until a boy's fifteen, I suppose you can do something for him,' he said wearily. 'After that there's not a lot any father can do.'

They still loved their mother as devotedly as ever. Violet and the twins were now adopting the rationalizations

Before the corporal could explain what was so special about the Royal Fusiliers the two recruits in the identical blue suits started walking towards the door.

The corporal stopped. He was not the man to take nonsense from recruits but had never faced a situation quite like this before.

'And where might you be going?'

The twins paused, faces expressionless except for a faint but identical raising of the eyebrows.

'I said, where d'you think you're off to, you lovely pair?'

One of the twins spoke then, as quietly as if telling somebody the time.

'We don't care for it here. We're off home to see our mum.' They continued to walk towards the door.

The corporal felt the two boys were trying to make a fool of him, and grabbed one by the arm.

There was something strange about what happened then. Violence is usually accompanied by some sign of emotion but the faces of the twins remained expressionless. There was a thud. The corporal staggered back against the wall, holding his jaw – and still unspeaking, still unhurrying, the twins, in their dark blue suits, walked down the stairs and out across the square where the ravens perched and the last of the afternoon sightseers was being shown the spot where Queen Anne Boleyn lost her head four hundred years or so before.

Ronald and Reginald Kray of the Royal Fusiliers were back at Vallance Road in time for tea.

The ending of National Service is often seen as a factor in the rise of lawlessness among the young. Perhaps. But for the Kray twins it is undeniable that without the two years they were now to spend in contact with the army, they would never have been able to take over the East End with the speed and ruthlessness they showed when finally released in the spring of 1954.

Next morning, just before daybreak, the police called at

Vallance Road. The twins, who had spent their first night of service to Queen and Country at a dance-hall in Tottenham, were asleep. But they had been expecting the police. They yawned, dressed, made no attempt to resist, and telling their mother not to worry as they'd soon be back, went downstairs and into the police car which carried them to Bethnal Green Police Station where a military escort returned them to the Tower. They were placed in a cell, presented with a fresh uniform apiece, told to get shaved, given a slice of bread and mug of army tea, and informed they would be appearing in the Commanding Officer's orderly room next morning charged with being absent without leave.

From the day the Fusiliers tried teaching them the rudiments of discipline and military training, the twins found something they could never really do without – an enemy. They also discovered certain skills they needed from the army – lessons in organization and morale, of leadership and weaponry and propaganda which were to prove invaluable when the time came to organize a private army of their own. They learned about themselves as well – how much they could take and just how tough they really were; together with the advantages of being twins. They learned how vulnerable a large organization can be, and taught themselves new ways of making officials ridiculous. They tested out their powers of resistance – and found them more than adequate.

Next morning the twins were lined up among the other petty offenders to face the charge of absence without leave and striking an NCO in the lawful exercise of his duty. By army standards these were serious charges. The corporal gave his evidence and normally this would have led to a court-martial. But there would have been something faintly ridiculous about court-martialling a pair of boys for knocking out an NCO on their first afternoon in the army. There was also a practical difficulty which no one had thought of until that moment. Which of these identical young tearaways landed the actual blow?

The corporal wasn't sure, but thought it was the one on the far left.

'Were you the one who attacked the corporal?' the CO asked Private Ronald Kray.

'No, sir.'

'Then it must have been you.'

'Oh no, sir.'

'Well, one of you did it.'

This was a situation the twins had faced since childhood and they knew exactly how to act.

'Did what, sir?'

'Struck this NCO.'

'But which one of us are you accusing, sir?'

'Whichever of you made this cowardly assault. Who did?'

The twins shrugged their shoulders – an impertinent gesture and a slightly uncanny one, for they did it together.

The next seven days were spent back in the guardroom. Wisely perhaps, the Commanding Officer had decided to temper justice with discretion and rather than become embroiled in interminable questions of identification, contented himself with reading the twins a lecture on doing their duty and awarded them the most moderate punishment he could in the circumstances.

The twins showed no sign of objecting. The guardroom was icy, the food just eatable and instead of a mattress they slept on the bare boards of a punishment cell. But this was what they wanted, for it proved how right they were to be contracting out of an organization that could treat anyone like this. There was also a certain satisfaction in the very harshness of the regime. Bare boards and bad food were a challenge. The better they resisted, the manlier they felt.

Apart from a visit from their father – still on the wanted list as a deserter, wily old Charlie Kray had the nerve to bluff his way to see them by pretending to be their uncle – the only event of importance was the arrival in the guardroom of a grey-faced, battered-looking thief from Mile End who had been drafted to the Fusiliers straight from a four-year sentence at Portland Borstal. He introduced himself as Dickie Morgan. One of five sons of an Australian sailor father and part-German mother, he had begun his criminal career at eight by stealing from the orthodox Jews of Whitechapel who paid him a halfpenny a time to light the gas for them during the Sabbath. He had been in and out of approved schools and Borstals ever since and had a triangular dent just below the hairline where he had smashed his skull falling into a chalk quarry escaping from Ardale Approved School.

Dickie Morgan was the first of an invaluable set of criminal acquaintances the army would introduce to the twins in the months to come. His twisted smile, his gaol humour, his habitual-criminal's cynicism made a particular impression on them. For like the twins, he lived in a world of his own – in which the chief aim was to grab and spend as much as possible before the next inevitable spell inside. Already life had taught him a philosophy which matched the conclusions the twins were reaching on their own account.

'Ordinary straight life's just not for the likes of us. That's why we're in a separate world. You see, we get bored with most of the stupid things straight people seem to enjoy, when they could be out drinking or doing a spot of villainy. What's the best thing in life? Getting money. And after that? Spending it.'

A week later, when the twins had been released from the guardroom and went on the run the second time, Richard Morgan went with them. And this time they employed a little more finesse.

* * *

In their first escape they had been acting out of sheer bravado. Now, thanks to Morgan, they had a clearer idea of what they wanted. Dickie Morgan didn't merely talk and dream about the 'separate world' of the habitual criminal. He lived in it, and the twins were swift to see its possibilities.

The Morgan house in Clinton Road – one of a warren of grey little terraces coiling away from the western end of London Docks – was something the twins had never really known before: a truly extraordinary household. The barrel-chested sailor father had just been sentenced for his part in a raid on the warehouse where he was night-watchman. 'Chunky' the elder brother, who was in Parkhurst Gaol, had made a name for himself in a riot at Portland Borstal organized by an immensely strong young giant from Hackney called Frank Mitchell. And one of the younger brothers was already serving his apprenticeship in Borstal.

Somehow in the midst of all this, with her straight hair, her full-moon spectacles and her text of 'Bless this House' on the kitchen wall, stood the eternally worried, uncomplaining figure of Richard Morgan's mother, bringing up the two youngest boys, and cooking eggs and bacon for the unceasing traffic of 'friends on the run' who made for Clinton Road, snatched a few hours' sleep on the front-room sofa, and dodged off over the garden wall before the police knocked on the door as dawn was breaking.

At Vallance Road the twins' actual home-life had been curiously sheltered, and Violet and her parents were an influence against dishonesty. The Lees were 'respectable'. Here it was different, and at Clinton Road the twins found what they had always wanted – lawlessness and adventure. And as fellow deserters and friends of a youthful old lag like Richard Morgan, they had a guide to the exclusive and caste-ridden maquis of petty East London criminals.

Previously as dedicated young professional boxers they had been ascetic to a degree – non-smoking and -drinking and continuing to get up at six each morning for their training runs almost until the day they entered the army. Overnight this went. For the first time in their lives they smoked and drank. Instead of training spins and early nights they adopted thieves' hours, out most of the night and cat-napping during the day. And they made their first actual money out of crime – a few pounds which was their share from a raid on a Clerkenwell dress wholesaler when they joined forces with an old-time thief from Mile End and got away with seven rolls of cloth.

And just as Morgan introduced them to the criminals of Mile End, so they enjoyed taking him surreptitiously to the places where they were known. The fantasy of being wanted criminals on the run gripped them all, particularly Ronnie, who was to play the same game with spectacular variations in years to come.

Now that the police were after them in earnest, they could play out this fantasy for all it was worth; the two of them, alone, uncaring, wanted by a society they despised yet always able to survive, fight back, and vanish like the Scarlet Pimpernel himself.

They always had been natural actors – particularly Ronnie, who had inherited his showman's instincts from Grandfather Lee, and the first night they took Dickie to the Royal Ballroom at Tottenham they had the role they wanted.

The Royal is still one place in the East End where the young can meet, pick each other up and show off with impunity. A great barn of a place off the Kingsland Road, with brass and mahogany swing doors, and a façade that looks like mouldy marzipan, it usually boasts two separate bands, and the noise inside is deafening. In early evening it is a ballroom pure and simple, but when the pubs close it becomes something more. The noise increases, coloured spotlights flicker high above the crowd, and on hot, early summer nights, the Royal becomes a living showcase of the East End. In the days when the Kray twins were there, it was also a good place for fights.

The girls and the dancing were unimportant, except for background and the sense of occasion they gave the place. The crowd was the sort of audience the twins enjoyed, and the real attraction of the Royal was as a place where the local tearaways could come 'on show'. It was the tribal proving ground, where the self-appointed 'rulers' of the neighbourhood would make their ritual appearance like the young bloods of some primitive society. And just as in a primitive society, the entry of someone from another territory into the group of sharp-eyed youths around the bar carried inevitable overtones of challenge.

But the night the twins took Dickie there, none of the wild young men of Tottenham was in the mood to pick a fight.

Three brothers – all good amateur boxers – led the reigning local gang of Tottenham, and were in the bar. They knew the twins and understood that their appearance was a challenge – particularly when everybody knew they were absent from the army. There were a tense few minutes as the twins and the Tottenham gang sized each other up. Then the local gang quietly surrendered. One of the boxers offered the twins a drink, asked how they were doing, and offered to lend them a fiver – which Ronnie grudgingly accepted. Dickie was impressed. He and the twins remained for half an hour, drinking at the Tottenham gang's expense, then caught a bus to Clinton Road, feeling they had won a useful victory – and that their great adventure was progressing.

It continued for the next fortnight. A fourth member joined their team of young escapers – a wild boy on the run from Rochester Borstal. The twins already had a knack of gathering people round them in the most unlikely situations, and at the boy's suggestion they decided it was time for a little expedition. Unlike Dickie and the twins, the boy could drive, so they stole a car, and drove to Southend for a holiday. For a few hours they enjoyed themselves and took a lot of trouble choosing a rude post-card which they posted to their CO at the Tower, saying, 'Having a good time. Best of luck. Ron, Reg and Dick.'

The twins were always rather proud of this and Reggie insisted, 'The CO had a sense of humour and put the card on the board in the officers' mess.' But once they had made their little gesture, what else was there to do in Southend? Drink. Visit the cinema. Walk along the pier. With Southend full of ordinary straight people having their boring summer holidays it was no place for the twins, so they slept the night in the car then drove back to the one place where they could be happy and where they were certain to be picked up in the end – Bethnal Green. They were getting bored – and for the twins, boredom was worse than the army or the Law or any rival gang.

A few more visits to the Royal, one of which ended with a brawl in which the twins gave Morgan an exhibition of bar-fighting he was never to forget. A couple of attempts, neither successful, to steal from lorries parked up for the night on the bomb-sites along the Commercial Road. But petty thieving wasn't the twins' style at all, and their hearts weren't in it. All that really mattered was the next round in their running battle with the Fusiliers. They were ready for the fray. So when a keen young constable called Fisher recognized them in a Mile End caff, they came along without a murmur. It was a relief to have something to fight against once more.

Back in the Tower the detention cells in the Waterloo Building almost seemed like home. The Commanding Officer gave them a stiffer sentence and a stronger warning. It was boring for him and boring for the twins, but until they decided to settle down and soldier, this absurd cat-and-mouse game would continue.

For the rest of early summer, the pattern of escape, recapture and imprisonment continued. And just occasionally it looked as if the twins would settle down and soldier. Once they got as far as the .303 range at Purfleet where both proved unusually bad shots. When they beat up a sergeant who had tried teaching them a lesson on his own account, the CO decided to separate the twins. Reggie was sent to the punishment cells at Purfleet and Ronnie to the tender mercies of Wellington Guards Barracks.

It did no good. They were worse parted than together. At Purfleet Reggie spent his time perfecting his left hook on a stream of obligingly aggressive NCOs until he was left alone. Ronnie among the Guards found fewer opportunities for self-expression, weeded the barrack square and resorted to his earliest form of protest – refusing to shave or wear a uniform.

The month they spent together after this at Colchester military detention barracks marked the turning point of their military career. Until then, with an optimism that does them credit, the Fusiliers had clung to the belief that the twins were redeemable private soldier material. Now it was plain they never would be, and this month at Colchester was to bring them face to face with some of the toughest delinquents in the army and strengthened their resolve to get out of the army the hard way. It was now too that they began forming rather more precise ideas about their own future when they were discharged. Reggie said:

'I can remember discussing armed robbery seriously with someone for the first time at Colchester. You see, by then, Ron and I had decided that when we came out we wanted the good life and that there was only one way to get it.'

'The Good Life' – but where was it? When they had served their month at Colchester, they were back together at the Tower, and nothing was easier than to forget about the army, change into a jacket and an old pair of trousers and slip out through the Shrewsbury Gate among the tourists any afternoon. Which, very soon, they did and faithful grey-faced Dickie Morgan followed them.

From Tower Hill you can turn right into Cable Street, left up Backchurch Lane and you find yourself in Whitechapel. It was tempting, but this time the twins had no wish to be caught, and instead of turning right at the top of Tower Hill, they went left, down through the City and into the West End where their friends from Colchester had told them 'the Good Life' was waiting for them. They had been told that, in the West, anyone prepared to fight could make himself an easy living. There were mugs there to be conned, ponces to be preyed on, gambling clubs waiting to be tapped, armed robberies to be executed. Provided you weren't fussy there were no limits in this villains' Eldorado – and the twins were not feeling particularly fussy now.

Their only problem was that this particular Eldorado was already occupied. In the 1950s the whole West End had been neatly tied up by that pair of self-styled 'Kings of the Underworld', Mr Jack 'Spot' Comer, and Mr Billy Hill. Very little happened here without their knowledge and assent and the primary interest of this double monarchy lay in the prevention of the sort of high Chicago-style villainy the twins had set their hearts on. As they soon found out, this tattered pair of eighteen-year-old army absentees had as much chance of horning in on the rich pastures of West End crime as of joining the Stock Exchange.

This hardly seemed to matter at the time. Confident of their talents and modest enough to know they had a lot to learn, the Kray twins understood that time was on their side and they were prepared to wait. In the meantime they soon found themselves one part of the West End where they were accepted and appreciated and *could* make their presence undeniably felt.

* * *

In the early fifties a large hotel off Piccadilly Circus was leading one of the strangest double lives of any eating place in London.

During the day the tea-rooms and the downstairs restaurants with their Odeon-style décor and absolute respectability were a great place for children's teas and maiden-ladies' outings with the most reliable poached egg in Central London.

But around midnight with the aunts and school children safely in their beds, their places in the Lloyd-Loom chairs would be taken by a very different clientele. And by one o'clock the downstairs tea-room, which stayed open through the night, was transformed into an informal club – part sanctuary, part labour exchange – for half the petty thieves and criminals in London.

'A regular den of thieves,' is how one of the regulars remembers it. It was certainly convenient, and cheap – and close to all the places where criminals could work.

It was not the place for the upper echelons of crime. They had more exclusive social territory. But in the old days, after midnight in the big downstairs lounge of the hotel, one saw the social side of West End crime – the small-time fences and ponces, the informers and thieves and pickpockets, the villains and the bouncers who required work or a chat and the society of their own kind. This was where the twins were brought by Dickie Morgan, and they soon began to make their mark on this nocturnal criminal society.

Almost everyone who met them now agrees there was a strange air of innocence about them which marked them out from other villains round about them. Some thought them shy. They were extraordinarily polite to anyone older who took the trouble to talk to them. They never bragged, were never loud-mouthed, never seemed to swear. Among a race of almost universal gamblers they never gambled. Among womanizers and ponces they showed no interest in women. Among hard-drinkers they were never drunk.

Most of the time they would just sit – slightly apart from everybody else – usually silent and impassive, watching and listening to what went on. Several who knew them now remark upon their eyes. 'There was something about them that bored right through you, especially if you were lying to them. You always felt they knew.'

They also had an air of weirdness and danger, which everybody noticed from the start. Some say they cultivated this quite consciously. Certainly they did so later. Natural actors that they were, they picked up all the tricks of instilling fear with an economy of effort and projecting their presence to maximum effect. But what distinguished them even now from all the other violent characters around them, is that they had an extraordinary presence to project.

It remains something of a mystery. Part of it was due to their behaviour as identical twins. With their telepathy and uncanny similarity their effect was literally double that of a normal individual, and this certainly explains much of their effectiveness. So does their imperviousness to pain and danger. They were so fit and vicious that they had already perfected a technique of synchronized and ruthless combat which rendered them invulnerable as long as they stayed together.

But there was something else. 'They were,' says one old villain who came up against them shortly afterwards, 'a thoroughly evil pair of bastards.' And from now on in their story, the idea continually recurs that they were uniquely and positively 'evil'.

Largely because of this the twins were accepted as true villains from the start. Without knowing exactly why, older and more experienced thugs were wary of them. One or two who weren't were dealt with efficiently and unemotionally, but these were 'unimportant nobodies' – 'liberty-takers' who hadn't the good sense to understand the twins for what they were. There was an old wrestler, working as a doorman at a club in Berwick Street, who had the stupidity to refer to the twins as 'boys' and whose jaw was nearly broken by a punch that sent all sixteen stone of him down the stairs to the men's room.

People who befriended them were shrewder. 'You never knew who you'd be needing next time. You weren't getting any tougher or any younger and it was common sense to keep on the right side of a pair of up-and-coming youngsters like the twins.'

One of the first freelance villains to befriend the twins during their Piccadilly days was Tommy Smithson from Hackney – gambler, tearaway and non-caring fighting man, he remained one of the twins' extremely few real-life heroes. Smithson was the supreme non-carer of the London gang-world. A loner, too independent and irresponsible to accept the authority of the Spot–Hill kingship, he went through life with a masochistic desperation never to give in to anyone. A smallish man and an indifferent fighter, he could be rash to the point of lunacy. His lean, dark face cut to ribbons, he would fight and lose and go on fighting. He was free with his money, off-hand with his women, game to the last and unimpressed by anything the 'straight' world values.

That summer he was running a snooker hall and illicit gambling club above a restaurant in Archer Street, Soho. When he met the twins he offered them the hospitality of his club, and they spent a few nights sleeping on the snooker tables when the last customers had gone.

A few months later Smithson was slashed and left for dead in Regent's Park at three in the morning by a gang he had had the rashness to challenge. Somehow he survived, refused to name his assailants, and swathed in bandages, his right arm paralysed, was back in his snooker hall before the week was out. He finally died of gunshot wounds in 1958 after a Maltese fired a shotgun into his stomach from such close range that not even Smithson could survive. Years later, Reg Kray was to describe his death in a short obituary of his own.

'As he was dying he followed his enemy to the street

door where he collapsed and died. This last effort on Smithson's part was typical. He always fought on until he died. Ron and I went to his funeral, for we admired him.'

Violent and early death would be the fate of many of the villains the twins befriended now. One was Tony Mulla, another East Ender of Greek and German descent, a big good-looking psychopath given to outbursts of wild rage, and fits of weeping and self-pity. When the twins met him in 1952 his state of mind had hardly been improved by having had his flat at the Elephant and Castle broken into at three in the morning by members of the same gang Smithson challenged. Mulla was in bed with his wife. Realizing his visitors meant business and that if he resisted his wife certainly would be hurt, he begged them to leave his face and his wife alone. They agreed and sliced him up the back with cut-throat razors.

Mulla always had a devoted friend – a large, not over-intelligent ex-boxer from Tottenham called Melvin. In the late fifties Mulla and Melvin were to stage a come-back by taking over a number of the new strip clubs in Soho, and suddenly becoming rich. Then at the height of their success, Mulla and Melvin had the sort of sudden, pointless disagreement such criminals are always prone to. Mulla insulted Melvin. Melvin shot Mulla through the head and when he realized what he had done, turned his gun on himself.

Doomed, desperate men like Mulla, Smithson and Melvin made a great impression on the Kray twins and as much as they ever modelled themselves on anyone they probably did on them. But these non-caring villains were by no means the only people the twins met now who were to influence their future. There were also smarter, cannier men who were in an altogether different league, men like Bobby Ramsey, with his black coat, pig-skin gloves and Irish profile, who had been associated with one of Billy Hill's less successful ventures in South Africa and was still in close touch with the man who was to tell an Old Bailey jury – 'I am the King of the Underworld.' The Kray twins were to hear from Mr Ramsey later.

Summer turned to autumn and the twins were still seeking the elusive 'Good Life' – and still on the run from the Fusiliers.

They weren't bored any longer. They had friends, and were getting quite a reputation.

For a while they even took a room – in a condemned tenement block in Finsbury Park – rat-infested, uncarpeted, the ceiling down, with a wash-stand and an ancient brass double bed where they would sleep together. When they felt it was time to move they followed their father's example and, feeling safer in that foreign country that lay 'across the water', they crossed the Thames and spent the next few weeks in Peckham. Among the drearier late-Victorian London suburbs, Peckham was hardly Kray country, but it served its purpose. The police weren't looking for them here and they picked up one more item of practical information now that produced dividends in the years to come. For want of anywhere to go they spent several evenings in a snooker hall and grew quite enthusiastic about the game. Not as players. It was the economics of the game that interested them, and how the hall proprietors protected themselves against trouble. Billiard-table cloths were vulnerable to wilful damage. They would rip quite easily.

The snow came early that year, and it proved their undoing. They had nowhere warm to go except back to Vallance Road. But Sergeant Silvers from Bethnal Green Police Station spotted them at once. He was round with a squad car before breakfast and had a job waking the twins before taking them back to the station.

Another period in the guardroom. Another lecture from an officer on the lines of 'I hope you've learned your lesson' – which they had, of course, except that it wasn't the one the army wanted and the twins escaped again in time for Christmas.

They drifted back to Mile End and on Christmas Eve were sitting in the Red Caff at about nine o'clock in the evening. Normally they would have been more careful, but a thick fog had come up from the river and no one was likely to be out on such a night. No one, except the police who were beginning to take an interest in the will-o'-the-wisp lives of the Kray twins, and in from the fog came Police Constable Fisher who had arrested them six months earlier.

It was all quite amiable. The twins asked if he'd like a cup of tea, but he refused politely. Then Ronnie said that seeing it was Christmas and he was an understanding chap couldn't he forget he'd seen them and let them have Christmas Day at home with their old mother if they gave their word to give themselves up on Boxing Day. Police Constable Fisher was sorry but Christmas was one thing – duty another.

They promised to come quietly, but there was just one thing Reggie would like to tell Police Constable Fisher if he'd come outside. The constable agreed, and as Reggie stood talking to him Ronnie shoved him from behind and sent him sprawling across the pavement. By the time he was back on his feet the twins were away into the fog.

The twins missed their Christmas dinner back at Vallance Road, and were caught a few weeks later. They were tried for assaulting the police.

Constable Fisher was commended by the magistrate and received the princely sum of seven shillings and sixpence, though whether as reward for zeal or compensation for discomfort was never made clear. And the twins received a month apiece in Wormwood Scrubs, along with their picture in the *East London Advertiser* and the headline, 'Kray Brothers beat up PC.' It was fame of a sort, a testimonial to their rising status, and the newspaper cutting and the photograph duly found their way into the cuttings book at Vallance Road, along with their boxing photographs and the reports of earlier misdemeanours. Boxing or crime, it scarcely mattered. They were on their way, their name was getting known. From nobodies they were emerging into somebodies.

As the twins were the first to admit, they had been lucky over their month's sentence; and after life on the run, it was certainly no hardship. They were together on the same landing and saw each other during the day at exercise and in the prison workshops. Equally important, they were accepted as *ex officio* members of the small coterie of veteran professional criminals who form the top layer of the unofficial gaol élite – the men the warders are wary of and tend to leave alone, the ones with the extra tobacco and connections with the prison grapevine. The 'hard nuts who can get things done'.

This was an achievement, for they were barely nineteen and still had no genuine criminal record. What they did have was that presence which had so impressed the villains of the West and which made old lags accept them as 'their own kind'. And so the month in Wormwood Scrubs, far from being wasted time, was one more step up the criminal social register, widening still further the circle of names and faces on which the future of the twins would finally depend. More than with most careers, professional crime depends on knowing people – what they're worth, how far they can be relied on, and what they've done. The twins possessed a knack for remembering such details.

After their month in Wormwood Scrubs the twins were ready for their criminal life to come. There was not the faintest chance of their ever turning into soldiers, and the sooner the army was rid of them the better. But army regulations made it necessary that before they could be dishonourably discharged, they had to be tried and punished. The twins enjoyed this. They were kept awaiting trial in the guardroom of Howe Barracks, Canterbury, and made the most of their situation as private soldiers under close arrest awaiting a court-martial.

The twins were brought to Canterbury from Wormwood Scrubs. They arrived by train, handcuffed together, and passed the time by frequently asking the guard to let them use the lavatory, so that one twin had to stand in the corridor with his handcuffed arm around the door as the other twin relieved himself. The absurdity of this put them in good spirits and when they reached the guardroom they were greeted by an old friend – fellow Fusilier Richard Morgan, also under close arrest and awaiting court-martial. The three months they spent with him as the army prepared the details of their trial became a sort of three-man saturnalia, a holiday from the restraints of discipline and the worry of staying on the run. They had nothing to lose now and Ron explained how they turned all their ingenuity against authority.

'We did everything we could think of that would go against the army and they ended up a bit afraid of us. It was funny, but there seemed to be nothing we couldn't do if we felt like it. I started pretending to be a bit barmy – wouldn't shave or else shaved only half my face, and we treated most of the NCOs like pigs. Not that we really wanted to. Some of them were nice enough chaps. But if ever people like that think you're frightened of them they've got you where they want you. It was them or us. If we'd given in they'd have kept us in the army for ever.'

It was a performance once again, and a calculated one. The twins were natural actors, with a cockney underdog's instinct for those points where authority is particularly ridiculous. During the weeks at Canterbury they soon dominated the guardroom by losing all restraint when anyone attempted to control them. The result was a charade in which they acted out their secret inner life, with all its violence and conflict, its cruelty and cunning and anti-social humour. It also showed a touch of real madness, for Ronnie had a knack of appearing mentally unbalanced.

Less than three years later the act became reality when Ronnie would be certified insane.

It was not only Ronnie's madness which had its first rehearsal in this theatre of the absurd which the twins staged in the Canterbury guardroom. Almost everything which happened to them later was acted out in this military farce. At the time they thought it something of a joke. In retrospect it has a distinct touch of the macabre.

Scene one was a straightforward return to childhood with its wildest tantrums and uncontrolled rebellion – food thrown against walls and dishes smashed. A guard who tried stopping them was knocked against the wall. Shouts, screams, singing, hammering on cell doors. Uniforms were taken off and cut to pieces, bedding thrown around. By the end of the first day the twins had clearly made the point that they were uncontrolled and uncontrollable and safest left alone.

Scene two followed. Authority had to be slapped down as effectively as possible: which happened when the colour sergeant arrived to take charge of the situation. An immaculately turned out, not over-imaginative, regular soldier, he entered the guardroom from parade complete with his medals and scarlet sash, determined to take no more nonsense from three young hooligans. He had spoken perhaps six words to them when the latrine bucket was thrown over him. No one tried reading King's Rules and Regulations to the twins again.

Orders were given that they were to be more closely guarded than ever, and strictly confined to the caged-off area behind the guardroom. The twins seemed unconcerned but during the morning Private Ronald Kray did ask for a glass of water. Taking no chances the guard handed it through the bars; as he did this Private Reginald Kray produced a pair of military handcuffs he had borrowed several days before and snapped them around the guard's wrist and the bar of the cage. It took an hour to cut him loose.

Then they staged a protest against the closeness of their new confinement by burning their bedding and their uniforms. The fire hoses were turned on them but once again they didn't care, and next day the twins found a way on to the guardhouse roof where they sat most of the morning, shouting and singing and improvising tunes on a mouth-organ. By now the provost corporal had somehow got on good terms with them, and when all else failed he was able to persuade them down. But they had established what they wanted. They were invulnerable, they were the centre of attention, and a sort of truce ensued between the twins and the authorities. An uneasy truce, for Ronnie kept up his role of violence and madness. He would refuse to eat. He shaved only one side of his face. He would sit apparently brooding for hours on end and then erupt in a torrent of abuse and violence, throwing everything he could around his cell.

When Violet came to visit them, the guard offered her a cup of tea. Ronnie took it, tasted it and threw it against the wall shouting at the guard never to dare offer his mother such a filthy cup of tea again.

One can't help feeling that there must have been a touch of masochism in the way the guardroom staff at Canterbury left themselves so constantly exposed to the depredations of the twins. For somehow, the key to the NAAFI was left around in reach of Reggie Kray one night after the guard had locked it up as required in standing orders. It was the only key in existence, and when it couldn't be found the door finally had to be broken in.

And so it went on for the three months the Kray twins were awaiting their court-martial, and this period finally confirmed certain conclusions they had formed about life in general. If you are weak and worry about others you go to the wall. If you are tough and totally uncaring, you become invulnerable.

A few of the Canterbury staff did still try subduing them, including a guard corporal who set out to beat them on their own terms. He was a big man and a powerful fighter and when one of the twins called him something particularly insulting he went into their cell to teach them a lesson. Five minutes later he was standing tied to the pillar in the centre of the guardroom with the belt from his own trousers while Morgan and the twins spread a ring of lighted newspapers round him and performed an Indian war-dance until the rest of the guard arrived to drive them back into their cells.

So much for direct action.

A more effective method of controlling them was traditional upper-class disdain. The best example of this was provided by the adjutant, a tall languid cavalry captain, an ex-prisoner of the Japanese, who according to Morgan failed to rise to the three young hooligans.

'He was very much the old school tie – Eton and Sandhurst and all that. And when they tried shouting at him, and carrying on he just stood there and said, "I know perfectly well what you're up to and it's all right by me. But for God's sake, *do* stop making such a bloody row. You'll frighten the horses."'

Surprisingly this worked, and the twins did shut up. For one of the East End attitudes they had inherited was an old-fashioned respect for a gentleman. In the old East End there had always been affinities between the lower-class tearaway and the upper-class bounder. The true cockney tended to despise the respectable middle classes with their money and their moralizing. The twins themselves possessed an exaggerated hatred of middle-class respectability, but they also had a sort of envious respect for anyone like the adjutant who conformed to their image of what an upper-class man of action should be. It tied in with their admiration for Lawrence of Arabia and Gordon of Khartoum, and as someone who grew up with the twins explained, 'The one thing they would really have liked to be was a pair of genuine English gentlemen.'

The adjutant apart, there was one other person who

could more or less control them in the guardroom. This was the provost corporal, an easy-going, old campaigner who had dealt with enough tough customers in his time to know what he was up against. He never tried to order them about, and never lost his temper. He was kind and tolerant and adopted the line that he had a job to do and that if they would just remember this, life would be simpler for all concerned. On the whole this worked. Nothing else did.

For with the corporal and the adjutant away, the Kray twins established such a reign of terror and ridicule in the guardroom that they were practically invulnerable. They had all the money they needed. They did as they liked, and sometimes even managed to persuade the daytime guard to take them to a nearby pub for a drink. They presented an extraordinary sight, this pair of unkempt prisoners, with their dark identical faces, Ron with a walking stick and a half-shaven chin, as they walked into the saloon bar, bought the guard a drink and then trailed solemnly back to their cells.

They could have escaped almost any time, but for more than a month resisted the temptation, mainly because they realized that a further period on the run would simply put back their court-martial and the date of eventual discharge. But just before Easter the idea of a few days back in the East End became too strong to resist, especially as most of the camp seemed to be off on Easter leave. So they awarded themselves some leave as well. The Thursday morning before Easter the guard were surprised to see that Ron had finally shaved and that the twins and Morgan were actually looking quite smart for a change.

'Going anywhere?' asked one of the guard.

'Yes, home.'

For once they were not joking.

They had planned it rather well, and once again relied on that dapper old soldier and friend of the family, Harry Hopwood. The previous Sunday he had visited them and fixed a spot where he would leave a van near the main gates of the camp. Neither Morgan nor the twins could drive, but there was another prisoner in the guardroom who could: they arranged to take him with them.

Reg planned what would happen then. Ron and Dickie Morgan would ask to go to the lavatory. This involved a guard unlocking the cage, accompanying them to the ablutions and then bringing them back. This was the signal for action, and as the guard was fumbling with the keys Reg went to hit him and Ron put a necklock on him from behind. It was done so swiftly and silently that for several seconds the guard in the main room beyond had no idea what was happening and this delay allowed Dickie Morgan to get the keys from the guard and unlock the main gate to the guardroom.

From there it was each man for himself. The rest of the men in the guardroom had been playing cards and were unprepared for the whirlwind that burst in on them. A brief scuffle and a lot of shouting as the guardroom table was turned over: then the door was open and four soldiers were scurrying through the main gate with several of the guard in hot pursuit.

Then things started to go wrong. When planning the escape, Reg had not counted on pursuit. There was more shouting, and more joined in the chase. Ron and Dickie Morgan were out of training and were caught up with just past the gate. There was a fight and although they both broke free, they made a serious mistake. Hopwood had left the van on the left of the main gates, but in the confusion they went right – and ended up in Canterbury station goods yard. Here they played hide-and-seek between the shunting wagons as they dodged the guard. Then, more by luck than judgement, they escaped, clambered up a wall, waded a river, and threw off their pursuers.

Finally they found a parked coal lorry – which they commandeered. Their driver friend managed to start it up, and the four bedraggled soldiers were off on the road to

London. They were in high spirits as they thought of Bethnal Green, but a few miles out of Canterbury the lorry started showing signs of acute mechanical distress. It began slowing down. Steam billowed from the bonnet – and it stopped.

By now it was getting dark. They had no money and no transport. They were hungry and soaking wet. The police must have been alerted for them by now. If they stopped anywhere they were finished and their best hope was to get to London where there were friends and money and they could disappear for as long as they wanted. But London was sixty miles away.

'So we started walking and running, jumping in hedges to hide every time we saw headlights approaching. Dickie's feet were killing him, as he was lazy at the best of times, but Ron and I shouted encouragement and insults at him. We were used to walking from the days when we bought old clothes for a living and were knocking on doors all day, so it wasn't too bad for us.'

They continued the forced march for most of that night, with their clothes drying on them as they walked and Morgan's feet getting worse. Just before daybreak as they came limping into Eltham, three motor-cycle police were there to greet them.

'We were dead beat and gave up without a fight. We enjoyed a cup of tea at Eltham Police Station and a spot of sleep until the army escort arrived to take us back to the guardhouse to await court-martial for various offences. They never bothered to charge us with all the offences we had committed while we had been inside.'

The army had had enough of the Kray twins. The ritual of trial and punishment had to be played out, but it was something of a farce. By now there were enough charges on the book to have put the twins away for five years, but there was little point. The army would have to clothe them, feed them, guard them and at the end of it all the twins would be as far from soldiering as ever.

So when the court-martial was held on 11 June 1953, it was not so much a trial as an armistice between the army and the Krays. The prosecution officer confined himself to the fact that they had struck an NCO in the course of duty, had gone absent without leave and 'committed conduct prejudicial to good order and discipline'. The twins pleaded guilty, and the verdict was unanimous. Private Reginald Kray and Private Ronald Kray were to be confined to nine months' imprisonment at the army prison at Shepton Mallet and then ignominiously dismissed the service.

So the battle was over and the twins had won – after a fashion. The following nine months passed easily enough. They had no need to fight the army any more. The routine at Shepton Mallet proved no great hardship. Their parents and their brother Charlie visited regularly and although they were confined to their cells at night, much of the day passed in physical training and team games so that both could get back into peak physical condition. Morgan, who was with them, found the food uneatable. The twins didn't seem to notice.

By now they had both decided on their future. They knew their strength and they had learned a lot. After their release they would go all out to find that elusive something they had always wanted.

During these final months in prison they discussed their future life a lot and completed a further stage in the education thanks to which they hoped to reach it. For here at 'the Mallet' was a selection of the most promising and up-and-coming young criminals in the country. Previously the twins' criminal acquaintanceship had been confined to London. Anyone who was not a Londoner was dismissed as a 'foreigner' or a 'swede'.

But at Shepton Mallet this narrow-mindedness was rapidly dispelled. Here were young gangsters from the

Gorbals and the docklands of Cardiff, thugs from Liverpool, hooligans from Belfast. Military prison was a useful meeting ground and they soon found how much they had in common – so much indeed that in the years to come the Krays were to show a keen awareness of the nationwide possibilities of organized crime. Friendships made now were kept in good repair for many years to come, and the twins had an uncanny flair for never forgetting a face.

THREE

The Billiard Hall

The place had known much better days. All that remained of them now was the name – 'The Regal' – a relic of its grandiose beginnings as a cinema. During the snooker boom of the thirties The Regal in Eric Street was converted to a fourteen-table billiard hall. Now, like most of this part of Mile End, it seemed to have lost heart. Unpainted and unloved, it had become a target for the local small-time gangs who met here, fought here and tried cadging money from the manager. The insurance companies were wary of insuring it. There were rumours of its closing down.

These rumours reached the twins. Since they had left the army they had time on their hands and they paid the hall a visit. They felt at home at once. Reggie found someone to play snooker with. Ronnie, who disliked all games without exception, sat. He sat there all morning. There was no charge for sitting at The Regal. Next day the twins were there again. Within a week their friends knew this was where to find them. This suited them. They had always felt they needed a place of their own.

Around this time the violence at The Regal suddenly increased. The twins appeared to have no part in it, but there was trouble nearly every night. Tables were ripped. There were anonymous threats to burn the place down. Fireworks exploded. The manager decided he had had enough, and the twins made an offer to the owners of £5 a week to take The Regal over. The day their offer was accepted, the violence stopped as mysteriously as it had started.

For their weekly fiver the Kray twins became the legal tenants of the Regal Billiard Hall. They had to run the tables, the refreshment bar and keep the place in order. In return they had the takings from the tables. Soon these amounted to a tidy sum, for the twins showed a flair for business. Tables were brushed each morning. Reggie repainted the refreshment bar. The hall was open day and night. For the first time for years it began to show a profit. The Regal was becoming popular again.

People were always dropping in to see the twins – friends they had known from the army, men freshly out of prison who had been given their address, some of the local criminals, tough teenage boys from Mile End out for a night's excitement. The Kray twins' reputation had got round and from the very start they were the real attraction of the billiard hall. As one of their old friends says, 'Wherever that pair went, something would always happen. And if you missed a night at the old Regal, you'd be worrying all the time about what was going on without you. Next morning somebody'd be sure to say – "You should have been there last night. The things the twins got up to." Then you'd feel real choked for missing out.'

Sometimes it would simply be a fight. In these early days there were still people who would challenge one or other of the twins to a stand-up battle, like the old villain from the West End who kept calling Reggie 'son'. Reggie broke his jaw. Or like the Maltese gang who called demanding protection money from the hall's new management. The twins went after them with cutlasses. Violence was certainly important as a source of sheer excitement, but it was by no means all the twins could offer their admirers.

What they wanted from the hall was a headquarters, and like their grandfather, Cannonball Lee, the old music-hall performer, they both had a touch of the impresario about them. They enjoyed having people round them, and were true cockneys with their appetite for people, drink and scandal. They always seemed to have the latest piece of news from the underworld or to bring in some unexpected guest. Failing this, they livened things up with one of their practical jokes. 'Ronnie went for anything unusual. He found a giant from a circus once and brought him along for an evening. We got him drunk. Ron liked midgets too. One night he brought along a donkey with a straw hat. He said he was teaching him to talk.'

Now he had found his audience, Ronnie could start developing the self he dreamed of. For years he had read everything he could about Capone and the Chicago gangsters. He started dressing gangster-style – discreet, dark, double-breasted suit, tight knotted tie and shoulder-padded overcoat. 'I like conservative clothes,' he used to say. 'I can't stand anybody flash.' Despite this, he was developing his own small vanities and getting quite a taste for jewellery – a large gold ring, a gold bracelet watch and diamond cuff-links.

In the early evening he would be at the billiard hall playing his favourite part of ward boss organizing henchmen from some down-town poolroom. He had his private chair and used to sit facing the door and watching as the regulars arrived. As the play started lights would flicker on above the tables, leaving the remainder of the hall in shadow. 'Ron liked the atmosphere just like a den of thieves. He loved a lot of smoke and noise and people. He used to hand out cigarettes and say, "Smoke up. There's not enough smoke in here."'

Then, when the hall was full and play was going on at all the tables, with the air thick as any Limehouse fog, he would be satisfied. He would lean back slowly in his chair, smiling to himself, knowing quite well that everybody in the hall was waiting. He always kept them guessing for a while, calling now one and now another of the boys who hovered round him. He was beginning to talk to them like a screen gangster, muttering a few words over a cigarette as he stared into space. Then he lapsed into silence. These silences soon got him known as a deep one, an unpredictable leader. 'Always keep people guessing. Never treat them the same twice running,' an old West End gang leader told him once.

People were becoming slightly wary of the twins. One of their oldest friends, who knew them long before the army, noticed a change in them. 'I began to see that I could only go so far with them, and however friendly they were being, they seemed to keep themselves that little bit apart. Neither of them liked being touched. Put your hand on Reggie's shoulder and you'd feel him wince. You wouldn't do it twice.'

But it was Ronnie people really feared: 'We was all scared of him, to tell the truth – not just because of what he could get up to, but because of what he knew. He had a funny way of looking at you and yet not looking at you that always made you think he was reading your mind.'

Sometimes he spent the evening brooding in his chair and left early. At other times he decided he was drinking and picked a dozen hangers-on to go with him. 'It was always a bit of an event going to a pub with the twins. They used to like a crowded pub with a good singer and a lot of talent and perhaps the chance of trouble. When you went in with them people would stop talking and make room for you at the bar. We used to like that.' And sometimes at the billiard hall Ronnie would make his favourite announcement – 'Well, we've decided on a little row with so-and-so tonight. Who's for and who's against?'

It would be like a raiding-party with everyone bringing out his favourite weapon and piling into ancient battered cars outside the hall. The twins were always in the lead and would usually keep the destination secret. 'It was really all a bit of a lark. Sort of an outing. But it was a funny thing – wherever we went, to a pub or dance hall or another club, there was always trouble.' As for the fighting, friends of the twins insist that this was always deadly serious. 'They were a wicked couple really. They were frightened of no one and loved every minute of it. Something got into them once a fight started, and you could see they enjoyed their bit of violence, really enjoyed it. If I was cutting somebody or putting the boot in, I'd usually hold back a bit – never the twins though. If you watched their faces while they did it, you'd see real hate. They always went the limit.'

At this stage there was no clear purpose to those nightly gatherings. But gradually, behind the fooling, boozing and aimless brawling of this one small cockney gang, the outlines of something bigger started to appear. The gang began to change.

The key to this change lay in the twins and their power as fighters. They were not particularly big men. Ronnie was 5 feet 10 inches, Reggie half an inch shorter. Reggie tipped the scales at eleven stone, Ronnie at twelve and a half. Many of their fights were with much larger men, yet in the several hundred bar brawls, woundings, shootings, and punch-ups they were involved in, they never once appear to have come off second best. Neither was shot or cut or damaged seriously.

Both were abnormally tough; their teenage boxing training had left them strong in the arms and shoulders, and taught them both the precise use of their fists. They needed little sleep. Ronnie is reputed to have drunk fifty-five brown ales in one night at the billiard hall and carried on next day as usual. From the start they made it clear that they intended to become professionals of violence. They had their fantasies, their jokes, but behind the fooling there was one thing they took seriously – fighting. Here they knew their job, took no unnecessary risks and carefully refused to hamper themselves by effete conventions of fair play. These were for amateurs. If it was necessary to hit someone, they hit first and hardest and put the boot in afterwards. If they were cutting someone's face or backside, they used a knife or sharpened cutlass. 'Razors,' Ronnie used to say, 'are old-fashioned and strike us as babyish. You can't put any real power behind a razor.'

Reggie developed what was known as his 'cigarette punch'. With his right hand he would offer somebody a cigarette and as the man opened his mouth to take it, would hit him on the side of the jaw with a swift left. It required timing and you needed to know the exact spot to hit. Reggie practised it for hours on a punch-bag and the cigarette punch broke many jaws. An open jaw will fracture easily.

Similarly, the 'little wars' that everyone enjoyed against the neighbouring gangs were organized in deadly earnest by the twins. For most of their followers 'they were just a lark, an outing, a sort of club activity'. But for the twins there was too much at stake to leave anything to chance. They quickly learned the elements of leadership and imposed strict discipline. They began using many of the military principles they had avoided in the army; Ronnie's fantasies of Lawrence of Arabia started to make sense.

From the start he knew the importance of reliable intelligence about the enemy, and took trouble picking up facts about rival gangs. He had a following of small boys he used to meet in a café in the Bethnal Green Road. He was developing a taste for teenage boys, but these also acted as his 'spies'; he used to send them out to watch a house or club, or follow someone and report back to the hall. Payment was strictly by results. He used to call the boys 'my little information service'.

As a result of what they told him he often managed to plan out his battles in advance, banking on surprise and giving his followers their orders with cool military precision. Soon he was demonstrating more complex military skills. The billiard-hall wars became more ambitious. He would take trouble over 'propaganda' to mislead his enemy – usually in the form of rumours put round by his friends. Sometimes he used diversionary tactics during a raid, splitting his forces into two and timing his attack after the main body of the enemy had been drawn off by a false offensive. Secrecy became important.

A failure or an indiscretion by any follower was taken seriously. Sometimes the twins sat in judgement on an offender in the billiard hall late at night in a carefully staged court-martial. Evidence was heard, the prisoner was allowed to speak, the twins passed judgement. Ronnie was careful to make the punishment fit the crime. Sometimes it would be a simple beating, sometimes expulsion from the group. Several times members of the gang were awarded a day's solitary confinement and locked up in an empty house behind the billiard hall.

Reggie was an effective fighter and organizer, but the more serious the 'wars' became, the more the initiative and the ideas seemed to be coming now from Ronnie.

'Christ, Ron,' said one of the gang, after a preliminary briefing, 'you're just like a bloody colonel.'

'Am I?' he said. The name stuck.

Although short-sighted and an indifferent shot, Ronnie was obsessed with firearms. The twins had bought their first gun at sixteen. Since then their armoury had grown. Now it included a new Luger automatic, an old Mauser, revolvers of varying calibres and several sawn-off shotguns. Most of these were hidden under the floorboards of 178 Vallance Road. Ronnie dreamed of using all these guns, though at the moment they remained objects of fantasy. He still had his big Alsatian; he had trained it to be fierce and liked to think nobody else could handle it. He also had his ordinary weapons, a large collection of cavalry sabres, Gurkha knives, bayonets, anything that cut, most of them bought from antique shops. He enjoyed the feel of them and spent hours sharpening his swords on a big grindstone in the yard at Vallance Road. He filled his bedroom with them, saying that he slept more soundly surrounded by cold steel.

Reggie also saw the billiard hall as an important opportunity in life, but in a more practical way than Ronnie. With much of his father's sharpness, he was the businessman of the two and quickly realized that with the name the twins were getting, they had a chance of money. Possibly the good life was not so hard to find as they had thought.

Many of their friends were criminals, mostly thieves, and since the twins' fame had spread they started to play host to a fair slice of the up-and-coming criminals of the East End. Most thieves require a well-run base if they can find it, somewhere to relax, talk freely, pick up the latest gossip and know they are safe. For them the billiard hall was ideal. It was not yet known to the police, and the twins could guarantee the thief what he needed – order. They would see that no one tried to pay off old scores and no one preyed on those who were in luck. Thieves could leave the tools of their trade on the premises; in an emergency the twins might even look after a thief's takings for him.

The twins had connections everywhere: fences and other villains, con men and prisoners freshly released from gaol. If there was trouble they knew what was going on. If the Law started getting difficult, rumour said they could fix it. They had the natural con man's memory for faces and had begun inviting some of the choicer characters they had got to know in the West End and in the army.

Before long the billiard hall was offering local criminals a genuine service. It was organized efficiently. There were lock-up cubicles under the seats for the thieves' tools; stolen goods could be left round the back of the hall. If necessary the twins would arrange transport and worked an introductions bureau for criminals they knew. There might be a warehouseman they knew in Tottenham who had been getting in debt on the dogs and who wasn't fussy what he did for a couple of hundred pounds. Before the evening ended the twins would have contacted willing thieves, found customers for the goods and come to an understanding that when the warehouse was burgled they would be in for their percentage.

It would be an adequate percentage; Reggie always saw to that.

These growing business activities were certain to be challenged sooner or later. The twins had no real power yet. Each section of the East End had its own established 'guv'nors'. In serious criminal affairs the twins were interlopers, but for a while most of the serious local gangs seemed to ignore them. Three Poplar dockers who unofficially 'ruled' Poplar and Mile End finally decided to take them in hand. A challenge was sent out.

Not that it looked much like a challenge, simply an invitation to the twins for a drink at a certain Mile End pub the following Sunday morning. But in the East End there are ways of sending an invitation so that it becomes common knowledge. By the time the twins heard, everyone who mattered knew as well.

The twins' reaction to the dockers' challenge was unusual. All their friends at the hall knew about it and waited for the explosion; none came. Nobody liked to mention it. Nothing was said. By Saturday night the challenge had become the sole topic of conversation, out of earshot of the twins. At the billiard hall people were uneasy, suddenly remembering the dockers' records as amateur boxers. They were brothers, a good three inches taller than the twins, and all of them fought as heavyweights. No one could be surprised at the twins appearing shy of meeting them, but it would be the end of their reputation. Not even they could hope to bluff their way out of an affair like this. But they seemed unconcerned and the evening ended with a cheerful rumpus in a pub at Stoke Newington.

The following morning the billiard hall saw the largest Sunday morning turnout for years. Half the neighbourhood seemed to have arrived to see how Reggie and Ronnie were getting on. The twins seemed much as usual on a Sunday morning after a hard night's drinking: Ronnie unshaven and rubbing his eyes, Reggie neatly dressed in slacks and sports shirt, fixing a new counter to the bar. Both raised their eyes at all the visitors, but said nothing.

Reggie made tea. More of the regulars arrived. Conversation languished.

It was 11.50 when Reggie put down his cup and Ronnie nodded to him and they strolled out through the door. They continued their leisurely stroll along the Mile End Road and were ten minutes late when they reached the pub. Apart from the three large men drinking light ales in the private bar the pub was empty. One of them asked the twins if they were drinking. The twins nodded. The man had to call for the barman, who produced two drinks in half-pint tankards and scurried away. One of the large men passed Ronnie a glass.

'Beer mixed with lemonade. What little boys drink, or don't they let you yet?' he said.

The fight took place behind the closed doors of the private bar. While it lasted no one risked entering, but finally the manager thought the twins must have learned their lesson. There was blood and broken glass everywhere. Two of the dockers were out cold. Ronnie Kray had to be dragged off the third or he would have killed him.

FOUR

The Colonel

In most ways Ronnie led a simple life. At twenty-one he still lived at home, slept in the back bedroom of his parents' house in Vallance Road, ate all his meals in the kitchen and never seemed to have a penny in his pocket. His mother cooked for him, loved him, ironed his shirts and asked no questions. He was the dependent son he always had been. 'I used to hear things about my Ronnie, but I had learned by now never to trust what other people say. I knew him, others didn't. He was so kind, you see. Always made such a fuss of me, and that's more than most of the mothers round here can say of their boys.'

Apart from fighting and helping run the billiard hall he had no interests and no job. He couldn't thieve, understand betting or drive a car. His life was rooted in the village life of the East End. He had no taste for grand living nor, for that matter, for material success away from Bethnal Green. His only weakness was for the young boys he encouraged to come to the billiard hall. He had no interest in women, but with his boys he could become surprisingly sentimental. His favourite book round this time was *Boy's Town*. But he was wary of being known as homosexual and rarely took a boy out. Among his followers these boys were officially 'Ronnie's spies' and nothing else.

What Ronnie really wanted out of life was fame and notoriety. For years his dream-life had been peopled with successful gangsters, boxers, military men. Now he was 'the Colonel' he could at last invent a style of life that suited him. The billiard hall was his theatre; the house at

Vallance Road became his citadel. It contained everything he really loved – his swords, his suits, his mother and his dog. It was the one place he felt really safe. Somebody christened it 'Fort Vallance'.

He knew that big-time Chicago gangsters always had their private barbers. He would have the same. When he awoke now someone in the house would telephone the barber's shop in Whitechapel Road. Half an hour later the Colonel would be sitting in the kitchen in a purple dressing-gown, face smothered in lather, and while the barber stropped his razors Ronnie would hold the first conference of the day with his lieutenants. He also had his hair cut at home now, summoned his tailor here for fittings for his suits and ordered shirts and shoes by telephone. For a while a masseur called to give him massage every morning. He tried to practise yoga. Later he lived upon a diet of raw eggs, 'because raw eggs are strengthening and make you good at sex'.

At the same time his permanent suspicion of the police grew worse. From earliest boyhood he had hated them. Now he was certain they were always watching him. Outside his home he trusted no one and was convinced the telephone was tapped. At night he could sleep only with the light on and a gun beneath the pillow.

Reggie began to slip into his shadow. They still looked identical and were constantly together. One might have thought Reggie would have dominated Ronnie. He was the saner of the two – cleverer, more charming, more responsible. He was quite capable of living in the ordinary straight world. Yet it was Reggie who fell into second place and followed Ronnie's fantasies. He lacked the actor's instincts of his brother. Nobody thought of calling Reggie 'Colonel'.

Nevertheless he seemed quite happy now to follow Ronnie, dressing as he did, joining in his plans, even adopting the Chicago gangster role. He could be as suspicious now as Ronnie, on occasions just as violent; and he had problems

Ronnie never had to face. Ronnie accepted that the straight world was not for him and wanted no part in it. Reggie was not so sure. He had that hankering after what he still referred to as 'the good life'. Possessions and respect, a comfortable house, even a woman and a family – these were anathema for Ronnie, but for Reggie they were possibilities. One day he knew that he might leave the violent, homosexual world of Ronnie and go out to seek them on his own. But for the present, Reggie's duty was to stay with Ronnie and look after him. They could enjoy their life together, and Ronnie needed him. It would all work out in the end. In the meantime there was money to be made. Money is one thing that means much the same in both the straight world and the crooked.

'What is straight business, anyhow? Be honest. It's just a bloody racket, same as our way of life. All of that keeping in with the right people, going to the proper school, an' knowing how much you can fiddle an' get away with. All of those lawyers and accountants to squeeze you round the law. What's all of it except one great big bloody racket?' This was how the twins looked at life: business was a racket; rackets were business. By becoming something of a racketeer Reggie Kray had his first big chance to pick up some of the trappings of the good life he had heard about. If it was necessary he would take it seriously, dress the part, become methodical, even keep accounts. So he cut down his drinking, kept to more regular hours, bought himself single-breasted suits and started making money. Ronnie could be the Colonel. They would still have each other.

Now on their twenty-second birthday they were a formidable pair and there suddenly seemed no stopping them. They were the ideal complementary couple. Ronnie would bring the crowds in, Reggie would fleece them. Ronnie would make their 'name' for violence. Reggie would market it. When there was a serious fight they could still join in together.

It was now that Reggie started to be known as the 'live wire' of the two. He was terrier-like in his eagerness to worry out cash from any situation. There were already certain dues ready for the taking. In the East End it had been taken for granted that the reigning 'guv'nor of the manor' had his legitimate sources of income. Each week he could count on a few pounds from every betting shop in the district as insurance against lesser hooligans. If trouble did occur the guv'nor was expected to deal with it; it was the same with some pubs, cafés, and various tradesmen. The arrangement was usually informal; sometimes a loan, sometimes some infinitely extended credit. Anyone vulnerable to trouble was a potential source of income. Sometimes it needed tact to get it, but Reggie knew how to ask a careful question and never take no for an answer.

Minor protection was the bread-and-butter of villainy; there were far bigger pickings to be had from other criminals. With honest men there always comes a point when they will rather call in the police and take the consequences. Crooks can't. The reigning local villain has them at his mercy. Illicit bookmakers and unlicensed gambling clubs had always been fair game for a pension to the local guv'nor. Working methodically, Reggie made the rounds of all of them in Bethnal Green and Mile End and upped the contributions. It was the same with the local rackets that he heard about; and the twins were making sure they heard about most of them. The billiard hall was a good receiving ground for criminal information, a word from a fence, a tip-off from a taxi-driver, a telephone call from a barman. The twins would always pay well for any information they could use, and they had a sixth sense about what was going on in their district.

Mile End has a lot of thieves. Few of them are very good. A big haul is rare and any thief who has one tries to keep news of it to himself. This is hard. Others are usually involved and goods have to be disposed of. Somehow the

Kray twins always seemed to discover in the end; when they did, the thief would get an invitation to the billiard hall and it would usually be Reggie who discussed their percentage. Thieves are vulnerable, and they would usually pay up more or less what the twins demanded. Those who didn't finally wished they had.

'You know who I met the other night?' said Reggie Kray to a small man with a squint, after losing a game of snooker to him at the billiard hall. The man was a successful fence from Shepherd's Bush. 'Old so-and-so from Islington, asking if I wanted ten thousand quid's worth of forged fivers. Just shows how barmy people are. What could I do with all them snide fivers? Even if I could afford 'em, which I can't.'

'Some people's like that, Reg. How much he want for 'em?'

'Yeah. A right bloody nutter. Thirty bob I think.'

'Thirty bob for a snide fiver? You do pick 'em, Reg boy. I'll say that for you. What're they like?'

'Looked fine to me. But as you know that's not my game, and he said he was selling the lot. Three thousand quid, take it or leave it. Must think I'm rolling in it.'

'He's off his chump, Reg. Stark staring. Still, there's one born every minute.'

They played another game of snooker, had a drink, and the man went back to Shepherd's Bush. Two days later, Reggie received an inquiry about forged £5 notes. It came from a friend of a friend who wanted Reggie to meet a man with a maroon Rover in a pub in Dalston. The man was brisk, well-spoken and wore a neatly trimmed moustache. After a couple of drinks he said he might be interested in some goods that Reggie had for sale. Reggie was non-committal. He said the goods weren't his, and he wasn't particularly interested in the idea.

The man became more enthusiastic. If these were quality goods, he would be very keen; naturally he'd have to see them first. Reggie said so would he. Finally they arranged to meet again the next night at the Terminus Café in Mile End Road. Reggie would bring the man with the goods; if they both liked his work they would split the lot between them. Reggie would bring £1,500. If he were genuinely interested the man with the moustache should do the same.

There used to be a tall, lugubrious thief called Ozzie who was often around the billiard hall. He had been in prison so many times that his nerve had gone, but he was always glad to be of use to the twins, and the following night Reggie took him with him to the Terminus Café. The maroon Rover was parked outside; Reggie was soon introducing Ozzie to its owner as a master forger. Reggie called for tea and something to eat, paying with a fiver which was automatically accepted.

'One of his?' asked the man with the moustache.

'One of his,' said Reggie.

'Any more I can see?'

Ozzie produced a roll of fivers from his back pocket. Examining them, the man said that he couldn't tell them from the real thing, which was hardly surprising as Reggie had drawn them just that afternoon from the Mile End branch of Barclays Bank.

Where were the rest of the notes that were for sale? In Ozzie's flat off the Commercial Road. Why not collect them straight away and settle the deal? Five minutes later the Rover was drawing up outside the tenement where Ozzie lived with a lady pickpocket from Stoke Newington. This was the crucial point of the operation. The man with the moustache opened the door and started to get out of the car.

'No,' said Ozzie. 'If you don't object, I'd rather bring them down to you. My dear wife knows nothing of my activities. I prefer to keep my business and my private life apart.'

'Quite right,' said Reggie. The man closed the door, and Ozzie walked up the stairs to his flat. As soon as he was there, he rang Limehouse Police Station, gave his address and asked them to send round a squad car as the man in the flat below was murdering his wife. Three minutes later he came down the stairs holding a solid-looking brown paper parcel.

Reggie had £1,500 in his hand, ready to pay. So had the man with the moustache. All that remained to do was to examine the parcel of fivers.

The string was stiff and tightly knotted. Inside the first parcel was another, also tightly tied with string. Reggie had nearly undone it when the squad car came from Limehouse, klaxon wailing, blue lights flashing.

'Christ,' said Ozzie, 'they've twigged. I'm off,' and shoved the parcel into the man's lap.

'Don't go without your money,' shouted Reggie, giving him his money.

'Here's mine,' said the man with the moustache, who had already got his car in gear.

'Thanks,' shouted Ozzie. 'See yer,' and the Rover hurtled off down the Commercial Road. By Aldgate Underground Reggie remembered an important appointment.

'Sorry, I gotta go. But remember, I'm trusting you with my share of the notes.'

'You know you can trust me, Reg.'

When the man with the moustache got back to his large house in Barnet and found that his parcel contained wads of neatly guillotined newspaper he was angry. But he should have had more sense than turn up at the billiard hall with a loaded shotgun, looking for Reggie Kray. Apart from the beating he received when he found him, he was also charged by the police later in the evening, when they picked him up, still clutching his loaded gun, from an alley in Whitechapel. He was fined £25 plus costs.

Reggie was philosophical about it all when he met Ozzie to collect his £1,500 and tipped the old thief £50 for his part in the affair. 'Just goes to show. If people weren't greedy and always thinking about getting something for nothing, Ozz, they wouldn't come unstuck.'

There were old-style cockney con tricks too: some of the ways Reggie Kray made money were as ancient and dishonest as the East End itself. There was the 'tweedle', for instance, one of the classic cockney tricks in which the victim was sold a valuable ring at bargain price. The ring was genuine and the victim was actually encouraged to have it valued, but there always came a point, just before the money was handed over, where the con man on the tweedle switched the real ring for a replica. By the time the buyer had discovered his mistake, there was nothing he could do about it. Similarly with the 'jargoons', except that here the jewellery sold was fake from the start and the seller had to rely on faster talking and a quicker sale.

Reggie had a way with him. People trusted him, and he could always pick up a few pounds when he needed them from the jargoons and the tweedle. But these were small-time rackets, and Reggie Kray had no real wish to be a con man. He knew he lacked the polish and the self-deception to reach the top of this particular profession. He and Ronnie were agreed that their future would be as robber barons of crime rather than as hard-worked criminals.

FIVE

Gun Time

The 1955 Epsom Spring Meeting was a historic one for gangland and for the twins. Word had got round that the succession stakes of London villainy would shortly start as well and the twins felt a duty to be there to see what happened. Traditionally the Epsom races are an annual outing for the villains of London. Back in the days of 'Derby' Sabini and his gang this was where they made their biggest haul of the year. Whichever gang controlled the leading bookmakers' pitches was automatically guaranteed a percentage of the take from every bookie on the course.

By the fifties crime had outgrown the race-gangs, but tradition lasted. Anyone who wanted to could still work out the form sheet for London crime from what went on during these few days. A smile or a brush-off would show who was rising or on the way out; a handshake make it clear that an old grudge was forgotten or a new alliance in the offing. Little went unnoticed. The year 1955 was an exceptional one for London's criminals, and at the Spring Meeting attention was particularly focused on two of them.

One was a thin-faced gentleman called Billy Hill. He was an ex-thief and had spent seventeen of his thirty-eight years in places of detention. The other was a big, bombastic man with a large cigar who called himself Jack 'Spot'. He was Jewish and his real name Comer. As a young man he had fought against Mosley's black-shirts in the East End; since then he had organized his Upton Park Mob across many of the race-tracks in the country.

These two men had the complementary qualities of all natural double acts, and thanks to this they had become the Laurel and Hardy of London crime, or, as they liked to call themselves, 'kings of London's underworld'. For years they had been allies. From the mid forties, Spot with his gang of bruisers, Hill with his following of thieves had been raking over the criminal pickings of London's West End. They had faced little opposition. The pre-war gangsters had grown tired, but the West End was booming. Night clubs and drinking clubs, prostitution and illicit gambling clubs were producing fortunes. The rich underworld of London was there to be milked by anyone who guaranteed the one thing it required – peace to prosper and grow fatter still.

This Spot and Hill had done for more than ten profitable years: running the protection, taking their cut on the gambling and using their power for one main purpose – the survival of the *status quo*. They had never been a criminal 'brain' at the centre of a web of dangerous intrigue, nor were they Mafia-style organizers. If other gangs like the Italians or the Maltese wanted a stake in the West End, Spot and Hill would come to an arrangement with them. They acted very much like businessmen, drawing their profits from a discreet monopoly, carefully preserving good relations with the police, and becoming dangerous only when they felt their plastic empire threatened. The worst threat they had to face had come from non-caring tearaways, but these could be dealt with, and it seemed that nothing but old age would stop the coalition of Spot and Hill continuing for ever. Then the unthinkable occurred. Spot and Hill fell out.

Hill, who is now agreeably retired in a large white villa on the Mediterranean, is inclined to be charitable over what happened. 'Jack was becoming insecure and a bit jealous of me. He was an older man, you see, and once he got this persecution complex he was impossible to work with any more.' Spot says he should have shot Hill while he had the chance. Certainly their friendship had already gone very sour by the time the twins took over the billiard hall.

Once trouble started between gangland's two 'kings' the odds were against Spot. The August before, in the so-called 'Battle of Frith Street', Spot had already been badly cut in the face. He was beginning to get too old for this sort of thing, and if it came to a showdown Jack Spot would need much younger, tougher allies – like the Krays. He had known of them for several years, but had kept clear of them: he could recognize trouble when he saw it.

Now things had changed, and just before the Epsom Spring Meeting Jack Spot had swallowed his pride and called on them at the billiard hall. The twins were most polite but not effusive. This was their territory. Jack Spot was asking to see them. When he offered them a pitch at Epsom races, they said they'd think about it. It was unheard of for two boys like them to have their own pitch among the country's leading villains, but they were not impressed. 'We never had liked Spotty. Never thought much of him.' Finally they accepted for the hell of it. It might be interesting. 'Interesting' had become a favourite word of Ronnie's.

Spot saw to everything. The twins knew nothing about racing. This did not matter. Spotty had found them a good bookmaker to 'mind'; they simply had to stand by his pitch keeping an eye on their percentage. They also had to keep an eye on Billy Hill. He had the number-one pitch up by the winning-post, and was surrounded by some 'interesting' friends. There was a dark young man who smiled a lot – already one of London's leading hatchet men, 'Mad' Frankie Fraser. He, like Ronnie Kray, would stop at nothing in a fight. Next to him was Billie Blythe, a wild little man with a conviction for cutting a Flying Squad officer in the face; and there were others like them.

Against men like these, Jack Spot had little but his fat cigar. Five years before the men round him might have made a fight of it – not now. Several had just returned from prison. For them nothing was worth the price of going back; their softness showed. This brought everyone's attention to the twins. Young as they were, they suddenly seemed to be challenging the toughest criminals in London. They also had a chance of seeing just how vulnerable and weak their allies were. But their behaviour puzzled everyone. It was hard to tell if it was sheer bravado or stupidity. For the twins seemed to be making a point of totally ignoring their danger. They appeared as unimpressed by Hill's men as by Spot's.

Most of the Italian gang were there, intent as usual upon weighing up the odds between the two sides. One of them knew Reggie well enough to feel he should warn him what he was taking on.

'This lot mean business. You two must be stark staring mad to show up here with Spotty. If you want to kill yourselves, there are less painful ways of doing it.'

The twins laughed and offered him a drink. When he had gone, Ronnie turned to his brother. 'The way these old men worry, Reg. Fair makes you sick.'

For the rest of that day the twins kept up their show of insolent indifference against the best-known gangsters in the country. They drank, they entertained their friends, they roared with laughter, they ignored the racing and the betting. Finally Ronnie yawned and rolled off to sleep. When the day ended they collected what was owed them, and without bothering to thank Spot drove off in their van.

In fact, of course, the whole performance had been carefully thought out. Their day at the races had been a conscious demonstration of contempt for the older generation of criminals, just as their alliance with Jack Spot had been a determined bid for power. 'It wasn't that we liked him. We despised him really. We just turned out with Spotty to show everyone that *we* was the up-and-coming firm and didn't give a fuck for anyone. Old Spotty understood.

Whatever else he may have been he wasn't stupid. He knew quite well that though we were there in theory as his friends, we meant to end up taking over from him.'

It was an exciting prospect, the big chance the twins had both been waiting for. For it to happen they had to stage the one thing all the other criminals at Epsom wanted to avoid – gang war, a real showdown with the enemy. Excitedly they prepared for total war, a running fight with the top West End gangsters where they could use their guns, and show how much tougher and more ruthless they and their followers could be against the old gangland kings. Ronnie was in his element collecting weapons, making plans, haranguing followers at the billiard hall. Fort Vallance was prepared as a redoubt and a headquarters. For several days the twins continued to mobilize. Then came the news that Blythe and Fraser and their friends wanted to fight it out in a pub near Islington. The twins were ready.

This was their moment, and that night London was very near a wave of gang-killing on a scale it had never seen before. Both the twins and their opponents finally meant business. Once shooting started it would be hard to stop; the retribution would inevitably roll on.

The twins filled their van with arms and a dozen of the best fighters from the billiard hall. Armed to the eyebrows they drove off to Islington. Ronnie had told them that their hour had come. But the pub was empty. They made themselves at home and waited for the enemy to come. This was a chance to ambush everyone and shoot it out with the advantage of surprise. Still no one came. Nobody entered the pub that night with the twins there and at closing time they could do nothing except call it a day and drive away. Ronnie was furious, and for several days he issued challenges and insults to the rival gang. They were entirely ignored. If the twins wanted action it was soon clear that no one else did.

Later they heard that Billy Hill had been alarmed to hear

about the challenge and had immediately called the battle off. The last thing he wanted now was bloodshed, Krays and trouble with the Law. Nor, when it came to it, did Spot. He too had had a little time to think. It was one thing to make a show at Epsom with the twins – quite another to become involved in a full-scale war where people would be killed. Spottie had always been a law-abiding monarch. He would far rather abdicate than hang.

And so the big war never came. The twins were carefully edged out from the dramatic role they wanted. For a while at least the old guard had succeeded in putting them firmly in their places. And 1955, which had begun so hopefully for the twins, ended with this setback, and neither was allowed to play a real part in the last rounds of the Spot–Hill feud that went on until the spring of 1956.

For a while they still had hopes. Nominal allies still of Spot, both twins and various followers did start coming west. Most evenings they would drop in at a club off the Tottenham Court Road where Spot still held court as in the old days. They had a certain status now, and found that they were getting talked about. One of Jack Spot's more genial lieutenants taught them a thing or two. Reggie began thinking of the money waiting to be picked up in the West End, Ronnie of machine-guns, bombs and full-scale war to exterminate Hill's following, leaving the Kray twins free to rule London as Capone ruled Chicago.

The only trouble was Jack Spot. True, he did take them racing once again to Leeds, but this was not what they required. He would not 'educate' them, as they hoped, about his rackets. These were *his* secret. Nor would he use them in a real fight. He wanted money, not machine-guns.

On the May night in 1956 when Frankie Fraser and Alf Warren waited for Jack Spot outside his flat in Bayswater, and put a second set of gashes in his face, the twins were not involved. They visited him in hospital next day. Now was the moment for the war they longed for. They guaranteed control of London within twenty-four hours. All that was needed was for Spot to give the word. Spottie rolled over in his bed and looked the other way.

Jack Spot retired and bought a bowler hat and a furniture business off the Gloucester Road. Billy Hill retired and bought a white Lincoln convertible and a house in southern Spain. An era of so-called organized crime was over. London was hotting up; no single organization could control it, certainly not with the old-fashioned methods of Spot and Hill. The twins went back to Bethnal Green. With Jack Spot's help they could have moved in on the rich rackets of the West End. Without him they were lost.

Had he done as they asked and 'educated' them, things could have been different, but they both lacked the knowledge and support to fight for the succession on their own. Control of West End crime was passing to a loose federation of existing gangs, the most important being the Italians. They were anxious to warn any of Spot's old allies against ideas of a comeback. A list was prepared. Various people on it were cut in various painful places. News reached the twins that it was their turn next.

For several days Fort Vallance was more fortress-like than usual. Nobody saw the twins and rumours started. They had been killed together and their bodies were laid out in Vallance Road, embalmed according to a secret clause in the Colonel's will. They had both fled the country, and were living it up in the Bahamas on the great fortune Billy Hill had paid to buy them off. They were in prison.

Finally they emerged. At around 10.00 at night their old van, filled once again with armed men from the billiard hall, collected them from the house and set off west along the Clerkenwell Road. It drew up opposite the social club the Italians used as their headquarters. Ronnie stepped out. As Colonel he possessed a medieval concept of the rules of war. The leader went in first. Reggie and the others watched through spy-holes cut in the side of the van. It was a dramatic entry. Several of the men who had put Ronnie on the list were standing at the bar.

'Some of you want to settle some business with me and my brother. We're here. Let's get it over with.'

No one replied.

'Can't yer speak English?'

Someone threw a bottle at his head; the Colonel drew his heavy Mauser automatic and fired three shots in return. Perhaps he aimed to hit the wall. Perhaps his marksmanship was bad. Nobody tried to stop him as he walked back to the van.

Ronnie Kray was never to forget this moment. It was an answer of a sort to the fiasco of the night at Islington. This was how life should be lived and victories won. This proved what he had always said – that the rich gangs of the west were soft and would collapse if anyone stood up to them. If someone like Jack Spot could govern the West End for ten years with a gang like his, think what the twins could do.

What they forgot was that Spot's power had come not out of violence but from its opposite – his skill in avoiding it. Like an old *condottiere*, his greatest battles had been those he never had to fight. His gang, his big cigars, the drink and the occasional brawls were his façade: behind it was a skilful fixer, an underworld diplomat who could negotiate between the clubs, the racketeers, the other gangs, and always fix a deal. Hill was the same, and ultimately a smarter man than Spot. But both took a lot of trouble not to offend the police. There was an unspoken understanding between them and the Law. Hill and Spot could keep their position provided there was no trouble to the general public and they kept their men in order. Behind this understanding lay a realistic old-time policeman's philosophy. Cities will always have a certain level of crime and there is something to be said for tolerating one gang that knows the rules rather than face a horde of unknown criminals.

This was anathema to the twins. In their way they were very honest. They both loved violence: they loathed the Law. By their lights Spot was a phoney: they would become the real thing. Spot's men had been the washouts of the West End: they would fight their battles with the toughest tearaways of the East End. And they would have none of the Spot–Hill understandings with the Law. 'Coppers is dirt.'

If it were necessary to fight, they'd go to the limit. If Ronnie had to kill, he'd kill. 'We weren't just playing kids' games any more.'

Now, as the twins aspired to greater power, many things changed, their gang included. It was still based on the billiard hall, but Ronnie was right. The kids' games were over. There were still jokes of course. Ronnie put on various acts, and there were as many guests and drunken evenings as ever. The twins remained good hosts and continued to have good parties. But they no longer seemed to have the old-style gang fights for the hell of it. Everything began to have a purpose. Even the hall seemed less of a club now, more of a business. Many old faces started to stay away.

This was inevitable. The twins' contemporaries were moving into their middle twenties. Many were thinking of marriage. Marriage meant settling to a steady job, keeping away from trouble, staying at home at night, saving and not spending. One of those who dropped out said, 'It's very sad, but if you're serious about a bird you just can't help yourself. You have to go straight – least for a while. One thing was certain – once I was courting I just had to choose. Either the twins or the girl I wanted to marry. And when I'd married her there was the flat to pay for and the hire purchase. Then the two kids arrived. I'd see the twins. Ronnie'd say, "When're you comin' out with us again?" I'd say I'd be around next week, but never went. Somehow there wasn't time.'

'Always it's bloody women,' Ronnie muttered. 'Women's our worstest enemy. Why can't they keep their places any more? They don't want men these days. What they want's lap-dogs.'

Lap-dogs or not, old friends were leaving as they were absorbed into the straight, female dominated world of the new East End. There had never been a style of life like this in Bethnal Green before – LCC maisonettes, new schools, television, supermarkets, car, and a wife determined to keep her looks and her husband. There was a demolition order on the billiard hall: new flats would soon go up in Eric Street. But the new middle-class East End was no life for the twins, even had they wanted it. Ronnie was openly homosexual by now; Reggie had no time for women. The new pattern of East End gang life fitted a younger age-group. Hooliganism ended by the early twenties. Now that the twins were planning a new war they needed other outcasts like themselves.

In the East End anyone serving a prison sentence is simply referred to as an 'away'. Any close friend of the twins who was 'away' had always been looked after. The twins had a keen sense of responsibility over such things. They wrote, they visited and did what they could to stop the man worrying about life outside. If there was trouble with the rent they'd see to it. If he had heard his woman was playing around, they made certain she was warned to be faithful or at least discreet. At Christmas time they sent a box of groceries to the family, and when release day came the twins would usually be outside the prison gates to offer a pound or two and a lift home in their car. They were genuinely kind to those they liked and had a knack of making kindness work.

But at the same time this concern for the 'aways' was a real source of loyalty. Now that their following was changing, it did as much as anything to place their organization on a professional footing. News travels nowhere faster than in prison, and it soon got round that the Kray twins were 'genuine guv'nors who looked after their own'. This gave them status, and their reputation spread through different gaols and into the wide world of working criminals outside.

This sort of reputation coupled with their 'name' offered the twins a useful reservoir of talent for the future. Once it was known that any villain on release had only to call in at the billiard hall to be sure of a fiver and some quick excitement, the twins could be sure of finding just the men they needed.

Discipline at the billiard hall was tighter now; the battles waged were more determined. Ronnie began thinking of what he called the 'politics of crime' and genuine criminals started to take the place of the happy tearaways of the year before. This new following became known as 'the Firm'. By 1956 its power had spread through Hackney and Mile End along to Walthamstow. South lay the river; to the north, Islington was being run by their old friends, the Nashes. Within the area they controlled, the twins were supreme. Each thief, each gambling club, most of the pubs and many businesses paid something to the Firm for the right to prosper. For the first time in their lives the twins looked like becoming rich. Reggie had his first big American car and a succession of good-looking chauffeurs. The big-time was beginning.

But although the fame of the twins was spreading and criminals talked about them as 'the most dangerous mob in London, the boys with the real future', one thing was lacking: the power to expand. Ronnie was planning his battles and hoped for alliances to carry the Firm into the West End. None of them quite worked. The Firm was just a little too dangerous for other gangs to want to know. Despite all Ronnie's challenges, not even Frankie Fraser wanted a real gunfight. The West End closed itself against the twins.

This was frustrating, especially to Ronnie. Though he had money now, a car, a thick gold wristwatch, these were not what counted. His best possessions were his guns.

When he went out he had a sword-stick and a .32 Beretta that scarcely showed beneath his well-cut suit. This was his personal weapon, although he had other guns as well. With the Beretta he took trouble filing the ends of the slugs and cutting them to make dum-dum bullets just like those with which Capone's men once blasted large holes in their enemies.

It was not only gang war that he wanted; he talked of 'doing' people all the time. Traitors were round him, and he began to make a list of 'those who'd have to go'. People would talk about the Colonel's list. Many would worry about it since he proclaimed that he was psychic and could read people's motives from their aura. He consulted a lady clairvoyant from Walthamstow. She told him he was under the protection of a powerful spirit guide, who guarded him and would tell him what to do through his inner voice. All the Colonel had to do was listen.

Even Reggie, who disapproved of 'all this spiritualist stuff and meddling with things you can't understand', was impressed.

That autumn a car-site owner in the Bethnal Green Road sold a young docker a second-hand Austin Eight for £120. It was a straight deal for cash, but the next day the man returned with the car saying it burned oil and that he wanted his money back. The dealer refused; shouting started.

'I'll be back tomorrow with my friends from over the water.'

'And I'll be ready for 'em.'

A few minutes later the dealer was on the telephone to Vallance Road; Ronnie's hour had come. For some while now the twins had made a tidy income out of the local car dealers, partly from ordinary protection (they went to work with paint-stripper and seven-pound hammers on the stock of one dealer who thought he didn't need them) and partly by helping out if a customer occasionally turned nasty. This rarely happened. When it did, the mention of the twins' name was usually enough to smooth things over or ensure prompt payment. The twins had no desire for trouble with the ordinary public. This case was different. The threat of a rival gang from south of the Thames was a direct challenge. Ronnie Kray's spirit voices told him he must act.

Early next morning one of the Firm was posted on the look-out by the car-site. When the docker arrived with all his friends he was to telephone the billiard hall. Whatever happened then, Ronnie would deal with personally. He had a long wait, and sat there in his chair in the empty hall steadily working himself into a rage. This was no time for weakness – this was war. Once an outside gang came on his territory he would show everyone the power of the Krays. He chose a Luger. He put on his big Capone-style overcoat. Then the call came. The docker had arrived.

In fact he'd come alone and wanted to apologize. So did the dealer. Both had calmed down since the day before and were discussing things when the door was kicked open and in stormed the Colonel and his driver. The driver had a knife. The docker tried to hit him, but before he could, the Luger fired twice and he was on the floor clutching his leg. No one spoke. The Colonel looked for the South Londoners; seeing they weren't there he left, slamming the door behind him. The only sign of his presence was the reek of cordite and the growing pool of blood on the floor. As someone said afterwards, 'it wasn't like real life. It was all straight out of a gangster film.'

Everyone realized the shooting was a big mistake – everyone but Ronnie, who had been thrilled to pull the trigger. Provided he was daring enough, he could get away with it. Provided he listened to his voices, he would never fail. Action was what counted. And everyone involved now rallied round to save him from trouble with the Law.

The dealer had to. Unless he hushed things up at once he knew he would rapidly end up in the dock with Ronnie

Kray on a charge of attempted murder. And so before the wounded man bled to death or the police arrived, he had him bundled into a car, and one of the men on the site rushed him to Bancroft Road Hospital. He dumped him in the outpatients', then drove off before anyone asked any questions. Half an hour later the docker was under surgery. Then the real game started, as the police arrived and tried to get someone talking.

Ronnie did nothing. Such was his privilege. After a long tirade, Reggie was taking care of him: within an hour of the shooting he was safely hidden in an anonymous flat in Walthamstow. He spent his time quite happily listening to operatic records, drinking bottled beer and trying to remember every detail of what it had been like to shoot a man. Soon he was working on his list and choosing who to deal with next.

All the real work fell on Reggie. He was the one who had to tie up every possible loose end if Ronnie were to be saved from joining the 'aways' for the next ten years. The dealer was no problem. Scared of the law and frightened of the Krays, he would do anything to avoid incriminating himself. So would his employees. The real problem was the wounded man, who was just coming round from the anaesthetic with a policeman by his bed. Once he really talked, Ronnie was in trouble. Reggie would have to see he didn't.

In any other part of London not even Reggie could have done this; but in the East End, if you knew the right man and had sufficient power, it was surprising what could still be done. Reggie knew many people, and the most useful was a portly man from Stepney with a stall in Brick Lane. His name was 'Red-face' Tommy Plumley, and he was the East End's fixer. He was an unlovable man. 'Slimy old devil, Tommy. Just like an old fat snake.' The one thing he knew was everybody's price. Reggie Kray telephoned. Red-face took over.

It was too late to stop the docker talking to the police.

Dazed though he was from the anaesthetic, he had given an account of what had happened. But later that afternoon several friends visited him in hospital, all of them suddenly concerned with his safety. If he knew what was good for him he would do nothing rash. Despite the police guard by his bed, the docker was soon distinctly worried.

Next day the police swooped and arrested a man on suspicion of the shooting. An identity parade was held that afternoon inside the hospital; the docker identified the suspect as the man who shot him, and the police went to charge him under the name of Ronald Kray. Now for the first time the arrested man objected. He wasn't Ronald Kray. His name was Reginald. His driving licence proved it; he could also prove conclusively that on the morning of the shooting he was nowhere near the car-site.

Prove it he did. Reggie's alibis were so unshakeable that the police at Arbour Square could do nothing but apologize and send him home next morning. After a blunder like this by the police, Ronnie was safe; the only people to be taken care of now were the site-owner and Ronnie's driver. Here Red-face fixed things personally, paying a visit to the hospital in Bancroft Road. During his short chat with the docker he stressed that the Krays were valuable friends and hard enemies and that if he knew what was good for him he would no longer be quite so positive about the morning he was shot. When the police pressed charges against the site-owner, their chief witness's memory suddenly turned vague – so vague that he could no longer state for sure where he'd been shot or who was present or what really happened. Finally the case had to be dismissed for lack of evidence.

Red-face was a tidy-minded man who liked to keep his promises. A policeman was discreetly rewarded – so were the docker's friends who warned him and the car-site man who drove him to hospital. Finally there was the docker to be taken care of, or rather, the ex-docker. With his left leg now an inch shorter than his right, it was clear that he would dock no more. Red-face discussed it with him very amicably. The man's wife had always dreamed of opening a sweet-shop and tobacconist's of their own, but they had never had the capital. Red-face understood.

Thanks to him, Ronnie's first shooting ended happily for everyone involved. The docker lost an inch of leg but gained a sweet-shop; Red-face drew a good commission on the settlements, and the twins became more feared than ever, particularly Ronnie. The only man to lose was the car-site owner, who paid well over £3,000 before he was through. As usual Reggie was swift to point the moral. 'If you're a straight man and start playing with fire you must expect to burn your fingers once in a while,' he said solemnly.

'After the shooting, Ronnie seemed a bit like Superman,' says a member of the Firm. 'We were in awe of him. It seemed that there was nothing that he couldn't do and get away with. Reggie was different. Never knew where you were with him. Most of the time as good as gold. Talk anything over with you; understanding as you like. Then he'd turn vicious. Hard to know exactly why he did. Just get these moods, he would – he could be wickeder than Ronnie.'

Tension between the twins increased; their rows worsened. Ronnie was proud of what he had done, and took delight in telling friends exactly how the shooting felt. It was obvious that he could hardly wait to repeat it. But Reggie's attitude was contradictory. Sometimes he seemed appalled by Ronnie's action. 'You must be raving mad,' he would shout. 'You shoot a man, and then you leave it all to me to clear up. One day you'll get us hanged.'

But Reggie could appreciate his twin's excitement better than anyone and he was vulnerable to Ronnie's taunts about his cowardice. 'All you're fit for's clearing up,' Ronnie would mutter at him. 'You couldn't shoot a man if you tried. You haven't got the guts of a flea.'

Reggie was torn as usual. Part of him wanted to steer clear of trouble, but another part longed for the chance to prove himself his brother's equal. When trouble started with a gang from Watney Street, Reggie did nothing to prevent it.

Like most gangland feuds, this one appeared a fuss about nothing, but had its roots in deep resentment from the past. The Watney Streeters were no real threat to the Krays. Most of them were Irish dockers. The twins called them 'weekend gangsters'. They were young toughs who had grown up together, worked and drank together and operated various small rackets around the docks. They enjoyed a good Saturday night brawl when they had been on the beer. But they were descendants of the old-time Watney Street gang which had always been the enemy of the ancient villains of Bethnal Green. That summer Ronnie decided to shoot one of them, a boy called Charlie. Charlie was smart, and had devised a foolproof little racket with a number of local post office drivers, who relabelled parcels for him, sending them on to addresses where he could pick them up. Ronnie heard about it and, as usual, demanded fifty per cent of the profits. Charlie agreed, but there was constant trouble over payments; Charlie went on the list.

In the middle of 1956, the twins seemed to have achieved what they had always really wanted – a foothold in the West End at last. A man called Billie Jones, who worked in the docks, had taken over a West End drinking club off Cambridge Circus called The Stragglers. It was a good club, but also a popular place for fights. These were expensive and they upset the Law. To stop them Jones's associate, the boxer Bobby Ramsey, suggested calling in the twins as informal partners. Ramsey had known them both for years. They were delighted, and Reggie Kray's cigarette punch soon put an end to trouble. The Stragglers started to make money. Then there was suddenly a war.

Jones had a fight with Charlie in the docks and was

beaten up. The following night Ramsey drove down to Limehouse in his large Buick and beat up Charlie. Two nights later, Charlie and a full gathering of Watney Streeters cornered Ramsey in an East End pub called The Artichoke, dragged him outside, kicked and punched him unconscious and hit him over the head with an iron bar.

Ramsey recovered, but Ronnie felt that he was personally involved. Jones and Ramsey were both known to be friends of the twins. Charlie was taking an extreme 'liberty' attacking them after the trouble there had already been over the mail business. The Kray name was in jeopardy. Ronnie wanted another shooting, but Jones and Ramsey lacked the Colonel's single-mindedness. Finally they agreed to make an example of Charlie and the Watney Streeters with the biggest straightforward beating one gang had inflicted on another in living memory. The twins did the planning together.

Ronnie's secret service of small boys kept Charlie under constant watch. The Colonel could not resist choosing a gun for himself, just in case things went wrong – a 'Young America' revolver with dum-dum bullets. According to reports, the Watney Streeters would be drinking at a pub called The Britannia the following Saturday. Cars were laid on from Eric Street for 9 P.M.

That night Ronnie was very much the Colonel – calm, all-powerful, full of the excitement of knowing that he would soon be going into action. He would become a soldier glorying in the fray. He was invulnerable. He was the leader, a great man joining the ranks of other great men of history. He had chosen his raiding-party from his dozen best men. Ramsey and Jones joined them. They set off, but just for once the Colonel's secret service failed him; or Charlie was smarter than they knew. As the large cars drew up in front of The Britannia he and his friends escaped by the back entrance, leaving their drinks on the bar – when the Colonel entered the only person to be seen was a boy called Terry Martin who had rashly stayed behind to finish a hand of gin rummy with three friends.

For the man of action one thing is worse than a defeat – fiasco. After all the preparations, the Krays had been made fools of by a bunch of Irish dockers. Still, they had someone. Ramsey believed that Martin had been there when he was beaten up. He would do, and was dragged out into the street.

According to police evidence, Ramsey took over then. Gangland protocol demanded it. He had the right to his revenge. The others stood by as he slashed Martin twice over the back of the head with a bayonet and stabbed him in the shoulder. Then they closed in to kick him unconscious. It might easily have been murder. According to medical evidence given in court, 'it was only by luck that he survived'.

When Reggie called off the gang they drove away, leaving Martin in the gutter. Someone bolted the front door of The Britannia and peered out.

'It's all right. They've gone.'

The three men who were playing cards with Terry Martin trooped out and picked him up and drove him to the London Hospital.

The Colonel behaved very much in character. Anyone at all concerned with safety would have disappeared and concentrated on an alibi for the evening. But Ronnie was beginning his revenge. Blood had been shed and the excitement was only starting. He had to find the whole of Watney Street. Ramsey was driving his black Buick, Ronnie beside him directing operations, and the hunt went on round Stepney until the car was stopped by a police patrol soon after midnight.

At first the Colonel seemed to trust in his invulnerability. When the police found his 'Young America' revolver he said, 'Careful with it. Can't you see it's loaded?' When they brought in the crowbar and machete from the car and pointed to the bloodstains on his shirt, Ronnie shrugged. 'I 'ad a nose-bleed.'

The twins had both escaped the Law so many times. It must be possible again. Ronnie was not worried. Red-face would fix things as before.

But Terry Martin was not willing to be fixed. For once the East End's code of silence was not working. At the Old Bailey he would be the leading witness for the prosecution. Against this there was not much to be done, and the most the defence could manage for the twins was to play the old game of tripping up witnesses over their identities. Reggie, who had been arrested with a bloodstained jacket, offered to take the blame, exonerating Ronnie. Ronnie pointed out that he had been found with a gun, and so had better take the whole rap. Reggie could keep things going while he was away. In the end a clever defence counsel managed to create so much uncertainty over identifying the twins that the judge had no alternative to accepting Reggie's story that the bloodstains on his jacket 'might have come from watching sparring between boxers at the billiard hall, where he was employed' and dismissing him from the case.

For the Colonel there was no escape. On 5 November, Guy Fawkes's Day, the majesty of the law descended upon Ronald Kray, and the recorder, Sir Gerald Dodson, sentenced him to three years' imprisonment for causing grievous bodily harm to Terence Martin of Chapman Street, Stepney.

SIX

Twins Apart

Two pairs of grey denim trousers, three blue-and-white-striped shirts, a grey flannel prison jacket, prison-issue woollen socks, boots and cotton underwear, communal bath once a week with yellow soap and a regulation short back and sides. A day that began at 6.30 A.M. with the bell clanging on the landing and ended when lights went out at 9.30 P.M.

From 5 November 1956, a wet Friday, when the gates of Wandsworth Gaol closed behind the black Maria bringing the latest batch of prisoners down from the Central Criminal Court, this became the new life of Ronnie Kray. Nothing could have been further from the old life of drink and fights and easy money than the dingy monastery of Wandsworth Gaol; nothing more at odds with the dream world the Colonel had built round the Eric Street billiard hall and Fort Vallance. Yet he took to it surprisingly well. His mother worried that it would be terrible for him to be parted from his Reggie, but Reggie came in to see him on visits, and neither twin seemed unduly concerned at being parted. After the first days' gloom of settling in, the Colonel appeared very much his old self.

This was partly because he had so many friends in prison that Wandsworth was something of a home from home, and although he was locked in a single cell on the ground floor of the main prison block after lights out, he had plenty of opportunity for renewing old acquaintances during the remainder of the day. Next to him in the workshop, where he sat five hours supposedly making brushes, was his one-time cell-mate and comrade-in-arms, ex-Fusilier Dickie Morgan, currently serving a four-year sentence for hijacking a lorry-load of meat. The same day at exercise he met his boyhood friend Checker Berry, son of old Teddy 'Kid' Berry who gave him his first professional boxing lessons.

The ordinary man who finds himself in prison gets his worst shock from the sudden contact with a gaol world alien to life outside. For the professional criminal this is not the case: his society is one that stretches both sides of the prison wall. There is liberty one side, restriction the other, but the gossip and friendships are there in common, and Ronnie Kray had much the same status among the small core of professional criminals in Wandsworth Gaol that he had enjoyed in the billiard hall and Bethnal Green. The great majority of prisoners were beneath his contempt and unworthy of his attention. They were essentially straight people who had come unstuck, as Ronnie said, by 'pinching somebody's bicycle or fiddling the books at the local fish-shop'. He wasn't interested in such riff-raff and they took good care not to get involved with him.

But there were a few professionals in Wandsworth who regarded their spell away as an interlude in their normal way of life. These men had heard about the Colonel and his private 'Returned Prisoners' Aid Society'. They knew he had a brother outside who commanded considerable power. And when their spell inside was over they knew how useful the friendship of a gang like the Krays' could be. Soon Ronnie's life in Wandsworth Gaol was cosily buttoned up.

Reggie helped: he had never shown himself more practical and efficient than when he set about organizing the well-being of his twin brother inside Wandsworth Gaol. In theory all prisoners are equal, apart from the privileges they earn by hard work and good behaviour. No extra food or comforts can be sent in and what money they earn by prison work goes into an account at the canteen to be spent on sweets or extra tobacco. But no society is able to survive without a currency, even if a forbidden one. Once there is a currency it can be manipulated to acquire privilege and power.

The unofficial currency of every gaol is tobacco, and Reggie Kray saw to it that his brother was tobacco rich from the day his sentence started. This was simple, but required organizing. The first move was for Ronnie to find a number of non-smoking married men serving their sentence with him who had families somewhere in London – then to suggest a deal. If they would supply him with their spare tobacco, he'd arrange for their wives to be put on the Kray pension scheme. An ounce of tobacco would rate a £1 note for the wife outside. Reggie made certain that the money was paid regularly each week.

Once Ronnie had all the tobacco he needed he began using it to build himself a life apart from the rest of prison society. In his own eyes he remained someone exceptional. Even in prison he could adopt a lordly attitude towards the petty chores of servitude. There was the question of work. Canteen earnings were geared to the number of brushes turned out each day and a straight prisoner soon learned the knack of managing the pitch and bristles and earning a reasonable wage. Ronnie never bothered. Straight work was even more contemptible within prison than without, and he would buy brushes off other men in the brush workshop to fill in his minimum quota by the end of the day.

Similarly with food: whenever he considered the food below standard – particularly the fish, which is universally loathed in prison – Ronnie would just refuse it, filling up instead with cakes and biscuits bought from the canteen by one of his paid followers.

So Ronnie kept his private dream alive during these first months in Wandsworth by turning prison life into a replica of life outside. A fantasy can be lived anywhere. He had his batman and his servants to look after him. He had his group of followers who endlessly discussed the villainy they'd start when they were free. He had his silences, his moods, his periods when people whispered that the Colonel was thinking and had best not be disturbed.

Reggie survived the separation too. He missed Ronnie: Vallance Road was a lonely place without him, and nobody could take his place within the Firm. 'There didn't seem much point in doing things without the Colonel there.' Reggie was no substitute for his brother and didn't try. Ronnie's dream world vanished with him: no more vendettas, sudden shootings, wars to the death. Without the daily contact of his twin, Reggie calmed down. Suddenly he was free from the suspicions and fears he had always shared with Ronnie. Gradually he relaxed, became more confident, and the old charm, which had been wearing thin, started to reappear. Now he was head of the Firm he came into his own as leader and chief 'money-getter'.

'Reg was the live wire and Ron was the lazy bastard. All that Ron wanted was the glory, but Reg was after anything that spelled money.'

He had an idea how to get it now. 'I'd always felt that what the East End needed was a decent, properly run club of its own so that the East End people could come and listen to some music and buy their women a drink without having to worry about some hooligan making trouble.'

Reggie had dreamt of this for years. The billiard hall and then The Stragglers had given him a taste for playing host and meeting people. As long as Ronnie was around, any club of the twins' would be restricted to a hardened clientele. With him away, Reggie had his chance. He took considerable trouble finding the right place before deciding on an empty shop along the Bow Road. It was completely derelict but it was central and the rent was cheap. Reggie and two of the Firm did the redecorating themselves, building a stage and putting up red flock wallpaper in the bar. All the ideas were Reggie's; he had never been happier than he was now, making this place entirely his own. A few months after Ronnie began his three-year sentence Reggie was putting on his brand-new smoking jacket for the opening of 'the finest drinking club the East End's ever known'.

It was a success from the start. Reggie had a flair for knowing what cockneys wanted and was smart enough to see that the new affluent East End needed a West-End-style club of its own. He soon showed real talent for club life. He said 'no hooligans' and meant it; the few who came were quickly dealt with. He said he wanted men to be able to bring their girl-friends; they did. Soon he had regulars who came because of him and suddenly the club was getting known as one of the 'in' places on the East End circuit for people from the west. The first few lesser-known celebrities started to arrive in the Bow Road – a playboy or two, an up-and-coming starlet, journalists, an occasional film man in search of new locations. For them, this was the authentic East End they were looking for. For Reggie they were ambassadors of the good life, and started him on a love affair with the famous which the twins would share in the years ahead. The success was Reggie's, but Ronnie was not forgotten. The club combined their joint initials. Reggie christened it The Double R.

Unlike his brother, Reggie Kray had the makings of a first-rate businessman-gangster of the old school. Without his brother, he would have made a definite success of crime and almost certainly have been a rich man and a free one to this day. During his period of freedom from his twin Reggie took few risks, did nothing for the hell of it and shrewdly chose to work with just a few rich, semi-honest clients who needed him. He also showed that, without Ronnie there, he could hold on to his money.

During this period with The Double R, as Reggie got established as a character and showed that he was thoroughly at home in the limbo-land of crime and club life, he rationalized his criminal affairs. There was no need to grab at anything to bring in £50. Crime and the club life went together. He could confine himself to working with a few men at a time who could be thoroughly exploited; he found he had a talent for spotting them. They were the men with money and with something else – greed, boredom with the straight world, a weakness for dishonesty. According to Reggie, 'It's odd how you can pick 'em out at once. There's some rich people can't resist the idea of crime. You see them getting all worked up when they think they're with criminals. I s'pose it's because they've always longed to do something forbidden. But they seem to get a kick like sex out of the idea of crime.'

The way it was developing, The Double R was the ideal place for meeting men like this. The corrupt moneyed world could mingle easily with the criminal one; Reggie began exploiting both.

He could be vicious still – when necessary. On the few occasions when there were fights at The Double R he was as lethal as before. He was still cunning, too, and not the man to forget a grudge. Ronnie had to be avenged. A few months after Terry Martin went into the witness-box at the Old Bailey, fire swept through the drinking club owned by the Martin family in Poplar. At the time it happened, Reggie was fishing with a policeman friend in Suffolk. He had always been good with alibis; and he was clever about the threats that sometimes came his way. These usually came from people he had tricked out of money. One day he heard that someone who had threatened him was trying to buy a gun from one of the East End's illicit arms dealers. He spoke to the dealer, who sold the man the gun he wanted, but it was a special one – so special that when the man waited outside The Double R and took a shot at Reggie as he left, it exploded in his hand. He was in hospital a month, and nearly lost his hand.

Photographs of this period show Reggie smiling: the wariness has left his face. Despite the hours he was keeping, he looked fit and well. He kept himself in trim, drank moderately and lived a very normal life. He liked young children, enjoyed the country, began riding at weekends.

Before long The Double R was bringing in a steady income and it was clear that he had hit on the formula for success – the orderly raucousness, the sentimental cockney songs of Queenie Watts, the villains mixing with celebrities and the regular presence of several large but well-behaved old boxers like handsome Tommy Brown, the 'Bear of Tottenham', and 'Big Pat' Connolly, the Glasgow doorman, who weighed twenty-one stone in his prime. Sometimes the gipsies came, and Reggie, remembering his own Romany blood, stood them drinks and told them they could stay. He now had real celebrities among The Double R's visitors – Jackie Collins, Sybil Burton, Barbara Windsor: he called them by their first names and drew a certain glamour from their presence. He looked like turning into something of a playboy, dressing well, enjoying an evening in a West End nightclub and, for the first time in his life, taking an interest in women.

This was the biggest break of all from Ronnie, who had always managed to keep him away from women. Bound by the ties that link a homosexual with his identical twin, Ronnie had always seen any show of interest in a girl by Reggie as rebellion – which it was – and treated it accordingly.

'What you thinking of, goin' with a bloody woman? You're gettin' soft. Don't you know that women smell and give you diseases?'

Now things were different without Ronnie there, Reggie realized he was good-looking and that women found him attractive. Life at The Double R taught him what he had never understood before – that women are part of the good life and not to be ashamed of. Now, for the first time, Charlie Kray, the elder brother, really entered Reggie's life. He and his blonde wife, Dolly, fitted in naturally with the new life of The Double R. Reggie got on well with him, although the relationship was different from the one he had with Ronnie. Charlie had nothing of Ronnie's viciousness or showmanship or dreams of glory; he was an easy-going man whose wife didn't get on with her in-laws, and so he had built a separate family life of his own with their two children in a modern flat in Stepney. He and his wife enjoyed themselves. He did well as a wardrobe-dealer. They often had a night out in the West End together. Dolly danced well, and Charlie was something of a gambler, like his father.

Now, with The Double R flourishing, Charlie Kray joined in the success. Had Ronnie been around, the money would have gone as fast as it was earned; the club would have become another battleground, and Reggie's energy would soon have gone into fresh wars and further gang alliances. With Charlie there, things were different. Charlie was shrewd. They found another drinking club at Stratford and bought it. They began their own car-site on the empty plot beside the billiard hall. Then Charlie heard of an empty house going for a nominal rent next to the car park of Bow Police Station. It was typical of Reggie to decide that this would be an ideal place for an illicit gambling club. Despite their neighbours, the Wellington Way Club, which they opened in the spring of 1957, became their biggest money-spinner so far. Blackjack, rummy and faro were bringing in a minimum of £50 a night in house money. The profits doubled when Reggie installed an illegal book-making business on the premises.

Despite the close proximity of Bow Police Station the only threat to the gathering enrichment of Reggie and Charlie Kray was not the Law but the prisoner in Wandsworth Gaol, who was just entering the fifteenth month of his sentence.

Ronnie Kray seemed fine. Now he had his small world under his control he was quite happily sitting out his sentence and hoping for remission for good conduct. He was no trouble. He read a lot. *Boy's Town* was still his favourite book. 'It's a lovely story. I used to dream of doing something like that for homeless boys when I came out. Not just because I like boys either. I wanted to do some good. Something that I could be remembered for.' He kept to himself, apart from his 'pensioners' and a few close friends. The warders treated him warily. Reggie and the family wrote regularly. And he made a new friend, a good-looking giant of a man called Frank Mitchell. Ronnie had been reading *Of Mice and Men*. Mitchell reminded him of Lennie. He was a gentle psychopath, immensely strong, childlike with those he trusted, violent against authority. Warders kept clear of him, and although he had spent most of his life in institutions he was proud of taking any punishment he got. Ronnie admired this. He admired his body and his looks. He also liked to feel that he could care for him. He would try to cheer him up during recreation; when Frank was depressed Ronnie would send him presents of food and tobacco. Few people visited him, so Ronnie arranged with Reggie to get members of the Firm to come to see him. When they talked, Ronnie always promised Mitchell that he and his brother would look after him in the years ahead.

Then Ronnie Kray's routine was broken. Without intending it, his good behaviour had made him eligible for the easier life of a first offenders' prison and he found himself aboard the Solent ferry, bound for the Isle of Wight. The prison at Camp Hill was more humane than Wandsworth. There was a liberal-minded governor, prisoners mixed freely most of the day, and the whole prison staff made an attempt to teach these first offenders trades and stop them turning into hardened criminals. Ronnie hated it.

There were too many games, and far too many straight prisoners for his liking. In Wandsworth the old lags respected him. He had had prestige. Here he was nothing.

The Wandsworth tobacco circuit didn't operate. Instead of prisoners needing his help, most of these new ones kept clear of someone smelling so patently of trouble. He was still shy, still vulnerable, and found it hard to start a normal friendship. All his relationships beyond the family had been with the weird, the cowed or the small group of Bethnal Greeners he had grown up with. New friends appeared impossible.

He was entirely alone here: his family and followers were a continent away across the Solent. He had no aptitude to learn a trade. And for the first time he sensed that he was losing touch with the one being who had always been his firm link with reality. Reggie's success started to obsess him.

Gradually he withdrew into himself. He gave up the effort of talking to people. He stopped writing letters and seemed to lose the power to read. All he could do was watch, and he gradually became convinced that everyone was hostile to him. In the past he had controlled events; now he was helpless. People had feared him; now they were getting their revenge. During the night he would lie awake for hours, brooding on what he'd seen, trying to work out what had happened to turn everyone against him.

'If Reggie'd been there, I'd have been all right. But there was no one. I started thinking there was someone there all set to do me in.'

The worst thing was not knowing what he had done.

'Then I worked out what was behind it all. I was a bit barmy now. But I thought everyone was thinking I had grassed.'

This explained everything – the silences, the lack of friends, the sudden isolation. But it was terrible. Ronnie had spent his life loathing the Law: an informer was the lowest of the low. No one could seriously believe this of him. The suspicion turned to certainty. What other reason would a group of prisoners have for making him an outcast? He tried to face it calmly. If people thought like that, so what? He knew the truth. He had less than a year to serve now; then he'd be back among people who loved him and respected him. The year soon proved too long.

'I don't know what it was set me off, but I thought there was agents everywhere working a big plot to torture me.'

His only hope was vigilance – never trust a soul or give himself away. Somehow at night he had to keep himself awake. His survival depended on it now. He talked to no one, did nothing except concentrate on his battle to stay alive. People ignored him, but he knew that they were watching.

Then came the thought that finished him. Just suppose all his enemies were right – suppose he *had* been an informer without knowing it? How could he prove he wasn't? If only Reggie had been there, he would have known, but on his own like this how could he be sure of anything? Perhaps there was someone else inside him forcing him to do things he never knew. How could he know that he was Ronnie Kray at all?

Hardly sleeping now, barely eating for fear that someone might have poisoned his food, Ronnie spent most of each day huddled in his cell facing the door. The warders, worried that he might kill himself, kept him under observation, making him more nervous still. They noticed that the only time he moved was to go to the mirror. He spent hours on end watching himself. They thought it vanity. It wasn't. He was attempting to keep sane with the sight of the one familiar thing remaining – his own face. Even that was changing: there was a puffiness around the eyes, a faint thickening along the jaw-line.

This was the point at which he broke. The watching game could last no longer. If they were all against him, he would face them and get it over with. That evening, instead of staying in his cell he walked down to the recreation room. He stood apart from all the others, watching for a while. There were all enemies – he could see that now.

They were pretending to ignore him with their silly games, but he had had enough.

He began breathing deeply as he had done between rounds as a boxer to gain strength. He screamed, then charged, arms flailing, punching at everyone he could. He tipped a table over and hurt several prisoners before he was safely put into a straitjacket.

Later that night he thought he saw the man who had been plotting everything against him from the start. The governor of Camp Hill Prison had heard of the trouble at recreation and called into the sick bay to see if prisoner Kray were feeling any better.

'Filthy old bastard,' screamed Ronnie, and spat at him. He felt better then.

Ronnie was moved to the psychiatric wing of Winchester Gaol for observation. The medical officer diagnosed an attack of 'prison psychosis' – a term covering almost any form of violent mental disorder brought on by confinement – and had him heavily sedated. For a while he seemed to recover. He answered questions coherently, was pleased with news of the family and began eating again. Then came the news about Aunt Rose. The family had known that she had leukaemia for nearly two years, but had kept it from Ronnie for fear of upsetting him. Wild Aunt Rose who once beat two women in a straight fight in Vallance Road fought death as she had fought everything. Twice she dragged herself home when the doctors had given her less than a year to live. When she was too weak to stand, the family refused to let her back into hospital.

Violet insisted, 'It wasn't right to allow our Rose to die in a place like that. So we took turns, sitting up with her every night. She was in the big bed in the front room where our mum and dad sleep now. The doctors warned us that her end would come with a haemorrhage and that it wouldn't be nice to see. Her feet swelled up and the rest of her went thin as a rake. Then on Christmas Eve the bleeding started. She went on Christmas Day.'

Two days later, in the psychiatric wing of Winchester Gaol, Ronnie received the letter from Reggie telling him 'Aunt Rawse' was dead. By evening he was incoherent and had to be placed in the straitjacket again for his own safety.

Reggie had nightmares all that night. So did Violet Kray. She dreamt that two men in white coats were dragging Ronnie across a courtyard to a building without windows. The following morning she received an official telegram from the governor of Winchester Gaol:

'Your son Ronald Kray certified insane.'

SEVEN

Flight from Long Grove

According to the board by the gate the place is simply Long Grove Hospital, a peaceful spot within the Surrey countryside. By the main entrance is a marmalade-pot lodge, lace curtains at the windows. Forsythia flanks the drive; no one is about. Epsom lies a mile and a half away across the fields but all the forsythia in the world will never alter the outline of the old lunatic asylums built to an identical pattern round London at the turn of the century. All have the same red, Aldershot-style wards and office blocks, the same high water-tower that peers like an enormous head across the country. And Long Grove still receives most of its patients from the same part of London as when the London County Council erected it in 1907 to cope with the growing number of the mentally disordered from the slums of Hackney and Bethnal Green. Ronnie was driven here from Winchester Prison on 20 February 1958. He was never to forget the terror of those first few days. He was placed in Napier Ward, a locked ward; trained nurses kept each patient under day and night supervision.

'I wouldn't move, but sat all day huddled round the radiator. I wasn't quite sure who I was. The radiator seemed the only friend I had because it was warm. I was completely on my own, and funny things used to come and go in my mind. I thought the man opposite me was a dog, and if I got his name right he'd come and jump in my lap. I'd have a friend then, but I never got his name. I didn't recognize anyone, although Reggie and my mother visited me. Sometimes I thought I'd kill myself to stop someone else doing it first.'

According to his medical report he had 'put his hand through a glass window' and showed signs of 'verbigeration and marked thought blocking'. He was 'unstable and in fear of bodily change'. He believed people were still plotting against him, tampering with his letters and censoring them for sinister purposes. No intelligence test was carried out, and there was nothing on his report about his criminal case history. But the doctor had wide experience of the mentally sick and seems to have had no difficulty summing up the patient's character: 'A simple man of low intelligence, poorly in touch with the outside world.'

For the Long Grove doctors, this was all he was – a simple man, a fairly simple case of schizophrenic breakdown. He would never be entirely cured, but could be helped over the breakdown and then stabilized on regular doses of the new tranquillizers that were revolutionizing the treatment of the mentally sick. At Long Grove they were performing these miracles every day and the doctors set to work on Ronnie, placing him on Stematol – a drug which damps down neurotic symptoms without doping the patient completely.

Out of the eighteen hundred patients at the time, six were from prisons, and the hospital made a point of insisting to the Home Office that they would be treated exactly like ordinary patients. So Ronnie Kray became a routine case – nothing to make a fuss about. His family agreed, although for slightly different reasons. They knew their Ronnie: he was simply 'acting up a bit to kid the authorities into giving him a change of scene'. Reggie had seen him 'acting barmy' once already in the army and knew the lengths he'd go. If the medical officer at Winchester Gaol had been taken in and sent him to this comfortable little hospital near London, that just showed what a good actor Ronnie was. Within a week the treatment had begun to take effect. Ronnie had left his radiator and there was no longer a dog in the bed opposite. He began to read again, to recognize his family. The doctors were so pleased with his progress that by the end of March they had him moved from Napier Ward to MI Block. The doors were left unlocked there.

Although schizophrenics form by far the largest single group in Britain's mental hospitals the disease remains something of a mystery. Kraepelin described it in the 1890s under the name *dementia praecox* but medical research is still scratching at its origins and true nature. It can take many forms, although the disease usually develops over a long period and is sparked off by a final crisis. There is no known 'cure' as such, but sufferers can be helped over the 'florid' state of a schizophrenic breakdown by various modern drugs; after-effects vary enormously.

In Ronnie's case the medical reports show considerable vagueness over the form of his disease. He was in Long Grove to be treated, and here he was responding rather more quickly than most. But had the Long Grove doctors taken the trouble to find out a little of his history of violence and delusion, it is hard to believe that they would have moved him quite so promptly out of Napier Ward. The hospital's policy of treating mentally sick criminals like ordinary patients was a worthy one as far as it went; but it was patently absurd if it led doctors to ignore the fact that a man like Ronnie was a criminal.

For Ronnie was no ordinary schizophrenic whose problems could be tidied up with three capsules of Stematol a day. Crime formed an important part of his disease, and had his doctors had the time to study his history they could not have failed to recognize him for what he really was and treated him accordingly. Among the different types of schizophrenics there is a small group who are potentially dangerous and the most difficult to spot – the paranoid schizophrenics. Most schizophrenics find it hard to face the world and finally collapse through inability to reconcile their delusions with the world outside. The paranoid schizophrenic is different. Even if he has a breakdown, his obsessions can persist despite it. He has the strange power to direct all his mental faculties to the protection of his distorted world. This means that outwardly he can often appear completely logical and normal; inwardly he is ruled by his obsession as he 'continues in his vicious circle of ill-advised aggressiveness, self-protection, misinterpretation, spread of delusional ideas and increasing watchfulness'.

There are certain symptoms that usually reveal themselves: lack of feeling for others, difficulty in communicating, erratic behaviour, extreme moodiness. Often delusions of grandeur are combined with extreme feelings of persecution. Sometimes the paranoid schizophrenic suffers what is called 'double orientation': he follows the normal world, yet simultaneously identifies with Christ, Napoleon or some great figure of the past. Frequently he believes himself to be directed by a fate or personality somewhere beyond him. At the same time the blunting of the emotions can lead to 'callous and apparently motiveless crimes of violence' if his obsession demands it for its defence. Sometimes such violence would seem the only way he could survive. 'A trifling affair may arouse wild fury and an incident pregnant with pathos be treated with levity.'

Qualities like these appear in many of history's great religious leaders – also in its most notorious criminals. Jack the Ripper, Al Capone and the Boston Strangler are textbook cases of the violent paranoid schizophrenic. So, as the Long Grove doctors might have discovered, was Ronnie Kray.

But he was recovering so fast that no one did. Stematol was working. Ronnie appeared quite normal, reading, joking, writing letters home. The doctors thought that they had done their job. By the beginning of May, Ronnie appeared so well that he applied to be discharged from hospital and allowed to return to prison.

This request was not as strange as it may seem. Ronnie

was haunted by the fate of his Wandsworth friend, Frank Mitchell, who was considered such a public menace that the authorities had refused him a definite release date. Mitchell saw year follow year in prison, never quite knowing when it would all end. Officially certified insane, Ronnie could end up in the same position.

The hospital considered his request; at the end of May, two doctors examined him. They were both optimistic about his general condition. He showed no marked psychotic symptoms now, answered intelligently and was, they wrote, 'quiet, co-operative and mentally subnormal'.

But he still showed signs of depression. A swift return to prison could bring a recurrence of his trouble. Reggie was told that for his brother's own good he should stay where he was a while longer. Ronnie was upset at the news. He thought he would never be released. Reggie calmed him down. He wouldn't let that happen. He had a bright idea that ought to work; it always had done in the past.

At Long Grove the main visiting hours are on Sunday afternoon. East Enders take their families seriously; by three o'clock the wards are crammed with cockney relatives and friends. This is the high-spot of the patients' week; the hospital provides tea and biscuits to make everyone feel at home. Not that the Krays and all their friends ever let Ronnie feel neglected. Each Sunday he always had the two visitors he was allowed. But during one visiting-time after Ronnie's application had been rejected an extra lot turned up – two large American car-loads of them. The first car, an electric-blue Lincoln, contained Reggie and an old friend of the family called Georgie Osborne. The second, a black Ford, held several characters from The Double R. One was a safe-blower, two were ex-boxers, and the man at the wheel was known for his skill as a smash-and-grab-raid driver. Both cars parked just outside Ronnie's block. The men in the Ford told the hospital porter that they hadn't realized visitors were restricted to two at a time; they would wait and see Ronnie later. Reggie slipped on a light-fawn raincoat and he and Osborne walked into Ronnie's ward.

On visiting afternoons there was always a male nurse on duty; on that afternoon there was nothing about Ronnie to give the nurse particular concern. Ronnie was quite smartly dressed in a blue suit and maroon-coloured tie; if he was still upset at the doctor's decision, he was keeping it to himself. His brother in the fawn coat had brought a pile of holiday snaps and they were all enjoying them. The nurse had never seen Ronnie laugh so much.

At 3.30 P.M. tea was brewed up in the scullery along the corridor. Regulations forbade patients to pass beyond the ward doors during visiting hours, so one of the visitors usually fetched it. That Sunday the Kray brother in the fawn coat went. The nurse nodded to him as he passed.

Twenty minutes must have elapsed before the nurse saw anything was wrong. Young Kray was still there, laughing with his visitor, who seemed to have an endless store of snapshots. Why hadn't his brother come back with the tea?

'Where's your brother?'

'Which brother?'

'Your brother Reggie who went out to get the tea.'

'Reggie didn't go.'

''Course he did. I saw him myself.'

'He didn't. I'm Reg Kray. I'll prove it if you don't believe me. Here's my driving licence.'

'Then that was Ronnie went out for the tea?'

'Who d'you think it was? Thought you knew him by now.'

The nurse sounded the alarm-bell, but it was too late. The black Ford was on its way to London with Ronnie inside. Reggie had previously arranged with him to wear the same blue suit and tie, and switched the raincoat with him when the nurse wasn't looking. The police arrived and questioned Reggie and Osborne for over an hour, but there was nothing they could do once Reggie had proved his identity. As he said to one of the police, 'It's not as if we actually done anything. We've just been sitting here waiting for a cup of tea that never came.'

The track lay to the left of the road, a good half-mile before the farm. There was an ancient wooden gate-post and the track went trailing up between the fields and the nettle-beds towards the woods. Suffolk is a mysterious county, and this was a particularly hidden part of it. Borley Rectory, 'the most haunted house in England', was four miles distant. Even in high summer this countryside, with its decaying manor houses and lanes that lose themselves between the banks of hawthorn and cow-parsley, seems to be keeping out intruders.

A fortnight before Ronnie's escape Reggie had driven here towing a four-berth caravan. The owner of the farm was an old acquaintance, a London businessman the twins had often worked with in the past. He could hardly have refused them a small favour and at dusk he helped Reggie manoeuvre the caravan up the track and into the woods.

The escape was widely reported in the press; the police were combing London for 'this violent criminal'. They said, 'We know what type of person he is and are taking no chances.'

But Ronnie had vanished. Reggie continued working at The Double R as usual. Nearly a week after the escape, Reggie closed up his club and drove back to Vallance Road. By midnight the downstairs lights were out; soon the whole house was in darkness.

Just after one o'clock the back door opened. Reggie slipped out and scrambled over the yard wall. Then along Cheshire Street came the noise of a car starting and driving away; he had a long night's ride ahead. First stop was Walthamstow, where Ronnie was being looked after by friends; he came out muffled in a black overcoat. They arrived at the farm just before dawn.

When they had eaten, Reggie took a torch and led his brother out of the caravan. He had to show Ronnie all he had done for him and wanted to be back in Bethnal Green before anyone noticed his absence. The caravan was where he had left it. He unlocked the door, turned on the Calor gas lights and the heater and showed Ronnie how lovingly he had prepared the hideaway – the stacked provisions and the radio, the gramophone with all his favourite records, books, beer, a small gas refrigerator.

Under existing prison regulations, any prisoner certified insane who escaped and remained at liberty longer than six weeks had to be recertified on recapture. All Ronnie had to do was to behave himself and stay out of the way for a couple of months in the caravan. Then he could give himself up; the certification would have lapsed and he could complete his sentence with a minimum of fuss. Within a year he would be free.

Reggie had everything worked out for this. One reason he had chosen this part of Suffolk was so that Ronnie would feel at home; they had lived nearby as evacuees during the war and had often been back since. But Reggie realized his brother couldn't be left alone all day, and the third man who had travelled down with the twins was to be Ronnie Kray's companion, bodyguard and keeper for the period of his escape. Once again, Reggie had planned things well, for Teddy was one of the few people Ronnie trusted who was also capable of handling him. A young thief, slightly older than the twins, he had grown up in Bethnal Green and had been a trusted follower of the Colonel's in the days of the billiard hall. He was tough, single and heterosexual. Also, unlike most of the Colonel's admirers, he had a certain vein of humour and common sense.

Sitting in the Suffolk woods in early June, Teddy had no complaints: here he was earning £15 a week in luxury and idleness. The caravan was comfortable. There was all the food and beer he wanted. And the Colonel had never been in better spirits.

'He was a lazy bastard, but he always had been. He'd lie in bed all morning,' and Teddy had to cook and keep the caravan tidy. 'But Ronnie loved the country. It calmed him down, and when he was calm he was like a big child and no trouble at all.' They would spar together and run and do exercises to keep fit. Sometimes they took long walks at night and once they borrowed a car from the farmer up the road and drove to Sudbury to the cinema. Ronnie wanted to see *Dracula*.

For Teddy, being with the Colonel was like being a boy again, and there was one game in particular which Ronnie never tired of – the hunting game. It was Ronnie's idea to use loaded air rifles to make it more realistic, and since he didn't like the thought of hurting animals he suggested they should stalk each other. Teddy was the better shot, and hit Ronnie several times before Ronnie used his cunning and caught his friend in an ambush, hitting him in the eye with a pellet. Teddy had to go to Sudbury Hospital to have it removed.

Most weekends Reggie arrived at the caravan with a car-load of food and drink and a few friends who could be relied on to be discreet. They had some splendid parties. Ronnie would hear all the news from home and when there were visitors he would usually drink until he dropped off to sleep where he was. Reggie organized these parties to stop Ronnie feeling forgotten, but soon they were having the opposite effect. Talking of London made him realize how much he missed it, and when Reggie and his friends drove back on Sunday night he felt abandoned and confined within the four walls of the caravan. Teddy would get him out of his moods in the end and they would start their sparring and hunting and midnight walks. Then one more weekend would arrive, another party, and the following week Ronnie's moods were worse than ever.

For the first time now, sex became a problem. Had Ronnie liked women it would have been easier to keep him satisfied, but in the middle of Suffolk it was impossible to ensure the supply of young male 'prospects' he enjoyed in London, without arousing local suspicions. Reggie started bringing boys along at the weekends to keep the Colonel quiet. This was a mistake. Ronnie would always try and force the boy to stay. By Sunday afternoons terrible rows would start when Reggie insisted that the boy return with him. Jealous and frustrated, Ronnie would finally have to watch the boy he fancied driven back to London on a Sunday evening.

As usual, Reggie finally gave in. He knew that it was risky, but he let Ronnie have his night in London. It was a success. Reggie had borrowed a flat in Tottenham and the following day his mother and a few friends visited Ronnie there before he drove back to the country.

But if Reggie imagined that the Colonel would be satisfied with one visit, he should have known his brother better. He was soon clamouring for another; within a week Reggie had given in again, arranging a small party for the Colonel at a fresh address. The following week there was another, and in no time the comings and goings were being whispered round the East End. The Colonel's legend had begun again. One evening Ronnie would turn up at Vallance Road. Another, he materialized in the middle of the engagement party for his cousin Rita, who was marrying his old friend Ritchie Smith. He even visited The Double R. This was the Colonel's own Command Performance and the twins made the most of it. It was arranged for late at night, long after closing time, when the place had been cleared of all but the most trusted of their friends. As a special precaution a decoy car, similar to Ronnie's, was driven to the club first and someone of Ronnie's height and build hurried in with his collar up and face muffled. Everyone waited just in case the Law was watching. When nothing happened, Reggie had his moment of drama, lifting the telephone, dialling the number where Ronnie was waiting, allowing it to ring twice, and then replacing it. This was the signal that the coast was clear. Ten minutes later the Colonel arrived.

Soon they were famous, these fly-by-night visits of the Colonel to The Double R, a great 'in' secret for the 'other world' of London criminals, and Reggie was quick to draw maximum kudos from his now-notorious brother. Many of the top London villains were invited to The Double R after closing time to witness the Colonel's famous reappearing act. One night Billy Hill was there. Since he had retired from his 'kingship of the underworld' Billy Hill had changed. Wealth and exile had softened him and he was a reserved, softly spoken figure now, blinking from behind large magnifying spectacles and giving the impression of a certain shyness often adopted by those who have withdrawn from the power game. But although he had opted out, he had a nose for what was going on and who was rising. For him to turn up at The Double R on one of his occasional visits from abroad showed that the twins were in the news again.

Charlie Kray saw what was happening and did his best to warn Reggie. Ronnie should be thinking of surrendering and getting his sentence over, but by now the twins were far too busy enjoying the situation. One night Ronnie disguised himself and walked the length of the Whitechapel Road, laughing each time he passed the policemen who were still supposed to be searching for him. Another time he put on one of Reggie's suits and sat in a pub where the locals were used to seeing his brother.

'Evening, Reg. Any news of Ron?'

'No. Why? Seen him lately?'

'Heard he's about. Wish him luck if you meet him.'

Then Reggie had another bright idea. Through his doctor he found the name of a good Harley Street psychiatrist, and made an appointment for a Mr John Lee. Lee was their mother's maiden name, and on the day of the appointment it was Ronnie Kray who turned up at the Harley Street waiting-room. He was well-dressed, quite calm, and he and Reggie had carefully worked out beforehand what to say.

When he saw the doctor Ronnie explained his problem. He was engaged to be married. He and the girl were very much in love, but her family had raised an objection. Some way back in his family there had been a touch of insanity and they were worried that he might go the same way. His girl-friend wasn't worried, but could the doctor give him a test or two and write a letter saying he wasn't mad? It would set his future in-laws' minds at rest.

The psychiatrist was a good-natured man with a sense of humour. It was an unusual request but not unreasonable. Mr Lee seemed a normal, somewhat earnest young man. They talked for twenty minutes or so. The doctor asked various questions which Ronnie answered satisfactorily, and the doctor wrote a brief note on his headed paper giving it as his serious professional opinion that Mr John Lee of 178 Vallance Road, E1, was as sane as the next man.

The letter from the psychiatrist was one reason why Reggie wouldn't listen to Teddy when he told him that Ronnie was going mad again. During their adventures in London Reggie was seeing the Colonel he knew. But every time Ronnie returned to the caravan for a few days, Teddy saw someone different and was becoming frightened. Each trip to London now left Ronnie deeply depressed and he spent days in bed, drinking himself into a stupor. If he got up things were worse; anything in the outside world could start his fears. One day he saw someone passing down the road and spent the whole day worrying. By evening he was frantic, shouting that he had to get away to London. Teddy called in the farmer; between them they quietened him down, got him drunk and left him to sleep off his fears. They decided that until they could speak to Reggie, Ronnie and Teddy would both sleep at the farm. It would be easier to control him there if anything went wrong.

The rest of that day Ronnie seemed quite happy pottering round the farm; that evening after supper he and the farmer watched television. Suddenly the telephone rang. It was someone from the village reminding the farmer about some business he had forgotten. When he had promised to do it and replaced the telephone, he said, 'I wish he'd leave me alone. He's just a bloody menace, that man.'

Ronnie fell silent. They had a few drinks. Television ended, and as the farmer was going off to bed Ronnie stopped him. 'Listen,' he said, 'you've been a good friend, and I know just how you feel about that bastard getting at you on the phone. Just give me his address. I'll kill him for you. It's the only thing to do with scum like that.'

The farmer was no fool, and knew that Ronnie meant just what he said. That night the farmer rang a Harley Street psychiatrist he knew, explained the situation and arranged to take Ronnie to see him the next day. This time the examination was more probing than on Ronnie's previous visit to Harley Street. They drove back to the farm in time for supper. Ronnie was feeling tired. When he was in bed, the farmer rang the specialist for his verdict.

'I don't know who your friend is, but he's clearly homicidal. He shows all the symptoms of advanced paranoid schizophrenia. Get him to hospital or anything could happen.'

Reggie wouldn't hear of it, although the farmer rang him straight away; Ronnie was convinced that once he entered any institution his enemies would get him and he would be there for life. He could still present quite a coherent front to the world in general. Teddy and the farmer were the only friends who really knew how sick he was. And so the trips to London continued. When the farmer suggested getting Ronnie medical treatment, storms of resentment followed. Then for the farmer and for Teddy the problem solved itself.

The year of 1958 was a vintage one for gaol-breaks: Ronnie's departure from Long Grove was eclipsed by that virtuoso fugitive, Mr Alfred Hinds, who earlier that year had walked out of the law courts in the Strand and never been heard of since. Hinds was a bigger fish than Ronnie Kray: the police were still searching for him, and nearly picked up Ronnie Kray instead. Somebody had seen his midnight walks from the farm and reported them to the police. There was a slender chance that this was Hinds; early one morning the Sudbury police called at the farm to check in case it were.

Ronnie and Teddy by now slept permanently at the farm. Both were in bed, but the farmer handled the police perfectly, asking them in, explaining that his guest did like walking at night, then calling Teddy to meet them. This settled things at once. No one could possibly mistake this burly young tough for the gnome-like Mr Hinds. The police departed.

But Ronnie had been listening upstairs. He had been dreading the police for weeks. His fears now seemed confirmed. No one could reason with him. Either he got away at once or he would kill anyone who tried to stop him. The farmer agreed with him, rang through to Reggie at The Double R and left it to Ronnie to beg his brother to come and take him away. This time even Reggie was convinced. By the time he came, Ronnie was worse.

'You're not my brother, Reg. You're just a dirty Russian spy got up to look like him.'

''Course I'm Reg. You've known me all your life.'

'You just look like him. You're a dirty agent in disguise. Your police missed me this morning. You've come to take me off to kill me somewhere.'

'Don't you remember the old scar on my arm?' Ronnie did remember, and allowed himself to be led out to his brother's car and driven up to London. He insisted on making the whole journey in the boot.

For Reggie Kray the fantasy was over: he had to face the truth about his brother. The game they'd played was finished, Ronnie was no colonel but his mentally deranged twin brother. Now for the first time he was truly scared: 'For a while I really thought that I was going off my head myself.'

There was one person who might help – their mother. Once they were back at Vallance Road, Violet Kray managed to calm Ronnie for a while. But not for long. How did he *know* that this was Vallance Road? It looked like it, but that proved nothing. Similarly with this woman: she looked just like his mother, but possibly that went to prove just what a cunning lot they were.

'You're all a lot of dirty filthy murderers,' he sobbed.

That night the family called in a doctor they could trust and who had known the twins for many years. 'I knew that technically Ronnie was insane and did my best to get him into hospital. He was in a dreadful state. All I could do that night was give him sedatives and warn the family what would happen if he didn't get the treatment that he needed.'

Most of the family agreed with the doctor but Reggie was adamant: 'Just give him time and peace and quiet. He'll be all right.'

To give him this he moved with Ronnie into a third-floor luxury flat off the Bayswater Road. He never left his brother's side now and tried everything to cure him – fresh doctors, new drugs from America, trips to the country. But each day Ronnie seemed worse, and ultimately drink was all that kept him quiet. Sometimes he drank two bottles of gin a day.

According to the doctor, 'It was chiefly alcohol that produced the physical change that was so marked in him about this time. Alcohol in any quantity mixed with a drug affecting the central nervous system can have the most appalling oblique effect. I know that there were times when even he was scared. It must have been like DTs ten times over.' And by this time Reggie was drinking too. Soon he appeared as scared and anxious as his brother.

Then Ronnie got the idea that he would be all right if he could see an old friend who was now in Maidstone Gaol. Reggie would agree to anything by now and a few days later fixed a visit at the prison. One of the Firm took Ronnie, who entered the prison under an assumed name. For an hour this half-mad escapee sat in the visiting-room at Maidstone Gaol begging his friend to make a break from prison just to come and help him. The man refused. Ronnie wept, promised anything he wanted, but the man insisted that it was not possible.

This was the end for Ronnie. Back at the flat that night he tried to kill himself. Reggie prevented him, and then rang Charlie Kray. At last he agreed the family was right. Ronnie's one hope now was to get to hospital.

Next morning the Kray family called at Scotland Yard. This was against everything they believed in, but they were giving Ronnie up. By an ironic twist the duty sergeant could not find the name on the wanted list and there was a long wait before the police agreed to act at all. Finally it was arranged for them to call at Vallance Road at 2 A.M. the following morning. The brothers gave their word that there would be no trouble.

That evening the twins had supper with the family at Vallance Road. It was a tense meal and although Ronnie drank a lot, for once he seemed unable to get drunk. Somebody offered him two powerful sleeping tablets saying they would be good for his headache. He took them, but they had no effect. Sensing that something was not right, he started shouting and then weeping. His mother calmed him and he went on drinking until long past midnight. The police arrived as two o'clock was striking. Ronnie looked up as if expecting them and walked out to the car without a word or glance back at his family.

Strangely the original plan behind the whole escape now worked. By staying free from capture for so long, Ronnie was no longer certified insane. For a few weeks he returned to Long Grove. Here, with the treatment he received combined with Stematol, he calmed down. By September 1958 the doctors pronounced him fit to finish his prison sentence.

So he returned to Wandsworth Gaol, where he was treated like a normal prisoner. He was still suffering from delusions and at times became so violent that he was placed in a straitjacket for his own safety. Despite this, he was permitted to conclude his sentence. Ronnie complains that Stematol was now denied him. And in the spring of 1959 this sick young homicidal psychopath was released into the world outside. Dickie Morgan, Reg and Charlie were at the gates to meet him. He scurried to their car convinced that the Russians and the Mafia had combined to kill him. All the way back to Vallance Road he kept his head down in case someone shot at him. Once in the house, he felt he had to decide whom to kill first to save his own skin. Finally his old doctor was able to get him into St Clement's Hospital, where he spent the next three weeks under deep sedation.

Slowly he seemed to recover. First he became an out-patient. Violet Kray looked after him at Vallance Road. Stematol kept away the worst of his nightmares and permitted him to coast along the borderlines of normality. Those who had known him before his breakdown recognized that the Colonel had changed and changed for good. He was far moodier, more erratic now and more suspicious. He was more frightening too. Physically he seemed more dangerous than before.

The change in his appearance which he had first noticed in the mirror in his cell at Camp Hill had grown worse. No longer was he identical with Reggie. It may have been the combination of drink and drugs that did it; it may have been the physical change that sometimes goes with acute cases of schizophrenia. Whatever the cause, his features coarsened, neck and jaw-line thickened, flesh round the eyes closed in. Reggie would keep his looks; Ronnie would be a monster.

As for his mind, this had recovered from the breakdown. Soon he would cope again with life after a fashion. But all the dangerous tendencies of this time remained behind the thin veneer of drugs. Provided he kept calm he would survive. Faced with excitement or with stress he would lapse back to the paranoiac state of the previous summer. He would become abnormally suspicious. He would feel few of the emotional restraints of normal people. He would know little of fear or apprehension or regret. Given his previous history, he would almost certainly end up killing someone.

EIGHT

Comeback for the Colonel

Until their brother's breakdown, Reggie and Charlie Kray had been extremely smart. With Ronnie out of things they were quite free to use more subtlety than in the past. They had avoided trouble and had been quietly tying up their corner of the East End. Boom-time was just round the corner. They had made peace with everyone – even the twins' old enemies, the Italian gangs of Clerkenwell. The night the Colonel once shot up their social club was not referred to when his brothers drank with them at The Double R.

More important still was their new friendship with Billy Hill. This strange *entente* with their old enemy was partly due to sentiment. Criminals are often sentimental men and it pleased this rich but childless old gangster to find two respectful protégés. He could relive his life through theirs and they were always more than grateful for his sage advice. There was a practical reason, too, for Billy Hill's concern with the Krays. Although retired, he still had interests in London, mainly in gambling, and he needed people like the Krays to watch them for him. Quietly he began to back the Krays, showing them an opening here, fixing an introduction there, leading them to a new, rich world which promised to become an Eldorado of discreetly organized criminal activity.

Illicit gambling had always been the bedrock of the capitalism of London crime. When Spot and Hill 'ruled' London, their steadiest profits had come from the illegal

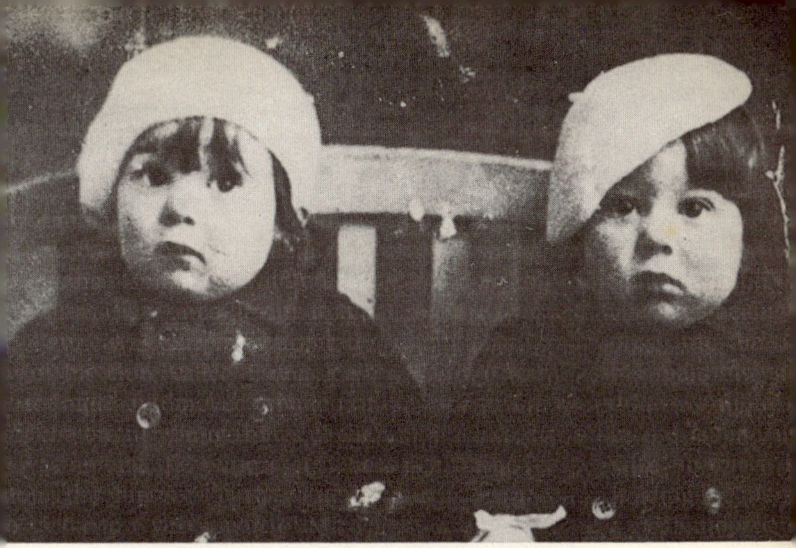

Violet's 'two little bunny rabbits', Reggie and Ronnie in their angora hats.

Reggie (left) and Ronnie, lightweight boxers, photographed before beginning National Service. *(Popperfoto)*

Ronnie (left), mother Vi, Reggie and grandfather Jimmy Lee. *(Popperfoto)*

The East End's wedding of the year – Reggie and Frances. *(Popperfoto)*

The Richardson brothers, Charles and Eddie, outside their Brixton scrapmetal yard. *(London Express)*

The upstairs sitting room at Vallance Road became the twins' operations room. This is one of the few occasions they were photographed with their brother Charles. *(Sunday Times)*

After Frances' death, the twins seemed closer than ever. For a while their life revolved around Ronnie's decidedly middle-class flat at Cedra Court. *(Daily Express)*

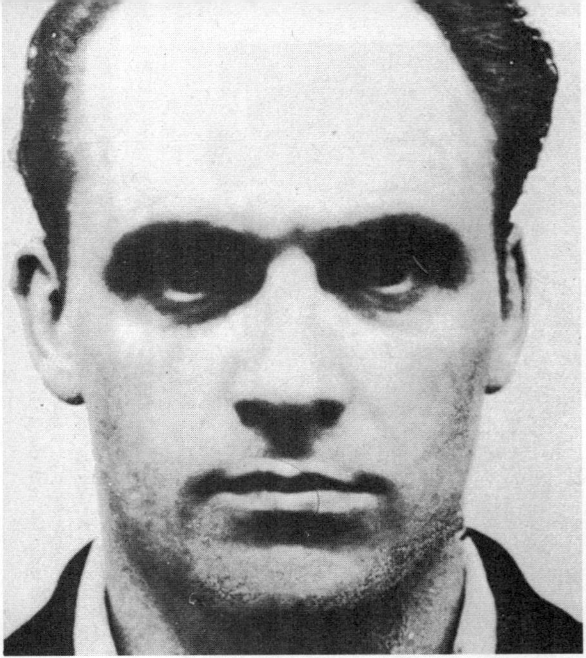

Jack McVitie was an old-style East End villain who claimed to be afraid of nobody. He should have known better than threaten Ronnie Kray. *(Syndication International)*

George Cornell, who worked for the Richardson gang. With the Richardsons arrested he became the number one target for the Krays. *(Syndication International)*

Reggie arriving from Parkhurst Prison for his mother's funeral, August 1982. He was indignant at the way he felt the authorities had deliberately chosen to have Ronnie and himself handcuffed to a pair of the tallest warders in the prison service, 'to try and make us look like a couple of dwarfs for the photographers'. *(Topham)*

Ronnie arriving at the
funeral from Broadmoor.
(Topham)

Floral tributes for Vi Kray. The arch is from Charlie, the two crosses in front are from Ronnie and Reggie. *(Topham)*

Charlie Kray with his father at the funeral. *(Topham)*

gambling clubs they controlled, and the Krays too made their modest livings from East End 'spielers'. By the mid fifties, gaming fever had hit London: illicit gambling was turning into a major industry, which was still effectively controlled by the underworld. Even the chemmy parties organized by well-publicized figures flitting from address to fashionable address around Belgravia were paying their nightly cut to someone in the background by whose permission play continued undisturbed. And through the influence of Billy Hill, Charlie and Reggie had been introduced to several of these parties as unofficial 'minders'. They showed promise, particularly Charlie. He looked well in a dinner-jacket. He was interested in gambling and had the right amount of toughness and deference to reassure the customers. More important still, the Krays were getting their first foothold in West End gambling; this, said Billy Hill, was where the fortunes of the future lay. As usual, Billy Hill was right.

Parliament was on the verge of legalizing gambling. The politicians claimed that this would hit the criminals, but Hill could see that it would really give the underworld the chance of a lifetime. With gambling legalized, the underworld would virtually be legalized as well. London could become the Las Vegas of Europe; and legalized casinos would have to be run by someone. Who better than the men who knew the work already, men like the Krays? Provided they were sensible, they could not go wrong.

Reggie and Charlie both agreed; already they were modelling themselves on Billy Hill and saw a golden future very near. They would polish up their image and concentrate on their clubs, leaving behind the rough and tumble of the East End dirty work. The understanding with the Italians would be consolidated, their entry into West End gambling exploited for all it was worth, and then with Billy Hill as adviser they would be set to take over a club or two in the West End once gaming was legalized. From then on life would be simple. No need for villainy. A good lawyer and accountant would handle their affairs and advise them where to invest their surplus earnings. They would be businessmen with a country house and a flat in town. They could move into property and betting shops and restaurants. Within a year or two they'd have their Rollses and live part of every year abroad like Billy Hill.

Ronnie could be taken care of properly. This was important. He could have everything he needed – the finest treatment, travel, boys, a discreet place in the country where he could be nursed during his attacks. Clearly he would need all this, for he was in a dreadful way. Most of his time was spent huddled by the fire at Vallance Road. The night Reggie brought him to The Double R he had blacked out. Everyone felt sorry for him. Charlie suggested they should treat him to a foreign cruise.

When he said this one night at Vallance Road, Ronnie was furious. He'd heard about these cruise ships: they could do anything they liked once you were aboard. Some people never came back at all. Charlie tried reasoning with him. He could go first-class to the Mediterranean or the West Indies. It would be good for him and get him well again. Charlie appealed to Reg, but Reg was suddenly unsure and looked away.

'If Ron doesn't want to go, he doesn't have to. Leave him alone. I'll look after him,' he muttered. Reggie kept his word and spent more time with Ronnie, drinking with him, driving him to the country and bringing friends to Vallance Road to meet him. The more he did, the more demanding Ronnie seemed. By weekends Reggie had usually had enough. He had his own life now. There was a girl he liked taking out; this was impossible with Ronnie around. So most weekends Reggie would send his twin to the country with their boyhood friend, Checker Berry. Ronnie still trusted him, and Checker was quite big enough to look after himself. Checker had a farmer friend in Wiltshire. He would book rooms in the village pub, and he and Ronnie stayed from Friday night to Monday morning.

Ronnie enjoyed the farm and got on perfectly with all the locals. He seemed a trifle slow, but otherwise quite normal; he didn't talk much, but was back on brown ale. He started riding; he was no stylish horseman, but enjoyed mastering his hefty mount. He took riding seriously, learning to canter, sitting the horse massively with ramrod back as if the whole point of riding were a continual battle of will between man and beast which he was determined to win.

One morning as he rode his weary nag back to the stable he reined in to talk to Checker.

'He's turned them all against me, hasn't he, Check?'

'Who?'

'My Reggie, while I've been away. He thinks I'm barmy, and that I can't see what he an' Charlie are up to. But I'm not barmy any more. They'd better both look out, those two.'

Violet was happy, Ronnie seemed better, and her twins reunited, just like the old days; Ronnie in the big back bedroom, Reggie in the smaller room off the landing. Nothing had really changed since they were boys. She was so grateful that she had them still to make a fuss of, and she was touched to notice that they had picked up their old habits, like taking off their watches and cuff-links every night and leaving them on the kitchen mantelpiece before they went to bed – Reggie's on the left, Ronnie's on the right. And Ronnie was soon starting all his old tricks, telephoning his barber in the morning and ordering his shirts just as he used to. He even bought himself another dog – a great brown Dobermann, which he kept in the yard and fed himself. When asked his occupation now, he would write 'dog breeder'. He even wrote this in his passport. It was good to see his sense of humour had not suffered with his troubles.

The rows had started up again between the twins, but this didn't worry Violet. Rather the reverse. They proved that Ronnie was back to normal. Years ago she had taught herself never to listen to what they said. They didn't mean it; it only upset her. But if Violet had listened to the arguments between the twins, she would have noticed something: Ronnie was more aggressive, Reggie continually on the defensive. Ronnie said he was going soft with all his smart new friends, that he was wasting all his time on women. It was degrading.

Reggie would try explaining all their plans for the future, but the arguments fell flat. Caution, economy, business prospects suddenly had no appeal. It was surprising how much Ronnie knew of what had gone on while he was away. There had been nothing disloyal about what Reggie and Charlie had done – but Ronnie made it sound disloyal: making allies with the Italians, listening to their old enemy, Billy Hill, straightening the Law, avoiding trouble.

'You're turning into just a little cry-baby. It must be all these dirty women you've been having.' Although Reggie shouted back, and knew that what Ronnie said was unfair, he had his first real doubts about the good life now.

Reggie felt guilty and gave Ronnie all the money he could squander, a wardrobe of expensive suits, a new blue Fairlane automatic to match Reggie's yellow one. He also paid for Ronnie's weekend trips to Jersey. Ronnie had two new boyfriends, brothers, and since he dreaded being caught for homosexuality in England he felt safer taking them to Jersey. Reggie imagined that these trips away were keeping Ronnie out of trouble in the East End, but Ronnie was emerging from his breakdown fast.

Reggie's first warning came when he heard that Ronnie had been into a gambling club in Vallance Road threatening to break it up and asking for a pension of £10 a week. This was absurd, since Reggie was part-owner of the club himself, but instead of facing Ronnie, he told the manager to pay him.

Then came more serious trouble. Ronnie persuaded Reggie to take him to a meeting with the Italians. There was a matter of some delicacy to be discussed, a compromise over their gambling interests. Diplomacy was needed. Ronnie lumbered to his feet and started shouting that the Krays had no need of a bunch of cheap Italians.

When he stormed out, Charlie attempted to apologize – their friends were sympathetic. Of course they understood about the poor boy and what he had been through in prison. But they all knew that nothing could be quite the same again: Ronnie had destroyed two years of carefully nurtured understanding. This was the first time Reggie showed he knew exactly what was happening. He drove to Vallance Road with an old friend and asked him wearily, 'What can I do about Ron? He's ruining us. I know we ought to drop him. But how can I? He's my brother and he's mad. Without me God knows what he'll do.'

A fortnight later there was a rally at the billiard hall. It was like old times with all the lights on and the smoke and crates of beer and the Colonel back in his favourite chair opposite the door. There were a few old faces but many more had come from other parts of London. The Colonel had been busier than anyone suspected. He looked delighted with himself. He wore a new blue suit, new spectacles and held a gleaming cutlass. A huge dog slobbered at his feet and growled when anybody came close. Ronnie's two boys were there; he'd never been with them on show like this before. Reggie glared at them when he entered. They grinned back at him. Ronnie smiled.

'All of the enemy will be at The Hospital Tavern tomorrow night,' said a white-faced boy with spots.

'All of them?' asked Ronnie.

'The whole of Watney Street. They'll be expecting you.'

'We'll be expecting them. It's time we got our own back for what happened when I went away. Some people think they can forget a thing like that. Some people have been getting soft. I think it's time we had a little war.'

Reggie said nothing.

Next night there was a full-scale bar fight at The Hospital

Tavern. Both gangs were armed with knives and chains and knuckle-dusters. But the twins proved invincible as ever: Reggie discovered something he had nearly forgotten – the strength that surged up in him as he and Ronnie lost themselves in a fight. He had no sense of danger – only of power and a driving impulse to destroy. Nobody could resist them, and when the bar was empty and the last of the Watney Streeters were scrapping in the street, Reggie was standing amid broken chairs and a carpet of smashed glass not realizing the fight was over. He took the microphone the singer used on Saturday nights, turned it full on and bawled through the loudspeakers that if Watney Street wanted any more, the Krays were ready for them. No one answered. He shouted again. But the police cars were screeching up outside and everybody was running. Then Ronnie was beside him, saying they must get away. As they slipped past the crowd, the ambulances had arrived, their blue lights flashing.

At Vallance Road they both went through the old routine of cleaning up at their Aunt May's house next door before saying good night to Violet. Next day the headlines said the East End had had its worst gang fight for years. Neither police nor crime writers seemed to know why.

That night, Reggie's divided life began again. He became thin-faced and his hunted look reappears in photographs. After a few gins he could usually convince himself that everything was as it had always been. He had his car, his friends, his money and his clubs. But however much he drank he never seemed able to bring back the future he and Charlie had planned so carefully together. In the old days he had been able to stand up to Ronnie. Now it was different. Ronnie was wilder; and once he was back with him all his other life seemed pointless and unreal.

In the late fifties London's gangland battlefields were changing. Violence was building up in Paddington and Notting Hill as rival groups horned in to milk the gambling, prostitution and rent rackets of West London. These were not Kray lands. There was no money for them here and from the press exposés of the time it was clear the law would soon be cracking down.

But Ronnie had been thinking about Paddington. It appealed to him. It was 'interesting', with so many rackets, so many chances of new villainy, that the East End seemed quite tame by comparison. Just past the Edgware Road an authentic whiff of old Chicago hung in the air, with drinking clubs burned out with petrol bombs and tough young men in overcoats shooting at each other from moving cars.

Ronnie was planning an alliance of gangsters to control London – something more grandiose than the timid plans his brothers had had with the Italians. Ronnie's idea was for a warlike federation, using violence to get power. One man would have to be the leader, somebody respected and feared so that his name was law. This was a worthwhile role at last for the admirer of Capone: with Reggie he knew he could do it, but not if they stayed tamely in the East End. One gang in Paddington required help; if the twins gave it, they would have instant allies and the chance to move on to the West End.

The planning and discussions of his great idea occupied the Colonel's energies – deals, secret meetings, pay-offs, promises – and when the time for action came he kept his word, leading his cockneys into several of the bloodthirstiest gang fights West London had ever seen in the summer of 1959. Reggie complained that they were wasting their time, but he was always there when Ronnie needed him.

The Colonel felt his scheme was working; but financially it was a disaster. By alienating all those business-minded gangsters the Krays relied on for their income, Ronnie destroyed three years' careful work in as many months. Certainly they had no chance now of the neat slice of Mayfair gambling they had hoped for. The billiard hall closed down; the takings from The Double R and the spieler in Wellington Way barely met Ronnie's extravagances. The Colonel's dreams of empire were expensive. The new gang needed to be paid, but Reggie's richer clients stayed clear now, thanks to the twins' new reputation.

Ronnie had his own ways now of making money. Often he just asked for it – a loan, a contribution, an investment – and since people were frightened of him, he invariably received. A publican, a shopkeeper, an illegal bookmaker – anybody who was vulnerable was likely to be tapped for £50 or £100 to pay for his evening out. One of his favourite methods was to 'pawn' his big gold watch with a publican for £200 and a week later to ask for the watch back. No one ever had the nerve to refuse him or demand repayment. This suited Ronnie as a means of money-grabbing; it kept life simple and flattered his vanity. But there were better ways of making money.

The twins knew all about capitalizing on violence: in the past they had peddled it like any other commodity. This had been Reggie's speciality. If someone needed hurting or protecting, if a business had to be wrecked or a club destroyed, Reggie had arranged the details like a professional providing any normal service. The twins invariably gave value for money.

Ronnie gave his clients something more – excitement. Some businessmen enjoyed sharing the twins' wildness. Ronnie cashed in on this and in the process some of these action-loving friends acted extremely stupidly.

Perhaps the stupidest of all was a man called Daniel Shay. In the summer of 1959 he owned his own car business and was living in an expensive flat in Edgware. He was not particularly honest. According to evidence later produced in court, he already had thirteen convictions for various types of fraud. But he was not a dangerous man. Quite the reverse. Everyone who knew him found him charming, perhaps a little too easy to do business with, and rather kind. He lived well, gambled, but not to excess, and was devoted to his wife. Then he met Ronnie Kray and began boasting of his friendship with the twins.

This suited Ronnie. He never minded businessmen using his 'name' provided they paid for the privilege; Shay paid. On several occasions Ronnie borrowed from him and the money never seemed to be returned. Then Shay began to change. This friend of the twins began believing he could act as they did. By then Ronnie was earning a considerable income each week from shopkeepers he 'protected'. At the beginning of February 1960, kindly Mr Shay did something out of character.

At the Hampstead end of the Finchley Road was a small shop called Swiss Travel Goods run by a Pole called Murray Podro. Shay had already met him playing cards, and when he called at the shop and chose a briefcase, leaving his card and saying he would pay later, Podro permitted him to take it. A few days later Shay returned, bringing the twins and telling Mr Podro that he had taken a 'diabolical liberty' overcharging him for the briefcase. He grabbed him, hit him and demanded £100, otherwise he would be 'cut to pieces'.

It was a bungling attempt. Shay was no gangster, and as soon as he left the shop Podro telephoned the police. Two days later Shay returned to collect his money. He brought Reggie with him; as they entered the shop they walked straight into the police.

At the Old Bailey Shay was romantically described as 'running a Chicago-style protection racket' and sentenced to three years' imprisonment. Reggie got eighteen months. Ronnie was never mentioned.

And now with Reggie stuck in Wandsworth Gaol and Ronnie in command, the rampage started. The Double R lost money; the Firm was finally his private army; Fort Vallance was stocked up with arms. Nothing else mattered except the 'little wars'. The Colonel was convinced that he would soon rule London through the rattle of machine-guns and the blood of rivals flowing in the streets. He was quite happy. Reggie was safe behind bars; no women could reach him there. Charlie did not worry him. No one interfered with the strange war game he acted out, as he gathered information, planned his next moves and prepared to lead his fighting men to battle. He lived at home with Violet and had all he needed. Life would have continued from one battle to the next but for what occurred that autumn. Ronnie met Peter Rachman.

Rachman was not yet notorious as the extortionate West London landlord making his unsavoury fortune from rack-rented tenants. But he was stuffed with money and was vulnerable. This made him interesting to Ronnie, who had heard about him in Paddington. He tried to meet him. Rachman avoided him, but finally through Dickie Morgan, who worked for Rachman, Ronnie and several friends gate-crashed a party Rachman was giving at the old Latin Quarter Club in Soho.

It was a memorable occasion. Rachman had begun the evening in high spirits; everyone was laughing at his table. When Ronnie entered, Rachman and his girls tried to ignore him. Ronnie and his friends wore dinner-jackets, sat at a table and simply stared at Rachman. None of them spoke, or drank. Slowly the conversation died. When Peter Rachman went downstairs there was a scuffle by the door. Several Kray men joined in. Ronnie Kray yawned, said nothing and waited as the sound of fighting floated up the stairs. Then Dickie Morgan came up to him, grinning, and whispered in his ear. Ronnie nodded and stumped from the room.

Downstairs a Rolls was waiting, Rachman at the wheel. As Ronnie came from the club Rachman opened the door and asked where he was going. 'Vallance Road,' he grunted, and heaved himself in beside Rachman. He had his meeting.

There were no polite preliminaries as the Colonel delivered his terms: £5,000 immediately. Otherwise his men would be in Notting Hill every night of the week and would drive Rachman's rent-enforcers off the streets.

Rachman should know that he could put him out of business in a month.

At Vallance Road Rachman was invited in to meet Violet and afterwards to discuss things over tea in the upstairs sitting-room. Rachman had considerable charm, thanked Violet for the tea, called Ronnie by his first name and made no difficulties, when his host demanded an initial downpayment. He had £250 on him in cash, and wrote a cheque for £1,000. They parted on good terms. Next morning the cheque bounced. When Ronnie heard he drew a Luger from the armoury and went in search of Rachman; he had vanished.

Trouble began in Notting Hill exactly as the Colonel prophesied. Rachman's rent-collectors were methodically beaten up. Rachman's thugs faced fiercer thugs. Rachman's whole empire, which depended on intimidation of tenants, faced its one real time of crisis.

For Peter Rachman had made the mistake of underestimating Ronnie, thinking he would never have the skill or organization to upset his business. Now that Ronnie proved he had, something needed to be done. Rachman was a clever man. One thing he knew about was intimidation; and he knew that the more he tried to buy off Ronnie Kray, the more he would have to pay him later. Much money was at stake – rich influential people's money as well as his own. He had no intention of risking it for Ronnie Kray. What he needed was something big to offer Ronnie as a final payment to divert him from Notting Hill for good. Someone suggested Esmeralda's Barn.

NINE

Barn of Gold

On a fine autumn evening in 1960 a man called Stefan de Faye walked along Kensington Gore for an appointment with a retired naval commander at an address behind the Royal Albert Hall. De Faye was a tall, excitable man and was in something of a state: he knew that in the next hour or so he would have to make one of the most uncomfortable decisions of his life.

He was a club-owner, moderately rich, entirely honest and extremely smart. In his youth he had written a book entitled *Profitable Bar Management* and had recently secured control of the most promising gaming club in London. It was the sort of chance that comes once in a lifetime; being shrewd, Stefan de Faye had done his best to keep it to himself – not too successfully. Something had leaked out; there had been threats. Finally an invitation came from a certain ex-naval commander. De Faye knew all about him. He was a front man for a number of figures in the underworld. If he refused his invitation there would be less polite approaches later.

Had de Faye been a gangster or a gambler he might have risked this; as he was neither he continued walking down Kensington Gore until he found the address he wanted. He rang the bell.

The commander, a smiling gentleman with bright false teeth, answered the door and led de Faye into a long, brown sitting-room. Three men were waiting.

'Mr de Faye,' said the commander, 'my good friend, Leslie Payne.'

A big man with pale hair and eyes rose and shook hands. 'And these are the Kray twins, Reginald and Ronald. You'll find them very useful friends to have.'

Introductions over, the commander departed; business started. The twins both smoked and remained silent. The man called Payne did the talking – softly and with a hesitant, apologetic charm. It was as if he hated having to tell de Faye how much he knew; he was extremely accurate. He had the whole story of his club, called Esmeralda's Barn. It was in Wilton Place and had enjoyed a period of success as a night-club for the bright young things of the early fifties – Cy Grant was among the performers, the young Duke of Kent among the guests. What a waste to let a place like this go to seed. How very smart of Mr de Faye and his friends to see its possibilities now that the Gaming Act was law. The club looked very good, and with roulette and four chemmy tables in operation they should be clearing . . .

The big man paused, then named a figure so near the mark that de Faye could only nod in agreement. This was not all that Payne knew about the place: somehow he had gleaned details of the unusual company structure controlling it. He knew that there were four principal shareholders drawing profits from the gambling. He also knew the fact that caused Mr de Faye so much concern – that Esmeralda's Barn was controlled in turn by a holding company called Hotel Organisation Ltd. Hotel Organisation had one effective shareholder – Stefan de Faye. As Payne explained this, both twins smiled.

Payne's proposition was eminently reasonable. He had heard that Mr de Faye was no great gambler – why not exchange his vulnerable position for hard cash? In the long run it would save a lot of worry. Payne was offering £1,000 down. The sale could take place at once with a simple entry in the company minutes; it would be perfectly legal and would not affect de Faye and the two other directors, who could keep their directorships and profits from the

Barn. Once de Faye relinquished his control he would be surprised what a weight would be off his mind.

If he decided not to?

Leslie Payne made no reply, but looked towards the twins.

Stefan de Faye decided to take his £1,000.

At this point Leslie Payne becomes a key figure in the rise of the twins, and it was natural for Ronnie to go to him for advice when Rachman offered the information about Stefan de Faye's controlling interest in Esmeralda's Barn. Reggie had only just come out of Wandsworth on bail after nine months of his sentence. Thanks to the skill of his lawyers and a dispute about the evidence on which he had been convicted, his case had been reopened. In the meantime he was free. While he had been away Payne had become Ronnie's own personal adviser, fixer, front man and father figure. When Ronnie put his faith in anyone the trust was total while it lasted. Health, finance, sex life, business, law – whatever Ronnie's problem and whatever time of day or night, Checker Berry would be sent off in Ronnie's car and Leslie Payne, the omniscient 'man with the briefcase , brought back to Vallance Road to confer.

And yet in many ways Payne was a most unlikely man to have been mixed up with the Krays – a cultured, humorous character with a sharp brain, very pretty wife and two small daughters all living cosily in a suburban house in Dulwich. But Les Payne and the twins saw something that they thought they needed in each other. At that time Payne was a bankrupt and had watched fourteen of his associated companies float off into liquidation. He could see the twins' potential from the start. For Ronnie, who was often morbidly unsure of himself, Payne had the poise, the confidence and inside knowledge that he lacked. Some called him 'Payne the Brain'.

* * *

At about ten o'clock that evening Stefan de Faye met Payne and the twins, and the new proprietors of Hotel Organisation Ltd drove to Wilton Place to see their property. Everything had been legally tied up and signed: Payne didn't make mistakes. It was an interesting evening; interesting for the twins, who gazed with mounting avarice and awe as the earliest of the night's gamblers seated themselves at the rich baize of the tables and the chips began travelling; interesting for the club's manager and principal shareholder who was waiting to meet the night's big punters, ignorant of what had happened; most interesting of all for Leslie Payne, who held the company minutes of Hotel Organisation Ltd in his ever-present briefcase, and was waiting for a good moment to tell the manager and his co-directors that they had some new and unexpected partners.

Payne did it very well: nothing disturbed the ritual of the gaming-room as he informed the manager that the ownership of his club had changed for good. The manager showed no emotion as he glanced at de Faye's signature and casually remarked that he would fight the legality of the deal to the last lawyer in the land. Of course, said Payne (who had a pleasant smile for such occasions), by all means try, but he hardly thought that it would do much good. He had consulted the best company lawyers in London already.

He looked round him at the small bar, the softly lighted gaming-room, the restaurant where club members could eat well through the night, the roulette wheel in the anteroom. The place was filling fast now and he called a waiter, ordered a bottle of champagne, told him to put it on his account and asked his two friends what they'd like to drink.

The night the twins and Payne walked into Esmeralda's Barn the club seemed heading for success. It had been quicker off the mark than any other club when the new Gaming Act legalized gambling and had maintained its lead. Croupiers were still scarce – Esmeralda's Barn had the best in London. Gamblers were an unknown quantity, but the manager's personal friends, rich London restaurant-owners, were the one group who played big and always met their debts. The address was perfect.

This was the gold-mine that the twins suddenly found they owned a stake in. Payne and his lawyers soon restructured the business side of the Barn. De Faye's name stayed on the directors' list for two more years, but he never appeared and never collected a penny. The two junior directors were eased out, while the manager, the mainstay of the club and the one man to have invested real money in it, stayed on with a fifty per cent stake in the profits and the twins absorbed the rest.

During the first few months the twins made no great difference to the running of the club. For both of them it was a new toy. They had identical dark-blue dinner-jackets made in Savile Row and would arrive shortly before midnight, drink, order a steak in the restaurant, then watch the money roll in.

There were three chemmy tables, each with nine players, operating from 11 P.M. Until 3 A.M. each player paid at the rate of £3 per shoe to the house. From then to 6 A.M. shoe money rose to £6 each. After 6 A.M. it rose to £10. A good croupier takes roughly four minutes for a shoe. The senior croupier did it in less. Shoe money was straight profit to the house. When the twins came the Barn was drawing something over £10,000 a week from the tables. This meant that thanks to Rachman the twins suddenly possessed assured incomes of something like £40,000 each a year with nothing to do for them except wear dark-blue dinner-jackets.

Just before Christmas Reggie's appeal against conviction in the Shay case failed. Despite the efforts of his lawyers he went back to Wandsworth for the following six months.

Ronnie was left to make the most of wealth and Esmeralda's Barn alone.

He enjoyed sitting in the bar at night, knowing that people wondered who he was. He enjoyed the money. He enjoyed the sense of ownership. But there was nothing in the whole club for him to do: had there been, he might have learned just how delicate a business big-time gambling can be. He never did learn this. He was a villain, not a bank clerk. He hated gambling and despised the rich. He was incapable of sitting back and accepting £800 a week for doing nothing. For Ronnie there was something wrong with money that was not dishonestly acquired. He had to have a racket of his own. Not for the money; he had more than enough by now. But racketeering was a habit and a way of life. He could feel superior to those he cheated. Soon he was 'nipping' the cashier for small amounts and fleecing the occasional client. Then he found something neater. It was exactly what he wanted, since it enhanced his sense of private power.

Like any gambling club, Esmeralda's Barn was obliged to pay winnings straight away and bear any losers' cheques that bounced. Success depended on keeping the margin of dud losers' cheques to a minimum; the manager was extremely strict over the credit he would grant within the club. Ronnie was different. Whenever the manager was away or off duty, Ronnie as a director had the right to say who should have credit; he began granting it quite freely, seeing that it placed the gambler firmly in his debt. If the man won, Ronnie had done him a favour and would expect a good commission in return. If he lost, the house might have to carry the bad cheque; Ronnie would settle privately for whatever he could recover. Provided Ronnie could scare the man into paying him a few pounds, he would be satisfied.

The manager soon saw what was happening when cheques marked 'return to drawer' flooded the office. When they came to over £2,000 in one week, he mentioned it to Ronnie. Ronnie laughed. Why should the manager worry, when there was more play than ever across the tables? The manager tried explaining that no club could carry such losses. As a last gesture he offered the twins £1,000 a week to stay away. Reggie was still in Wandsworth; Ronnie replied that they weren't interested.

So the manager, good gambler that he was, saw that the time had come to cut his losses, forget the money he had invested in the club and place his bets elsewhere. He was scrupulously polite to Ronnie; he could afford to be. When he set up his new club in Curzon Street his richest clients followed; the cheques no longer bounced. Today his club remains what Esmeralda's Barn would have been – one of the four top gambling clubs in London. The twins could still have had a permanent share of the profits.

At the time, nobody worried. If the manager left, so much the better. His share of profit could now go to Leslie Payne and the twins. They had to bring a new manager in to run the gambling, but he had no say over credit; if something like £15,000 of bad cheques piled up in the cashier's office during the six months, who cared? Play was increasing all the time.

What Ronnie really wanted was a plushier version of the billiard hall, a headquarters where he could come on show with all his followers and be himself before an audience. This seemed impossible at first. Everybody in the Barn appeared so confident and rich. But Ronnie despised them. 'They're such a lot of cry-babies, frightened of what their old man will say when he finds out what they've been up to. So when they're in a mess they come crawling. They'll do anything then to save themselves, even pretend to like you. But they're not sincere like East End people. When it comes to it they always let you know your place.'

The chip on his shoulder showed; the urge to humiliate was irresistible. One of the Barn's most regular losers was a dead-beat peer. Ronnie knew he was on the edge of bankruptcy but always gave him credit to play. When he had lost again the old man would ring him up at Vallance Road and threaten suicide. Ronnie enjoyed this and would say, 'All right, you silly old bastard. Don't waste the gas by putting your head in the oven today. You can't afford it. Come round to Vallance Road when I've had my shave and I'll see what I can do. Don't be late.'

The clientele was changing as the dedicated, big-time gamblers started to keep away. Now came the playboy gamblers, gambling addicts, chancers and the chronically in debt, people the manager would have headed off; Ronnie welcomed them. If they got deeper into debt so much the better. The house could carry them and this would mean more people under his control. Violence crept in. Several drunken losers at the Barn were thrown down the stairs, and occasionally Ronnie instructed East End villains to call on members he considered 'cheeky' about their debts. What happened then was not his business: if somebody was hurt, an empty flat smashed up, this had nothing to do with him.

But on the whole Ronnie knew better than to use violence to get back money he was owed. He wanted power and status. There was a sort of devious flirtation in the way he played those who feared him: smiling one night, meeting them with a blank stare and a demand for money the next.

He began getting what he seemed to want – the pretence of friendship, the appearance of respect, even of social success; these were people who could introduce him to the smart life if he wanted it. They took him to their homes, their London clubs, dined him in the House of Lords, introduced him to celebrities. It was surprising how cheap the rich world was, and it gave Ronnie a new role – the playboy gangster in a sophisticated world.

As usual he began dressing for the part – sharper suits, heavier jewellery, better-cut overcoats. Then he moved into the West End, taking the lease on a top-floor Chelsea flat in payment for a gambling debt. He took the whole place over – furniture, pictures, the former tenant's young boyfriend. Then for a while he became something of a character on the Chelsea scene, the King's Road's own gangster-in-residence.

He was the showman once again, conscious of his public. Sometimes he played the heavy gangster, sometimes the clown. One night he brought a chimpanzee in evening dress into the Barn, sat him down at the tables and had him paid his winnings. Another night when things were dull he announced that he was marrying one of the girls in the club. This was a novelty at least; like everything with Ronnie it had to be done at once. Payne suggested holding the marriage aboard ship. He knew somebody with a boat moored off Chelsea Reach. It was 2 A.M. but the man was fetched, guests summoned; Payne was appointed best man, the wedding party started.

It was a great affair. Word soon got round that there was free champagne at Esmeralda's Barn; Ronnie was suddenly in earnest, drinking toasts and talking about the children he would have. The one thing he refused to do was kiss the bride. Not that this mattered. Long before dawn broke, Ronnie was slumbering quietly on a couch at the far end of the restaurant, the girl on one side and the man who was to have married them on the other. They woke up with the cleaners.

Despite a joke like this and an occasional experiment, Ronnie disliked women more than ever; now he was out of the East End he made no bones about his homosexuality. It was a relief to be able to admit it. Now he discovered its advantages. It was quite smart, a sort of eccentricity to be made the most of, and he had an entrée to the useful freemasonry of the similarly inclined.

There was no hint of effeminacy about him. 'I'm not a poof, I'm homosexual,' he would say, and was genuinely put out by the antics of effeminate males. 'Pansies,' he used to say, with the same cockney contempt with which he pronounced the word 'women'.

He liked boys, preferably with long lashes and a certain melting look round the eyes. He particularly enjoyed them if they had had no experience of men before. He liked teaching them and often gave them a fiver to take their girl-friends out on condition they slept with him the following night. He always asked them which they had preferred. He was something of a sadist, but was generous with his lovers. The gifts he gave them were his main extravagance. He never seems to have forced anyone into bed against his will and, as he proudly insisted, was free from colour prejudice, having tried Scandinavians, Latins, Anglo-Saxons, Arabs, Negroes, Chinese and a Tahitian. An important part of the compulsive pederasty which had begun to dominate his life was his growing fear of the dark. He dreaded sleeping alone.

During this period at the Barn he fell in love. This was not something he actually approved of: love, especially when combined with sex, was usually a means women employed to keep men at home and relieve them of their money. So it might be more accurate to say that Ronnie began living with a boy on a regular basis and permitted himself the luxury of continued tenderness for the first time in his life.

Vanity came into it. He enjoyed taking the boy out and being seen with him in the best restaurants: the boy was beautiful and behaved like a petulant young mistress. Ronnie enjoyed indulging these shows of temperament. He liked taking him to his tailors, selecting all his shirts and ties and doing what he could to curb the excesses of his youthful bad taste. He was extremely jealous: one man the boy had flirted with had his face cut open. The boy was 'his' boy.

He called him 'son', referring to himself as 'your old Dad'. Any extravagance was allowed him. One of Ronnie's greatest pleasures was taking him with a select party of 'interesting people' to the old Society Club in Jermyn Street. Ronnie loved the Society. With its dark panelling and pink silk-covered lamps, it was like something from a thirties film. This was where jovial businessmen brought their secretaries for a night out; an Israeli violinist called 'Gipsy' played Lehár at the tables; the champagne was expensive.

Never a great one for the swinging scene, Ronnie felt that the Society was somehow 'right', always tipped lavishly and paid his bill. When Gipsy came to his table, as he always did, Ronnie's eyes moistened at the music. Turning to his guests, he would point to his boy.

'Beautiful, isn't he? Don't you think he's beautiful? Don't you wish he was yours?'

During these six months with Reggie in prison Ronnie could finally enjoy worldly success himself – money, cars, boys, admirers, a West End flat, even social respect of a sort. He had achieved what every poor cockney boy longs for: freedom to be and do exactly as he liked.

But it was no good. Everybody round him seemed to find happiness; not Ronnie. Possessions meant nothing, friends could not be trusted, even his freedom made him feel an outcast. His spending orgies left him wardrobes full of suits, piles of shirts he never wore again. His new friends seemed to offer sympathy or flattery but he knew they laughed behind his back. Boys were like drink. They helped him to forget; next day the hopelessness returned.

His nightmares worsened. The world was slipping out of his control. His psychiatrist increased his daily dose of Stematol, and ordered him to rest. Somebody mentioned the Canary Islands: he booked at the best hotel, taking his boy-friend for a fortnight's holiday. This was no use either. How could he lie on the beach or waste his time swimming when there was always something to be done?

The boy soon became sullen at Ronnie's attitude, especially when he insisted on moving to a seedier hotel where he felt more at home. This didn't help: nothing on that sunny island interested Ronnie or could set his mind at rest. They returned to London six days early.

Reggie would help him. Reggie would soon be out of gaol. But when Reggie did return the unforgivable had occurred: he was in love, and with a girl. She was just sixteen, a schoolgirl – pretty and pert and innocent and earnest. Reggie was twenty-seven. She was called Frances Shea and was the sister of Frank Shea, a Hoxton boy the twins had known for years. Ronnie once admired his looks and there was a strong resemblance between Frank Shea and his sister. Her father once ran the gambling at The Regency Club in Stoke Newington, where the twins already had an interest. Reggie had noticed her during his period on bail from Wandsworth and taken her out then once or twice. She was in awe of him at first, but he was respectful, almost shy of her. He talked a lot about life, ideals, and 'seemed sort of sad, different from other boys,' she told her friend. He hadn't tried to kiss her yet.

It was when he returned to Wandsworth that Reggie really fell in love with her. During the previous period of his sentence he had been cheerful, 'one of the best, a laugh for everyone. When he came back he'd changed. All he could think about was this girl of his. He'd got it bad – you couldn't kid him about it.'

Each day he wrote to her. He was afraid she might fall in love with someone else before he was released. He wrote her poetry and was tormented by the memory of the brown eyes framed in the chestnut-coloured hair. Once he was free he could carry her off to a deserted bay beside a blue sea and build a house; the dark life with Ronnie would be buried and forgotten. She was his cockney Cinderella and he made her his princess.

This time with Reggie back the rows between the twins were the worst anyone remembered, with insults screamed about the girl and Ronnie's boys.

Ronnie soon realized his greatest danger of losing Reggie to Frances Shea would be through Esmeralda's Barn. Now that Reggie had his directorship and share of the profits, he had no need for crime. He could do what he had always dreamed of when away from Ronnie, living the good life and dazzling the girl.

The Barn was still bringing in big money throughout 1961. A discotheque was started in the basement. Lord Effingham joined the twins on the Barn's board of directors. There was still great potential; it would not be hard to make the most of it and use the contacts offered for expansion into other gambling clubs. Their brother Charlie had been doing well at the Barn on his own account. Anxious for this life to continue, he urged the twins to invest their profits in betting shops and clubs. Ronnie objected. He knew if Esmeralda's Barn became the centre of a thriving business chain, he would be quite superfluous.

Ronnie told Reggie it was time he brought his girl to meet him at the Barn. She was nervous when she came, a wide-eyed child in an unaccustomed world. But Ronnie seemed in a good mood, his big face beaming as he greeted her like one of the family.

'Hullo, Frances, my dear. I've heard a lot about you. 'Ow are you?'

And Frances Shea, who'd heard a lot about him, relaxed and was impressed. She met Lord Effingham. Ronnie insisted that she try her hand at roulette; she won a pound or two. She and the twins ate in the restaurant. But something about Ronnie scared her.

TEN

Organized Crime

Just eight weeks after Reggie emerged from Wandsworth, all three Kray brothers were in trouble with the Law. First Reggie – he was accused of petty house-breaking on the evidence of a woman who failed to identify him when she entered the witness-box of the East London Magistrates' Court. The case was dismissed; Reggie was awarded costs.

Then it was his brothers' turn; both were accused of 'loitering in the Queensbridge Road with intent to commit a felony' and of trying the door-handles of parked cars. The improbability of the charges gave Ronnie just the case he needed to stage a demonstration of the power of the Krays against the Law. It was something he'd been waiting for.

There was a combination of flair and thoroughness in the way he played it. The first thing he wanted was publicity; he briefed Nemone Lethbridge, the prettiest young female barrister in the country, to defend him. His case needed to be watertight so he hired a private detective and produced eight solid witnesses to swear to his alibi. Finally he wanted to teach the local police a lesson; this wasn't difficult. Through a contact on a local paper he made sure the East End press carried his allegations of victimization by the police under banner headlines: 'Detective called us "scum of the earth".'

In court the case could not stand up: on 8 May the Marylebone Magistrates' Court dismissed the charges. Now Ronnie could enjoy himself handling the publicity against the Law like an adroit public relations man. He held a full-scale party for the press at Esmeralda's Barn, where he proposed a toast to 'British justice'. There was a lot of free champagne and instant friendship. He got the full press coverage he wanted – the *Daily Express* carried a long article complete with pictures of the twins and ample quotes from them both under the headline: '"It's a vendetta," say freed boxing twins.'

The impression was of a pair of clean-living cockney sporting boys caught up in a sinister persecution by the police. From now on it would be a bold East End policeman who would risk his career tangling with them.

Photographed that night at their victory party as Esmeralda's Barn, both twins were smiling – Ronnie from a sense of triumph, Reggie with relief. For Ronnie the acquittal at Marylebone confirmed what he had always known – he was being picked out, persecuted, but had the power to beat his enemies. He was untouchable. Reggie felt none of this. He had loathed his time in prison and wanted no more risks. All he desired was peace and the chance to enjoy himself like any normal man. That summer he tried very hard to get it. His share of profit from Esmeralda's Barn had mounted in his absence. He was rich. He bought a new Mercedes, smart clothes, improved his dancing, rode, ran, kept himself fit. He spent weekends at Steeple Bay in Essex where the family had a caravan and he could swim and lie in the sun. He began seeing less of Ronnie; for once this didn't worry him. Frances was there. He was becoming a possessive lover. Neither had been in love before.

While he was in prison she had started a shorthand course. He didn't care for the idea of her being independent or seeing too many people. Each afternoon he would be waiting outside the college with the car. Since she was his princess she needed royal treatment – gifts, evenings out, all the respect the Krays enjoyed. She lived quite simply with her parents in a terraced house in Ormsby Street, just off the Kingsland Road. Suddenly neighbours noticed the expensive cars calling for her; word got round that she was Reggie's girl.

This turned her head at first. Reggie was very kind. Nothing was too much trouble and he never went too far like boys of her own age. He was proud of her and patiently possessive. She could be as temperamental and capricious as she pleased, but she was his for keeps. Her brother was in awe of him, even her father liked him. As Mr Shea says now, 'I respected Reggie as an athlete and a clean-living man. He never used bad language, even when talking to me on my own, and always had her home on time. We knew he never tried anything wrong with her, but treated her like a lady. We thought that was very nice.'

Reggie proposed to Frances in the autumn of 1961. She turned him down, saying that she was far too young to think of marriage. Reggie suspected that the real reason was that her parents secretly disapproved of him. To show how wrong they were and prove himself to Frances he decided to become a real success.

For some time now, Ronnie had been complaining that he was neglecting their business interests. Suddenly Reggie began attending to them. All his old energy and interest revived; he began keeping accounts in the laborious, backwards-sloping script that was such a contrast to Ronnie's ill-formed scrawl. Soon he was thinking of expansion. The new gambling clubs and betting shops were obvious targets. Provided he used his brain there was no need for unpleasantness or threats. The twins were businessmen, offering a service that these places needed. Their 'name' was an insurance policy against trouble and there was something of the insurance salesman about Reggie as he began whipping up fresh clients. He bought a black Crombie overcoat and started thinking of an office and a secretary. Les Payne gave him a briefcase like his own that Christmas; as Reggie drove from Vallance Road to the West End with it on the front seat of his Mercedes he felt he had a settled job at last with all the trappings of respectability –

Frances approved of that. And he was back with Ronnie in the only life he really understood. It seemed the perfect compromise to make everybody happy.

For a few months it worked: the twins made money and avoided trouble. Then Ronnie turned. Reggie and his briefcase – who did he think he was?

Nor did Frances seem to get much happiness from the new arrangement. Reggie was so on edge. They often danced late at The Hirondelle and called in at Esmeralda's Barn for a last drink. One night they found Ronnie there, drunker than usual; for the first time the twins had a slanging match with Frances present. She was terrified. All the old arguments and hatreds were brought out and finally Ronnie stumbled off, shouting that he had done with them for good. This had often happened in the past, only to be forgotten when he sobered up. This time he meant it and that evening marked a turning-point in his career.

He often used to spend the night in an old caravan on a bomb-site near Vallance Road. He went there now and stayed. Next day he sent his driver to the flat in Chelsea for his clothes. His West End life was over.

He still drew money from the Barn but rarely went there or bothered with its business. Suddenly he had other interests. One day it was a treasure hunt to the Congo. He had heard a rumour of several million dollars' worth of treasure buried by mercenaries in the jungle to the south of Brazzaville, and for a week or two talked of nothing else. Then he planned an English branch of Murder Incorporated. He thought of starting a crack regiment of London tearaways, equipping it at his own expense and personally leading it into action on behalf of a new African state. A religious mood followed: he announced he was sick of possessions and pain and hurting people and was leaving any day to work in a leper colony.

He could believe anything according to his mood. The visits to the lady clairvoyant increased, as he relied on her crystal ball for advice. His spirit guide was looking after him and she confirmed that he was the reincarnation of Attila the Hun and a Samurai warrior: he would achieve greatness through violence and then die young.

After a few weeks in his caravan he moved into Cedra Court, a block of thirtyish 'luxury flats' in Walthamstow, installing himself with a haphazard splendour which would have surprised his new middle-class neighbours. The décor was cockney Moroccan: rugs, leathercraft, silk hangings, brass trays had all been purchased on a recent visit to North Africa. Some of the rooms were without curtains or carpets, but in the living-room there was a large-screen television, several big bright-coloured china vases, gilt mirrors, a yard-long plaster figure of a recumbent Alsatian and an oil painting of a naked boy in a Victorian gold frame.

'I feel happy,' he told people, 'now I've got a place of my own.'

But the soft life was not for him.

'I've got to be someone, do something. Here am I nearly thirty, and going to die young.'

Because of this he had to hurry if he was to fulfil himself. He began building up another army in the East End. He could have had the pick of the top London villains, but he chose carefully. This time he wanted men dependent on him, men he could dominate. He already had a great range of contacts, 'useful' people he could count on to be 'with him' out of fear or obligation or self-interest in an emergency.

'If it was necessary I could have two hundred armed men in an hour anywhere in London.'

Previously the twins' closest followers had been cockneys; most of their new men came from outside London. Ian Barrie and 'Scotch Jack' Dickson were former Glasgow safe-blowers who learned to fight with the gangs of the Gorbals. Eighteen-stone 'Big Pat' Connolly, already in the Firm, was another Scot. Ronnie liked outsiders without London loyalties. For some time no one could be sure what new men were in the Firm. Ronnie was careful to find them legitimate employment. Some were installed as managers of East End drinking clubs and 'spielers': others moved round as strong-arm men in West End clubs the twins protected. He fixed up one man as sales representative with a big London engineering company; the managing director had been under obligation to Ronnie from the earliest days of the Barn. While Ronnie organized his army Reggie was busy building up protection among the freshly legalized West End gambling clubs. Thanks to his efforts, the twins' take more than doubled from this source in 1962.

The new casinos with their high profits and new middle-class clientele were far more vulnerable than the illicit gambling clubs of the past. Even the suggestion of police interest in a club could scare off the new-style customers. Club-owners seemed prepared for peace at any price – even Reggie's. So there was still no need for him to be involved in too much violence. With Ronnie in the background, the Kray name was quite enough. Clients began to come to him.

Reggie compared himself with other experts clubs required – lawyers or caterers or public relations firms. He was efficient and for what he had to offer no one could call his price excessive. He was the best around. A new club opening in Shepherd's Market felt it wise to ensure against trouble from the start by buying the protection of the Kray name for £150 a week. More followed: two in Knightsbridge, three in Chelsea, several in Mayfair. Reggie devised a tariff based on the club's profits. It was an inclusive charge. One night two young men threatened to bomb a club near Grosvenor Square. The manager wanted to keep the police out and asked Reggie's help. Next morning one of the men telephoned the club apologizing, and another £150 a week began to flow into the Kray funds.

Reggie was smart enough to see that foreign interests were becoming attracted to London gambling. He had heard rumours that the American Mafia, anxious to diversify investments, was trying to buy into several of the smartest Mayfair clubs. The French and Canadians were also busy. Reggie made sure that they contacted him early in negotiations. All these foreigners took it for granted that the conventions of smoothly organized protection on the American pattern operated in London, an assumption he was more than willing to encourage.

Reggie Kray's love for Frances changed with his success. She was not quite his Cinderella any more, but an important part of the business, the gangster's girl, taken for granted by the Firm. Her looks and youth went well with Reggie Kray the businessman around the West End. He bought her clothes, jewellery, a gold necklace, and liked to feel she was a credit to him. Ronnie became almost polite towards her.

She was the one who had the doubts, as the rich, claustrophobic gangster's world closed in on her. The large men and the large cars started to oppress her. She was becoming bored. Sometimes Reggie took her for a weekend by the sea. Here they would still enjoy themselves, but back in London he became impossible, especially when he drank. She tried to leave him several times, but soon found there were not that many boys willing to risk going out with Reg Kray's girl-friend – especially as he was still set on marrying her.

By this time Ronnie was ready for his greatest coup. He had the Firm assembled and had worked out his objectives. During his period at Esmeralda's Barn he had learned one important lesson – that Mayfair was not only richer but more vulnerable than Mile End. The sort of crime he had carried on in Whitechapel would work just as well in the swinging London of the sixties; he would use the methods of old-style cockney villainy to blackmail, trick and terrify his way into big business, smart society, credit-dealing, large-scale fraud.

He had considerable resources. There was the old myth of the twins' immunity from the Law and the carefully spread rumour that they had so many senior policemen bribed or blackmailed that any information offered to Scotland Yard about them came back to them. (There was, in fact, more than a grain of truth in this.) There was the code of silence, the assumption that it was unwise to talk about the twins because they always *knew* who had gone against them. There was the gaol network, bringing them information from the prisons and ensuring that while their associates were 'away' they would be looked after and their enemies discreetly dealt with. And there were the link-ups and pay-offs with a range of criminal allies throughout London – the Colonel's 'politics of crime'.

But Ronnie had been picking up some unusual fresh ideas about crime and violence. One of the few books he read at this time was *Mein Kampf*. Much of it bored him, but he understood the way Hitler insisted on the need for propaganda and a secret service as prerequisites of power in the modern State.

Eight years before, Ronnie had sat in the old billiard hall in Eric Street, paying his boys five shillings a time for scraps of information; now he had spies across the whole of London. In the East End he had his following of barmen, taxi-drivers, small-time criminals wishing to keep well in with the Krays and sending in regular reports to Vallance Road. In the West End he could use Esmeralda's Barn as a vantage-point and paid in fifties and hundreds for information he could use. The Barn was the ideal place for rumours from the world around him: anyone could be his spy – a businessman who had gambled too heavily and happened to know about a City fraud; a male prostitute with incriminating letters from a prominent politician who should have had more sense than to write them in the first place; a thief who knew the time and place when a rival gang would rob a bank. Ronnie had a surprising memory for facts. His mind was full of the crime and scandal of the city; sooner or later it invariably came in useful.

The information service was invaluable in other ways. In 1962 alone, at least three plans were made to murder the twins: one by a home-made bomb planted in their favourite pub, another by poison and a third by three Corsican gunmen hired by a West End club-owner with a grudge. The bomb, neatly defused, was delivered back to the man who ordered it. The intending poisoner had his jaw broken in a club in Old Compton Street. Three slightly worried Corsicans were met at Heathrow Airport by a reception committee who sent them straight home on the next flight to Paris.

With gangsters as with politicians, what they do counts far less than what they are thought to do: the twins had the politician's rare asset of perpetual credibility. People would always think the worst of them. Ronnie exploited this, using his followers and anyone he met to spread the wildest rumours of the twins' power. He loved to lard his conversation with hints of depravity and unspeakable wickedness, insinuating that the twins were behind every racket and maiming throughout London. It was even suggested that they killed for fun.

Every society seems to need a bogeyman. Ronnie began to play the part, living for the hush that fell across a room when he entered, the glances from other tables when he was at dinner, the tension in a bar until he left.

Vanity apart, notoriety was good for business. The twins' name for evil placed them above all competitors. Nobody wished to fight a legend.

In the first week of March 1962, the East End had its own royal film première. *Sparrers Can't Sing*, a sentimental cockney comedy of errors with Barbara Windsor, the East End's blonde bombshell, opened at the Empire Cinema in Bow Road before the Snowdons and a society audience. It was a gala night for Stepney. When the film ended and the royal couple drove off along Commercial Road in their Rolls, the film cast and their friends went to a celebration party at the new club opposite. It was called The Kentucky. Waiting to meet them were its young proprietors, immaculate in evening dress: the Kray twins.

The Kentucky was their latest venture, a plushier version of The Double R, designed to bring a smarter clientele to the East End. They had seen the publicity value of the première and arranged the grandest cockney party of the year. Queenie Watts was there to sing, Lord Effingham to mingle with the guests. There was all the brown ale anyone could drink; dancing went on till 3 A.M. The celebrities and the earlier presence of royalty made the occasion ideal for the twins, who were attempting to present themselves as local figures of success. Prestige had begun to matter. So had their local charities.

It would be wrong to be too cynical about the twins' philanthropy. They certainly enjoyed giving money away, but it is interesting that whenever they gave to charity, none of the local papers missed the fact. Back in July 1961 they had been photographed beaming beside the Mayor of Bethnal Green, Councillor Hare, at the St Matthew's Youth Club dance in aid of the organ fund. Since then their life as cockney worthies had been flourishing. Councillor Hare launched his Old Folks' Appeal: 'One of the first to make a donation, a gleaming television set, was "local businessman" Reginald Kray.'

So it went on – boys' clubs, cancer funds, hospitals and old people's homes never appealed in vain. This was becoming a key part of the twin's publicity, something to counterbalance all the tales of terror that were spread. Besides, the charities appeared to be a way of widening their circle of acquaintance. When the Repton Amateur Boxing Club put on a special show that November, 'local businessman Ronald Kray' donated all the trophies. The *East London Advertiser* ran a half-page tribute to the generosity of the twins, complete with photograph of Ronnie Kray with Billy Walker, the boxer, and the news that Ronnie had bought £220 worth of tickets. His guests included Joan Littlewood, Barbara Windsor, Victor Spinetti and Terry Spinks. According to the paper he had also invited Charlie Smirke, jockey, and Sir John Gielgud, actor.

This expansion of their public image brought the twins closer to each other. To all outsiders they were 'the Twins' now, firmly cemented in their double act by growing notoriety: fame, income, self-respect seemed to depend upon their togetherness.

Reggie was still the businessman: each minute of his day seemed to be filled with people to see, details to be taken care of. But it was Ronnie who was always there to force the pace, Ronnie who was unpredictable. He had the drive, the presence and the big ideas. Reggie was the one who usually toned down the violence, and tried to prevent Ronnie's excesses getting out of hand. Ronnie might dominate but Reggie felt that only he knew Ronnie well enough to hold him back.

That autumn they were together more than usual; there were fewer weekends away for Reggie, fewer nights out with Frances. The twins even dressed alike again, with identical gold jewellery, black gleaming shoes and tightly knotted ties. The light-heartedness of those first few months after Reggie's return from prison seemed over.

Just before Christmas, Reggie and Frances had their biggest row. She objected to the way Ronnie and his friends were taking over all their private life. He said her parents were trying to put her against him. At one point he was in tears, but finally agreed it would be best for them to see less of each other for a while.

'I saw that with the name the twins were getting, I could soon streamline crime and use them both to form a syndicate to ensure that things got done as in the States. I knew the Richardsons and the rest of the top villains: nothing could have been easier then than tying the whole thing together so that all the robbery with violence, all the fraud, protection, villainy came under one control.'

The idea of becoming the brain behind the twins struck several men besides Leslie Payne and proved their downfall. Payne was too shrewd for this. He hated violence; he knew the twins and was too moderate a man to cast himself as unifying genius of Britain's gangland. During the two years since he had changed their lives by organizing their entry into Esmeralda's Barn, he had been quietly co-directing the gambling in Wilton Place and doing nicely. He arranged the business side of their new club for them and that was all.

But while he could see the dangerous elements in the twins and had no wish to be the king of crime, they offered certain possibilities which it was hard to resist. With them there was a fortune to be made, and Leslie Payne started to use his brains and charm to work things out. This was when the rackets really started. There were endless possibilities in big business fraud; Payne and the twins began to make a lot of money.

The rackets varied but the twins' role remained the same. They were the source of fear, the men behind the scenes whose name ensured results. Few of their operations actually misfired; when they did, lesser men would take the rap. No one would risk denouncing the twins in court; it was understood that anyone going to prison for them would be suitably rewarded and his family looked after. Betrayal was unthinkable.

Thanks to the speed with which they worked, mistakes were rare. The twins and Leslie Payne ran a smooth operation. Their commonest racket was the 'long-firm' fraud, one of the simplest dishonest ways of making money ever devised. All that was needed was a little capital, an element of nerve, a front man and the threat of violence.

For a front man the twins usually chose someone they had a hold on from the past. Since he had a chance of ending up in prison, he was told to take a short, expensive holiday, settle his personal affairs, arrange to bank his share of the proceeds somewhere abroad, and then get down to work. For the next few weeks he would be busy. His job was to set up and manage a complete but fraudulent wholesale company; the success of the whole racket would depend upon the skill and credibility with which this was done. The twins had a set routine their front men followed. First, register the new company under a fictitious name; then rent a warehouse and an office and have stationery printed; finally, begin to write to the suppliers of wholesale goods. The twins would find the money for all this – also discreet employees for the warehouse. Once all the details were arranged, the 'long-firm' could start.

The twins' man would visit one of the local banks and see the manager. He would explain that he was starting a business and deposit a substantial sum of money as his firm's working capital. During the next few days some of this money would be withdrawn and redeposited to give the bank an impression of a thriving business. With the bank behind him, the front man would then make the rounds of the manufacturers, giving his orders for the goods he wanted, and start trading.

At this point the firm would act legitimately, paying suppliers on the dot, selling their goods cut-rate to shops and any likely customers and even placing small advertisements in trade papers. The aim was to establish instant credit. When this was done and the firm seemed to be flourishing, the twins would finally decide the time had come for their long-firm to realize its assets. Their man would be told to place maximum orders with all his suppliers. With the good name he had by now this would be easy, and when the goods had piled up in the warehouse the twins would give the order for them to 'hit the floor', being sold off in one grand slam. Everything would have to go, cut-rate and strictly for cash. The bargains would be remarkable – washing machines, refrigerators, crates of wine all offered at a third of the market price. In this way £30,000 or £40,000 could be cleared in a single day.

Once the warehouse was empty, the twins' man and his staff would disappear, drawing the last of their money from the bank and leaving the suppliers' bills to pile up in their empty office until the police arrived. If the police ever caught the long-firm manager, he would admit nothing, and go off to prison remembering the twins and his money safely banked in Switzerland.

There was big money in these long-firm frauds. In 1962 they cleared over £100,000 from this source alone. Before long they and Leslie Payne were talking of something more ambitious – a complex chain of fraudulent companies incorporating his know-how and their power. From there real possibilities began.

Payne had his own accountant, a pale, nervous man called Freddie Gore. He had originally kept the books at Esmeralda's Barn. He was a clever man and it was something new for the twins to have the advice of a trained accountant for their schemes. Gore owned a dormant company called Carston Securities. Soon it was decided that the twins required a central company of their own. Carston was ideal. Gore handled all the paperwork, revived it as the Carston Trading Company, and appointed Payne one of its new directors. Payne knew it was no use running a seedy operation. Carston soon had a well-run central office, with a receptionist and secretaries, in Great Portland Street. It had a warehouse, too, together with a trading account with the Bank of Valletta. Its file of references was impressive. 'The Carston Group of Companies' was ready to take wing.

It was a grandiose idea – a perfectly legitimate company to underpin a range of unconnected business frauds. It could be used to undertake all manner of deals, in England and abroad. Carston could easily become the twins' route into any firm in Europe.

The spring of 1963 was a good time for the twins as they

started to enjoy their public image as cockney benefactors and friends of the famous, together with their parallel success as organizing criminals. Behind the drunkenness and the disorder of their lives appeared a real sense of purpose. Now was the moment when everything seemed to boost their power. Ronnie's madness, Reggie's gift with people, the hidden violence, the open generosity and all their contacts through their clubs, their charities, the underground of criminals and the freemasonry of homosexuals.

Even their ancient love of boxing came in useful. That spring they made their bow as promoters, staging a bout between Ronnie's friend and former fellow-prisoner, Bobby Ramsey, and wrestler Roy 'Chopper' Levecq. That evening by the ringside of Bethnal Green's York Hall they sat like feudal chieftains with followers and friends and famous guests. They had three former world champions – Terry Downes, Ted 'Kid' Berg and Ted 'Kid' Lewis – in the audience. Also Councillor Hare. The local press gave the usual maximum publicity.

Now that the twins were learning to manipulate the law, the press and the social world, it was inevitable that they should turn their attentions next to politicians. Ronnie had read enough of Al Capone to realize that politicians had their uses for the criminal, but the few he met at Esmeralda's Barn or lunching at the House of Lords did not impress him. They smelled of trouble and he kept his distance. Now through their East End charities the twins were meeting a few MPs under different circumstances. Ronnie began to see that possibly Capone was right. Even in Britain it could be useful for a gangster to have a friend or two in the Mother of Parliaments.

The man who impressed them both was Tom Driberg, Labour MP for Barking. They met him through Joan Littlewood, who brought him to their new club one night for a drink. Reggie was particularly agreeable and chatted for some while about the changing East End. Driberg found the twins interested in his work as an MP; when he attempted to explain how MPs often worked behind the scenes alleviating hardship, they were both sceptical. Reggie mentioned that he had been trying to get a friend of his, a local man, shifted from Dartmoor to a London prison on grounds of ill-health. If Mr Driberg were sincere, perhaps he would look into the case. As a conscientious MP with an interest in prison conditions, Driberg promised to make inquiries. The Home Office examined the case and the man was moved.

For Driberg, this was one case among several hundred that he dealt with in a working year; for the twins it opened up an avenue of possibilities. Politicians had their uses which could be exploited; the twins were good at using human frailty to make men do as they were told. Quite suddenly they saw what could be done with a discreet gangsters' lobby of carefully fixed members in either House; for Parliament is the one place where the criminal's two main enemies – the police and prison services – are publicly accountable. Surprising things can be achieved behind the scenes by any member willing to put the right word at the right time to an obliging civil servant, and Driberg, who was immensely influential and corrupt, proved an invaluable ally of the twins. A future Chairman of the Labour Party, who found apotheosis in the House of Lords as Lord Bradwell-juxta-Mare, he was a pederast with a sophisticated taste in perversion, and a driving *nostalgie de la boue*. In return for his discreet support, Ronnie would always find him boys prepared for any performance he required.

There was something quite uncanny about the twins' success during the summer of 1963. Suddenly there seemed no limit to what they could achieve, and they had the confidence to match. Their protection rackets were expanding; the first long-firm frauds based on the Carston Group were ready to be milked. These were the 625 Centre, a radio and television business in the East End, and Dominion Refrigeration, a carefully built-up business in Brixton specializing in electrical goods. At the same time Payne and Gore were looking out for other business, some of it from overseas and some of it legitimate. America had shown how gangsters can invest their money in straight businesses; the twins were ready now to do the same. Reggie was anxious to buy betting shops, tobacconists and restaurants, and also a demolition business. His brightest idea was to take over a security firm specializing in the transport and protection of valuables. As he pointed out, this could be done through front men they controlled; the Kray name would be the best protection a security firm could hope for.

There were other ways in which the twins appeared intent on following the pattern of big organizing criminals in the United States. Ronnie had read about the way American crime syndicates brought in their gunmen from another city. He flew to Glasgow several times and, introduced by Big Pat Connolly, made an agreement with the leading Gorbals gang; later that summer two Scots flew down to Heathrow and shot a member of the Kray twins' rival gang – the Richardsons – in the legs. Similar deals followed. The twins also started to expand outside London; again they found it simple to use their name as London gangsters to move in on racketeers in other towns. The secret was to know exactly whom to squeeze. Knowledge of this sort was Ronnie's speciality. The favours and the endless drinking bouts with lesser villains were beginning to pay off. The twins found men anxious to work for them in the provinces; they took over two big clubs in Birmingham, another in Leicester and were soon organizing similar rackets to those in London. The formula of Kray power appeared universal.

Although Esmeralda's Barn was now losing money, they could afford to ignore it. 'You worry too much. Worry's for old women,' Ronnie told the latest manager, and put his uncle, Alf Kray, in his place. Since Ronnie was bored with the Barn, he moved his headquarters to a hotel in

Seven Sisters Road; this became the place where members of the Firm could sleep and drink and have their meetings. Then Ronnie felt they needed somewhere grander to entertain their followers and guests. The Cambridge Rooms, on the Kingston bypass, seemed exactly right – a big, pretentious restaurant close enough to London and the Surrey stockbroker belt. He interviewed the manager and made it plain that he would either ruin him or join him as his partner. In time he did both, but for a while The Cambridge Rooms became the focus for the twins' success. They staged a gala night early that autumn to celebrate their takeover, a grand Kray-style demonstration of the sort they loved. Ronnie had persuaded Sonny Liston, heavyweight champion of the world, to come as guest of honour. A telephoned message of goodwill from Billy Daniels, the singer, was broadcast over the loudspeakers, straight from Hollywood. Guests included journalists and criminals and fresh celebrities the twins were trying to impress; everything was on the house.

The high spot of the evening belonged to their mother. Recently the twins had bought her Solway Cross, a racehorse, for a thousand guineas – a touching gesture . . . but an unsuccessful horse. When Ronnie offered a 'grand raffle for charity', Violet gave Solway Cross as first prize. The horse was won by a comedian.

Reggie got very drunk that night but still insisted on driving the world champion to the Dorchester in the Mercedes. Later, Liston said he was more frightened during that half hour with Reggie Kray at the wheel, than at any time in the ring.

After his recent escapades it was inevitable that Ronnie should have been impressed by Ernest Shinwell. Shinwell, son of the distinguished Labour politician, dealt in dreams; his latest was to build a brand-new township costing several million pounds in the raw bush outside Enugu in Nigeria. The idea had possibilities: there had already been long conferences about it; the Nigerian government was interested; architects had been called in; Turif International, the construction company, had been consulted. But there were big financial difficulties: investors were wary of putting money into what was later to become Biafra and Ronnie soon appeared as one of Shinwell's last hopes of drumming up support.

There must have been misunderstanding on both sides. Shinwell was soon giving Ronnie the big treatment, lecturing him on Africa and promising fame and riches once the town was built. He took him to the House of Lords, where he introduced him to his father as a rich young businessman with an idealist's interest in black Africa. Lord Shinwell seemed impressed; so was Ronnie. Suddenly Enugu was his dream city and he saw himself becoming the grand young man of Africa. Shinwell arranged for him to fly out to Nigeria; an official car was waiting at the airport and at the hotel there was a delegation of Nigerian ministers and top officials to meet this strange young Englishman who had come to build them a new city. For three days Ronnie was a VIP and guest of the Nigerian government. The Minister of Health personally assured Ronnie that he would have all the help his government could give. He saw the land earmarked for what was now 'his' city. When asked what he would like to see he asked to look round Enugu's gaol.

Once they were back in London, Payne quickly set up a subsidiary of Carston to handle the financing of the new scheme; Ronnie, believing in a new life round the corner, put down the deposit on a brand-new Rolls.

It was a shade improbable: gangsters don't build cities, nor do penurious African politicians hand out instant fortunes. The idea of the town was viable; all that it needed now was long-term money. But it would be many years before it made Ronnie Kray the white king of Enugu. He wanted instant profits, and had no capital of his own to invest. A Nigerian contractor demanded £5,000, which he claimed was due to him under agreement. Payne, who was in Enugu, found himself suddenly in gaol. In England the twins had to find the money to get their friend released. This was not difficult, but they felt angry and betrayed – Ronnie in particular. Greatness had seemed so close.

Joe was a boxer and an old friend of the twins. He met Ronnie one night in a Fulham Road club just after his Nigerian hopes had folded; without knowing what had happened, he tried borrowing £5 – 'With all that weight you've put on, Ron, you look as if you could afford it.'

No one laughed: most people knew the signs when Ronnie was depressed. Ronnie said nothing, gulped his drink, called for his coat and left. He had his boy with him, his car outside ready to take him to The Cambridge Rooms for dinner. The car had reached the Kingston bypass when he changed his mind and told the driver to go back. Joe was still drinking at the bar.

'I want a word with you in private.'

'What about, Ron?'

'You'll see.'

Everyone in the club was watching now as Joe followed Ronnie into the washroom. Joe did nothing to defend himself. Ronnie used his favourite knife. Joe did not cry out. When Ronnie had finished he paused to wash his hands and straighten his tie before walking back through the bar. His car was waiting outside and he told the driver he had better hurry or they'd be late for supper.

When he had gone and the washroom door was opened, Joe was found in the corner, conscious and 'with half his face beside him on the floor'. The surgeons at St Stephen's Hospital used more than seventy stitches to sew it back in place. The police spent the whole night beside his bed waiting for him to talk.

Reggie heard what had happened straight away. He said that Ronnie must be off his head to do a thing like that. The police were waiting to pin something on the twins;

once Joe or any witness from the club talked to the police, Ronnie was finished.

'You'd better make sure no one does talk, then,' said Ronnie.

No one did, although it took Reggie and the Firm the whole night checking who was in the club and making sure that everyone understood just what was good for him. Joe knew this of his own accord. The policeman by his bedside was unlucky.

For a long while afterwards Joe was known as 'Tramlines' to his friends, and that autumn Ronnie forgot his politicians and his frauds and dreams of power to begin a brief and therapeutic splurge of sadism.

The Jonathan affair came soon after Joe's injury. Jonathan was a hard, good-looking little man, another old friend of the twins, and one night at the Barn the twins heard he had picked a fight with a young man who was the son of one of their allies. This was an indirect challenge. Jonathan should have known better. Reggie was for caution; Ronnie worked himself into a rage. There had to be a showdown. It was 3 A.M., but Ronnie rang Jonathan, saying there was something to discuss, and he would be grateful if he would take a taxi round to Wilton Place at once.

The Barn was closing, the gaming-room almost empty. Ronnie was in the kitchen. Jonathan was shown in. When he saw Ronnie he tried to run. Somebody tripped him and the kitchen door slammed in his face. There was a sturdy kitchen chair; Jonathan found himself dumped in it and heard Ronnie tell his brother to hold him down. Then Ronnie took a steel knife-sharpener which he had placed in the gas flame. Three men remaining in the gaming-room heard muffled screams as Ronnie branded Jonathan along each cheek.

Soon after this the twins left Esmeralda's Barn for good; the gold-mine was in debt, the tax-man at the door. The twins had other things to worry them. Ronnie was becoming dangerous again; Reggie was doing his lame best to keep him in control. This was hard. Sometimes he found himself involved in the excitement and needed all his strength to remind himself of where the twins' true interests lay.

Left to himself Ronnie would destroy all they had created. All he could think of was his enemies; all that he wanted was to murder them. Half-drugged or drunk, he spent his time trying to decide who was against him.

In Nigeria he had been fascinated by reports of the bestialities of the local Leopard Men. He began studying them, keeping the pictures of their mangled victims carefully mounted in his scrapbook, 'their livers and hearts removed', according to the caption, 'to make magic medicine'.

One night at The Kentucky he was drinking with two boys. One of them asked how he would like to suffer the sort of pain that he inflicted. Instead of answering, he took out his favourite knife and slowly sliced across his own hand. Someone had to drive him to hospital to have it stitched.

Reggie's chief problem was to keep Ronnie away from the police. Argument was useless. Much time that he could ill afford seemed to be spent in keeping him amused. Business began to suffer. There was the perpetual fear that Ronnie would land everyone in some appalling situation.

Ronnie's depressions were the greatest hazard; afterwards his nightmares started and he could easily go berserk. Reggie did all he could to keep him happy. There were his boys and there was drink; after sufficient gin or brown ale, Ronnie could forget his troubles and doze away safely in the big four-poster he had bought for Cedra Court. He also needed people round him, especially since he now enjoyed meeting celebrities. The parties started.

Soon they were getting known in certain circles. One night a well-known television don turned up at Cedra Court. So did a famous disc-jockey. Driberg was a regular visitor. Then came actors, a world-famous painter, several boxers, the chairman of an engineering firm, an assortment of men from the City, and two young men in dark suits who turned out to be Church of England clergymen.

During his Chelsea days Ronnie had learned enough of homosexual togetherness to know what was expected: entertainments were laid on. Some of the success of these 'at homes' must have been due to Ronnie's boys, some to the novelty of the locale. But by far the greatest draw was Ronnie himself. His appearance, his reputation as a criminal, his adroit mixture of sadism and perversion made him a creature of limitless appeal; he exploited the sexual overtones of violence with the same sly gusto that he brought to his more conventional acts of extortion.

None of the guests seemed put off by the chance of blackmail or by the dangers of flirting with a potential killer. Presumably this added to the excitement. Soon Ronnie was in demand as a guest at certain country houses round London. One he enjoyed was close to Brighton; it was after a weekend here that he first conceived the ambition for a country place of his own. The set-up of wealthy, upper-class country living appealed to him; he was enjoying his success and the surprising range of intimate friends in high places it afforded.

Around this time a different group of men was taking an interest in him: one was a small man called Read who had recently arrived in the East End. He had previously been in Paddington, where the name Kray occasionally cropped up among the criminals he knew. Now that he was a detective inspector at the early age of thirty-six and attached to Commercial Street Police Station, Leonard Read was anxious to meet the twins. He had found them elusive, yet the more he learned of local crime, the more important they appeared to be.

Witnesses were clamming up. Whenever he asked old East End informers about the twins, they changed the subject. A policeman likes to know what he is up against. When someone told Inspector Read that the twins often used The Grave Maurice, a pub by Whitechapel underground station, early in the evening, he decided to go along.

Normally the twins both had a sixth sense about the Law, and would never enter a pub where police were present. But Read was new to the district; and when Ronnie strode into the saloon bar of The Maurice, gazing round to check on unwelcome visitors, he didn't spare a glance for the man in the grey cap sitting in the corner with a Worthington and the racing edition of the *Evening News*.

ELEVEN

Twins Victorious

'PEER AND A GANGSTER: YARD INQUIRY' shouted the headlines, and the story, splashed across three quarters of the front page of the *Sunday Mirror*, explained that the Metropolitan Police Commissioner, Sir Joseph Simpson, had ordered a top-level investigation into the alleged homosexual relationship between a peer who was a 'household name' and a leading thug in the London underworld, who was involved in West End protection rackets. The investigation was being conducted by Detective Chief Superintendent Frederick Gerrard, who was inquiring into Mayfair parties the thug and the peer had been to, the peer's weekend visits to Brighton along with a number of 'prominent public men', his relationships with certain East End gangsters 'and a number of clergymen', and allegations of blackmail.

Within forty-eight hours, warned the *Sunday Mirror*, Sir Joseph would be meeting the Home Secretary to give him details of what the *Sunday Mirror* was revealing to its readers. Gerrard would get his marching orders; then the peer, the gangster and the erring clergy had better watch out.

With this front-page salvo in the *Sunday Mirror* the so-called 'Case of the Brighton Peer' began.

This was 12 July 1964. Things soon began to happen. Early next morning a photographer called Bernard Black from Clapton came to the *Mirror* picture desk claiming to have a reel of photographs of the peer and the gangster, and that day at New Scotland Yard, Sir Joseph Simpson prepared a public statement denying the suggestion that Her Majesty's Commissioner of Police was starting a private witch-hunt against titled homosexuals. It expressed pained surprise at the suggestion that he personally ordered an investigation into a relationship between 'a peer and a man with a criminal record'. It denied that he was giving the Home Secretary details from such an investigation. It denied that such an investigation had ever taken place.

Just after tea-time Bernard Black, the photographer, returned to the *Mirror* offices at Holborn Circus asking for his pictures back and saying that the copyright was not his to sell. The *Mirror* refused to return them. Next morning Black was in the High Court applying for an injunction forbidding the *Daily Mirror* or the *Sunday Mirror* to publish his pictures under any circumstances.

That Tuesday Superintendent Gerrard, the man the *Mirror* named as head of the officially denied investigation, asked to see the *Mirror*'s dossier in which the allegations were made. There was no dossier; editor Payne admitted as much, although a phalanx of reporters had been working hard since dawn trying to make good the deficiency.

On Thursday, 16 July, the *Mirror* led with massive headlines on 'THE PICTURE WE DARE NOT PRINT'. It described how this picture on its files showed 'a well-known member of the House of Lords seated on a sofa with a gangster who leads the biggest protection racket London has ever known'. Then an article appeared on 22 July in the West German *Stern* magazine, entitled 'Lord Bobby in Trouble'. Unworried by the distant hazards of the English libel law the magazine named Boothby and Ronnie Kray as the subjects of the *Mirror* story and published a picture of both twins in boxing kit alongside an early photograph of Boothby and Winston Churchill.

Lord Boothby retained Arnold Goodman, Harold Wilson's personal solicitor, now Lord Goodman, and Gerald Gardiner, QC, who later became the Labour government's Lord Chancellor.

Normally when an individual considers himself libelled, he seeks redress at law, but Lord Boothby's new advisers suggested a more direct course. Under their supervision he wrote a 500-word letter to *The Times*, which finally appeared on 2 August, openly identifying himself as the subject of the *Sunday Mirror*'s smear campaign and denying in detail all the allegations.

The letter was a model of precision, describing how Lord Boothby returned from France on 16 July to find Parliament, Fleet Street and other 'informed quarters' seething with rumours that he had had a homosexual relationship with a leading thug from the London underworld; that he had been to all-male Mayfair parties with him; that he had been photographed with him on a sofa in a compromising position; that there was a homosexual relationship between Lord Boothby, East End gangsters and a number of clergymen in Brighton; that various people knowing about these relationships were being blackmailed; and that Scotland Yard, after watching meetings between Lord Boothby and the thug for several months, had reported on them to the Commissioner of Police.

Lord Boothby went on to describe how he was once photographed 'with my full consent, in my flat (which is also my office) with a gentleman who came to see me, accompanied by two friends, in order to ask me to take an active part in a business venture which seemed to me of interest and importance.' He explained how he had turned the proposal down, said that anyone was welcome to publish any photographs taken of him, and added that although he had since learned that the man he was photographed with had been guilty of a criminal offence, he emphatically had no knowledge of this at the time.

He then refuted the *Sunday Mirror* allegations quite specifically. 'I am not a homosexual. I have not been to a Mayfair party of any kind for more than twenty years. I have met the man alleged to be "King of the Underworld" only three times, on business matters; and then by appointment in my flat, at his request, and in the company of other people.' He never had been to a party at Brighton with any gangsters – still less with clergymen. No one had ever tried to blackmail him. The police denied making any report to the Home Secretary in connection with him.

'In short, the whole affair is a tissue of atrocious lies.'

The letter concluded with a challenge to the *Mirror* newspapers. If either of them possessed documentary or photographic evidence against Lord Boothby, 'let them print it and take the consequences'.

The letter was signed, 'You obedient servant, Boothby.'

This attempt to clear his name by a direct challenge in *The Times* was unprecedented but was typical of Lord Boothby's directness. And it produced results. Just five days after the letter appeared, the *Daily Mirror* was carrying a new headline: 'LORD BOOTHBY. An unqualified apology.' All imputations made against Lord Boothby in the original *Sunday Mirror* article were unreservedly withdrawn. The International Publishing Corporation also paid Lord Boothby forty thousand pounds in compensation plus legal costs.

It was one of the largest settlements of the day – half a million pounds in today's devalued currency. And what made this so extraordinary was that the *Sunday Mirror* story had been broadly true, and Boothby had in fact lied repeatedly in his famous letter to *The Times*.

He was homosexual. He had a close connection with Ronnie Kray which extended back for at least a year before the *Sunday Mirror* broke its story. And behind the whole affair lay a scandal involving Ronnie Kray and Boothby almost exactly as the *Sunday Mirror* had suggested.

Had their story been substantiated, Boothby would have been a ruined man, and the Krays' criminal activities would have been seriously curtailed. Instead an extraordinary establishment cover-up occurred, which earned Lord Boothby a small fortune for his lies, stopped a Yard investigation in its tracks, and gave the Krays virtual immunity for several years – from the attentions of New Scotland Yard, from the British press, and from the politicians at Westminster.

Boothby had actually been introduced to Ronnie Kray early in 1963 by their mutual friend, and fellow homosexual, Tom Driberg (later Lord Driberg of Bradwell-Juxta-Mare and Chairman of the Labour Party). For Boothby, as for Driberg, the chief attraction of Ronnie's company was the excitement of being introduced to the boys he used to have around him.

In return Lord Boothby offered Ronnie Kray a somewhat different sort of excitement, by showing him the world of privilege and politics, even taking him on one occasion for dinner at the House of Lords, and on another dropping in for drinks at the most prestigious of London clubs – White's in St James's.

As a gangster in a Savile Row suit, Ronnie felt very much at home in White's.

'Nice place,' he said when telling me about it. 'Interesting people. Thought of joining it myself.'

He was always fairly cynical about Lord Boothby, knowing him for what he was, and sometimes calling him 'the Queen mother', or 'that daft old idiot'. But he undoubtedly enjoyed the smart life Boothby could offer him, and realized that in a crisis, a friendly member of the House of Lords might come in useful. Accordingly he made a fuss of him.

On one occasion he arranged a party in Boothby's honour at one of his favourite West End haunts, the old Society Club in Jermyn Street – at which Boothby was photographed with Ronnie sitting on either side of a teenage boy, along with two members of the Kray Firm, Billie Exley and Charlie Clark. On other occasions, he arranged for sex shows for Boothby and his friends in various locations in the East End of London.

Early in 1964 Scotland Yard's Criminal Intelligence

section, C11, began targeting the Krays' activities – and as well as details of their frauds and West End protection rackets, they inevitably picked up details of Ronnie Kray's relationships with men like Boothby. This was a matter of police concern because of the obvious possibility of blackmail.

The *Sunday Mirror*'s veteran crime reporter, Norman Lucas, had close connections with members of C11. One of these officers showed him C11's surveillance reports on the Krays, and told him that a full-scale Scotland Yard offensive against the gang would soon be mounted. This was the basis of the *Sunday Mirror* story, which Lucas wrote and which was published with the enthusiastic backing of its then proprietor, Cecil King.

Lord Boothby was on holiday in France when the story broke, and always claimed that he had no idea who the 'unknown peer' could possibly have been. On his return to London on 16 July he rang Tom Driberg to find out, and it was Driberg who told him – 'Bob, it's you.'

Driberg, of course, knew that the *Sunday Mirror* accusations were true. Boothby, staring ruin in the face, was suicidal. And Driberg, as a highly influential member of the Labour Party, seems to have done his best to save him.

As events were to prove, he was successful. A general election was in the offing which Labour, led by Harold Wilson, hoped to win. After the Profumo scandal the previous year, it was not in Labour's interests to be seen to be cashing in on an even murkier sexual scandal so soon after, involving as popular a former Tory as Lord Boothby.

So with Boothby now denying all the *Sunday Mirror* accusations, Driberg was able to convince his leader, Harold Wilson, to support what seemed to be a grossly libelled public figure. It clearly suited the Labour leadership to be strongly sympathetic to Lord Boothby's case, and to help him clear his name – which he did extremely quickly. On Harold Wilson's suggestion, Boothby consulted Wilson's personal 'Mr Fixit', Arnold Goodman, and assured him that the *Sunday Mirror* story was untrue. Believing him, Goodman took on the case, and brought in Labour's future Lord Chancellor – the celebrated barrister, Gerald Gardiner – as adviser.

With such extremely high-powered backing all the support for the *Sunday Mirror*'s accusations promptly faded. Scotland Yard denied all knowledge of C11's investigation, so that when the *Sunday Mirror* tried to get C11's evidence to back its story it was unsuccessful. It was equally unsuccessful when it sought evidence from those around the Krays. Hardly surprisingly, a wall of silence suddenly descended, leaving the *Sunday Mirror* defenceless.

It was then that Arnold Goodman suggested that, rather than engage in a lengthy libel action, Lord Boothby write his famous letter to *The Times*, which earned him £40,000. Once the original story was retracted, the *Sunday Mirror* editor, Reg Payne, was fired – and Cecil Harmsworth King apologized personally to Lord Boothby.

But for the Kray twins, this was by no means the end of the story. With their keen eye the twins had spotted some of the possibilities in the incident and did their best to make the most of them. Up to the point where the *Mirror* settled with Lord Boothby, Ronnie had not been named directly. Just as Lord Boothby had originally been 'a peer who was a household name' so Ronnie had remained 'a leading thug in the London underworld'.

When Ronnie was named it was entirely by his own decision and on his own terms. After the publication of the Boothby letter in *The Times*, Ronnie appeared to change his mind and personally selected the most flattering of the photographs which were then taken to the picture desk of the *Daily Express* – the hottest photograph in Fleet Street – the peer and the gangster sitting on the sofa in Lord Boothby's flat. The *Express* paid £100 for the right to publish and it appeared on 6 August on the front page beneath banner headlines. Nothing could have made it clearer that the 'leading thug' was Ronnie Kray.

Ronnie's main motive in having the picture published was undoubtedly to try to cash in on the settlement. He was considerably aggrieved when he had to content himself with an apology – and nothing more. But the indirect benefits the *Sunday Mirror* libel brought him were considerable.

The first was with the press. There had been the beginning of a press campaign on 'the frightening growth of lawlessness, extortion, blackmail and intimidating in London' in the *Sunday Mirror* in the week following the libel, and for the first time the twins were being brought to the attention of the public. Once the libel case came up, all this was over. Had the *Sunday Mirror* pursued its investigations of the Krays' criminal affairs it could have been legally dangerous for them, breaking the spirit of their apology to Ronnie, and bearing the appearance of revenge. Not surprisingly, the editors of other papers, having no desire for legal trouble either, kept off the subject of the twins as well. For the next three years the Krays were to be immune to press investigation, and on the few occasions when they were mentioned they found themselves referred to as 'those well-known East End sporting brothers'.

With the police the effects of the libel were more subtle and still more far-reaching. Though Sir Joseph Simpson had made a public denial of a police investigation into a relationship between 'a peer and a man with a criminal record', there emphatically had been an investigation of the Krays and their activities – protection, fraud, blackmail, wounding and intimidation. This had been in progress since the start of 1964, when Nipper Read had been promoted Detective Chief Inspector and attached to West End Central Police Station under Chief Superintendent Gerrard.

From all he had learned, Read had few illusions about the twins and knew that they were no ordinary gangsters. The flat at Cedra Court was under observation; their parties and unusual social connections had all been duly noted. With the people they were meeting and their backstairs influence at all levels of society, the twins were moving towards the invulnerability of the big-time organizing criminals of the States. If this continued Read feared they might soon be too powerful to touch. Unsuspected by the twins, the police had a case virtually prepared when the *Sunday Mirror* sounded the alarm with its first article. Once this had happened, the twins were warned. More important still, thanks to the Commissioner's denial of the investigation, much of the earlier evidence against the twins became unusable. Largely because of this, much police work against the twins and their organization had to stop.

Despite these difficulties, Superintendent Gerrard and Inspector Read still hoped for a chance to catch the twins, although since the *Sunday Mirror* libel, potential witnesses were warier than ever of speaking out against them.

Just after Christmas it seemed that the twins had suddenly slipped up and Gerrard and Read made ready to stake everything on one last throw; orders had reached them from above that the Kray case was to be settled one way or the other quickly.

Most of Read's hopes rested on a man called Hew McCowan. Son of a wealthy baronet, he was a well-known West End figure. The twins had known him at Esmeralda's Barn and tried to borrow money from him for their Nigerian scheme. McCowan put his money into a club instead – The Hideaway in Soho.

Soon afterwards he was in touch with Read, claiming that the twins were asking for a half-share in his profits. It was unique to find the owner of a club willing to stand up to the twins, but there was no corroboration of McCowan's story until one night in January 1965. There was an upset at The Hideaway with pictures smashed and threats before witnesses. Police were called and a man was arrested; Read sensed that here he had the basis of a charge against the twins at last, for the man who caused the trouble was their friend and drinking partner, 'Mad' Teddy Smith. Smith had given a firm impression that he had come on behalf of the twins and was demanding money for them. This, with McCowan's previous deposition, seemed enough. On 10 January the Kray twins were arrested and accused, 'with Edward Smith, writer', of demanding money with menaces from Hew Cargill McCowan at the Hideaway Club. Bail was refused.

It was a flimsy case, at best a feeble substitute for the full-scale police persecution ruined by the earlier publicity, but there was a good chance it would succeed. Read knew the odds, and as the policeman closest to the twins was banking something of his reputation on it. Similarly the twins prepared to make the case a final showdown with the Law.

The twins left nothing to chance. They engaged the finest criminal lawyers they could find – Petre Crowder and Paul Wrightson, QC: Wrightson had impressed Reggie when he prosecuted him in the Shay protection case four years earlier. They also hired one of the best private detectives in London; he was to find out all he could about the prosecution witnesses, particularly McCowan. Simultaneously messages were passing out of Brixton Gaol from the twins to all the members of the Firm, which was kept very busy in the next few weeks; it requires hard work and good organization to rig a trial at the Old Bailey.

Before the trial there was a battle over bail. The Old Street magistrate refused their first request; so did a judge in chambers, but the twins did not give up. They tried Judge Griffith-Jones at the Old Bailey and finally the Lord Chief Justice, offering him sureties of eighteen thousand pounds. He, too, refused and the trial was fixed to start on 28 February.

It was always a mystery where the twins were getting so much money from, and although both they and Lord Boothby always denied it, there seems little doubt that some of it must have come from him. As Ronnie had letters and photographs which proved their friendship, he could always threaten to expose him as a liar if he wanted to. Certainly some sort of outside pressure is the only explanation for Lord Boothby's irregular and highly suspect action when the twins took their bail application to the House of Lords. Against all precedent he intervened in a law debate to inquire if it was the government's intention to keep the Kray twins indefinitely without a trial.

At the time, Boothby was strongly reprimanded, and his intervention did nothing to prevent his former counsel, Gerald Gardiner, from rejecting the bail application out of hand. But it was a significant example of the growing power of the twins, when they could get a member of the House of Lords to ask a question in Parliament on their behalf.

There was still the trial. Juries are vulnerable and the jury's verdict had to be unanimous. Under the jury law of those days, one juryman dissenting from a verdict was enough to force a re-trial.

This was important. Jurors' addresses could be found: they could be followed home, watched, carefully approached. Out of twelve men there was a chance that one could be threatened or bribed. Once the trial started, the Firm was busy. The jury failed to reach agreement on its verdict; the inevitable re-trial followed. This suited both the twins. The private detective had had time to dig out more about the major witness for the prosecution. In Scotland several years before McCowan had appeared in various cases involving homosexuals and appeared with something of the character of an habitual police informer. For Paul Wrightson this was sufficient. McCowan was discredited as a witness; the judge stopped the trial before the final speeches; the twins and Teddy Smith went free.

That night the twins held the biggest celebration party of their lives. They were supreme by now and typically they chose the one place that would drive this message home. That very afternoon they bought McCowan's club, renamed it El Morocco, and invited everyone they knew, including the police from West End Central.

Read went along. One of the greatest problems a policeman has to face with organized criminals is simply knowing who is who – their clients, their dependants, their associates and friends. Such people constantly change, and a party of this sort offered a rare chance to learn about them. Read spent more than an hour in a telephone box opposite the club watching the arrivals; someone asked him in. It seemed a good idea to meet the twins at last on the basis of 'know thine enemy', and Read was soon face to face with them. It was the first time they had met. Ronnie was affability itself, laughing and pouring out champagne.

But soon afterwards, Scotland Yard – already sensitive about the twins – started receiving letters of complaint about Nipper's presence at the party. What nobody realized was that all these letters were prompted by the twins and intended to discredit the detective who had dared attack them. Even here it seemed they had succeeded. There was an immediate Yard inquiry. Read was cleared of any suggestion of improper contact with the twins. He was promoted but moved on to other duties, and Ronnie Kray boasted that with one glass of champagne he had chased his most dangerous enemy in the police out of the West End for good.

The police had been badly burnt by the Krays and a directive was issued from the Yard that in future detectives were not to frequent the haunts of known criminals; also to exercise caution when associating with anyone with a known police record.

And it was partly as a result of a report on the McCowan case that the jury law was changed. In future verdicts would be decided by a majority of the jury; one juryman dissenting would not secure a re-trial.

Police who knew the twins and understood the way their power was developing felt that the McCowan case had rendered them invulnerable. Press, politics, police – all had been used and all defeated by the twins. They were entrenched now: nobody wanted to risk trouble from them. Four years of fraud and murder were to pass before the spell was broken.

TWELVE

A Marriage in the Family

The two of them came arm-in-arm down the long steps of the Old Bailey when the McCowan case was over and they were free again. Frances was twenty-one and prettier than ever; Reggie was smiling the wry grin of his boxing days when he had out-fought someone in the ring. People were clustering round congratulating them, press photographers elbowing them for pictures. Ronnie was behind them. Like Reggie, he was pale after fifty-six days in custody. But it was Reggie and Frances everybody had to see, Frances especially. She had her happy ending after all.

There was a hired Daimler waiting at the kerb; they drove off like top celebrities, laughing at each other. A reporter had asked their plans for the future: for years it seemed that they had talked of nothing else, but they were suddenly embarrassed. Even in Brixton Gaol, when she agreed to marry him if he were acquitted, everything was in the future and a long way off; now it was happening. She was the star of the twins' acquittal, the prize the innocent man had waited for.

When the big, gleaming car drew up in Vallance Road there were still more congratulations – flags, neighbours, relatives and boyhood friends. Old Cannonball was beaming in his braces, wearing his best Sunday cap to welcome his boys home. Reggie was buying Frances a big engagement ring, a car, a gold pendant. There was no doubt of his love for her; she had convinced herself she loved him in return. Both were sincere in the way that human beings are at moments of extreme relief.

They talked a lot about their wedding. She wanted something quiet, Reggie was set on something grand. He was a public figure; his marriage could not avoid being an event. After the publicity of the Boothby case and the Old Bailey trials, he saw his wedding as a way to prove that he could still be good, respected, loved. The wedding would take place at St James's Bethnal Green, the red church opposite Pellici's Café where he and Ronnie went as boys. His old friend Father Hetherington would officiate.

They went to see the old priest. He had moved to Ealing, a quieter parish than Bethnal Green. Reggie carefully explained that he had come to ask him to marry them as he had been a true friend of his family and one of the few men he respected. For half an hour they sat talking in the front-room study with its books and crucifix in the red-brick terrace house in Ealing. Finally, as gently as he could, the priest refused, explaining that he could not perform a marriage which he felt should not take place. He would not give his reasons, but he was adamant. If they insisted on the wedding there were other priests.

There was young Father Foster, Father Hetherington's successor at St James's. A kindly man was spectacles, he felt no doubts about the couple's fitness to marry. On 20 April 1965 he conducted the East End's wedding of the year.

It had all the gusto of the Krays themselves: the Rollses gleaming down the Bethnal Green Road, heavy with guests; the women in their big hats like some cockney Ascot; the famous boxers in the church – Spinks, Allen, Ted 'Kid' Lewis; the young bride pale at the altar, as she became Mrs Reginald Kray. The wedding photographer was David Bailey.

His pictures are revealing. True to form, old Charles Kray has managed to duck out of them, but all the other central characters are there, immaculate in Bailey's *Vogue*-style camerawork. On one side are the Krays – Violet with hair swept back smiling regally, good-looking brother Charlie and his sleek wife, Dolly. And on the other – already the eternal cockney in-laws – stand the Sheas: Frank the father, Frankie the son and Elsie Shea with the dark eyes her daughter had inherited. She wears a dark velvet dress. Reggie was never to forgive her 'for wearing black at my wedding'.

Frances remains the perfect bride, serene, oblivious of everything except this one great moment. Reggie smiles nervously. Ronnie's grin is hardly the expression of a man seriously concerned at losing his twin brother to any silly woman.

Business was booming for the twins now that they were reaping the rich rewards of their acquittal. As long as they were sensible, they had a clear run for the future. The police had no wish for further trouble with the Krays; no other gang would challenge them, no one would enter a witness-box against them if he could help it. Once the McCowan case was over they were free to operate their frauds, protection and their various rackets as never before. There was something almost weird about the way their fortunes never seemed to falter. The next big step in their career had started.

Five days before Reggie and Frances married, $55,000 of instantly negotiable bearer bonds were stolen in an armed raid on the Royal Bank of Canada in Montreal. In May an even larger batch of bonds and valuable debentures vanished from a bank in Ontario. Both were sophisticated robberies; in neither case were the securities recovered, but the Canadian police and the American FBI were staying on the alert for somebody to cash them. No one did.

For some time the twins had had a working arrangement with a London-based front organization for the American Mafia over a group of Mayfair gambling clubs the Mafia controlled. Ronnie had met the top New York *Mafioso*, Angelo Bruno, when he was staying at the London Hilton the previous year. It had been a stormy interview, with Ronnie stating the terms on which the Krays were prepared to guarantee the Americans a peaceful life in London. There was an element of bluff involved, but as usual the twins had won: Bruno appeared impressed by the twins' Chicago-style approach to crime and tended to accept them as the nearest thing to a home-grown Mafia in England. This understanding was purely a local arrangement: the Mafia regarded them as one more London gang convenient to do business with. But the twins' publicity and success against the law were changing this. They were winning an international reputation; when any big-time foreign criminals were concerned with Britain the first name they thought of was the Krays.

The stolen Canadian securities were being held by a New York syndicate associated with the American Mafia. Professionals at disposing of this sort of loot, the syndicate knew they were too hot to handle in North America. As an experiment they decided to try them on the undercover European market. Shares could be stolen in America, then sold off in Europe. The syndicate had a backlog of $2 million of stolen securities waiting to be sold. Somebody suggested that the Krays might possibly be interested.

It was extremely tempting. Payne and his accountant Freddie Gore were ready with advice; both seemed quite confident that with the Krays behind them there would be no difficulty in disposing of the bonds in Europe. In July Payne flew to Canada. At a motel in Montreal he met a man sent by the Mafia. On the twins' behalf he purchased £20,000 of stolen bearer bonds at a quarter of face value, brought them to Paris, then helped the twins dispose of them in England. The twins pocketed three-quarters of the take. The traffic in American securities had started.

It appealed naturally to Ronnie, who had the instincts of a genuine tycoon – the love of power, the feeling for expansion, the monomaniac's obsession with himself. For him reality and fantasy were one so that the chance of dealing with the Mafia and entering the league of international big-time racketeers seemed quite inevitable. Soon he would have his private plane, his bank accounts in Switzerland, his foreign interests, his house like Billy Bill's in southern Spain.

Like all Ronnie's dreams, there was an element of truth in this. No other English racketeers had ever reached such heights: like royalty the twins could give their name to any scheme, knowing it would bring results. Other men would do the work, others supply the brains. On the strength of the Kray name a succession of con men, gun men, smugglers, fixers, forgers and international money men could begin to operate around the world. All that was required of the twins, it seemed, was to make sure everybody feared them.

Reggie and Frances spent their honeymoon in Athens. Frances disliked the food. Reggie could see nothing in the city. There was no one to talk to and the high-spot of the holiday came when some sailors invited them aboard a visiting American warship for the evening. Several nights running Reggie got very drunk.

Even so, he kept up his dream of living the good life with Frances. After the honeymoon he rented an expensive furnished flat off Lancaster Gate, but they had no real friends there, no interest in theatres, films, the life of the city. Reggie was out a lot. Frances was lonely and cut off. Reggie drank. The rows inevitably started. Finally they agreed they both wanted to live back in the East End where their real life lay; Reggie found a flat in Cedra Court, directly below Ronnie's. He might have chosen a more tactful place to live with a young wife.

Frequently the noise of Ronnie's parties kept Frances awake at night. She was never invited, but Reggie often went and in the early morning she would hear the sound of Ronnie's boys going down the stairs. When Reggie finally came home he was often bitter with her. Later he apologized. She blamed Ronnie and began to think he really hated her. She hardly ever saw him, but often heard him shouting in the night. Soon she refused to speak his name. For her, Ronnie became 'the other one'. Occasionally they passed each other on the stairs. The 'other one' would always be polite, smiling at her behind his spectacles.

'Hullo Frances, my dear. And how are you? Enjoying yourself in the family?'

Frances had never understood how joyless and oppressive the twins' private world could be. While he was courting her, Reggie had always been escaping from it; on their own he could seem gay and almost childlike. At Cedra Court there was little gaiety. There were still nights out with her husband to meet visiting celebrities. She dined with Judy Garland and George Raft, but rarely spoke at such occasions unless spoken to.

Her days were spent alone at Cedra Court, her evenings usually at clubs or parties where the guests were always criminals, the talk invariably of crime. A few of the regulars amused her. Mad Teddy Smith could make her laugh and she liked talking to him. The rest were not her type.

Everything was done for her: this was one way Reggie could still show his love, but when she suggested taking a job he was indignant. When she went shopping someone from the Firm was always with her. She had her own car – the smart red Triumph Reggie bought her when they became engaged – but she couldn't drive. She asked for driving lessons, but Reggie became jealous of the instructor. She stopped them before they were trouble. The car stayed outside in the street until the credit company reclaimed it.

She lasted eight weeks, then she left. Eight weeks were all the married life they knew and Frances finally returned to her parents in Ormsby Street.

But though she left her husband's roof she could not

get away from him, nor he from her. Each evening around six o'clock he would put on a clean shirt and his best suit, have two stiff gins and drive to Ormsby Street. The Sheas would not allow their son-in-law within the house, so he would stand on the pavement; she would talk to him from the bedroom window, often for an hour or so.

Apart from Frances, Reggie had one big problem on his mind that summer: how to provide a steady outlet for the stolen shares from North America. After the success of the first transaction, trade was booming, but there were technical problems which the twins could not hope to cope with on their own. The latest batch of $70,000 stolen Canadian government bonds needed forged registration certificates to make them negotiable. One of the twins' contacts spoke of a man to fix it. He was called Alan Cooper.

Cooper was thirty-six and rich. He owned a private bank off Wigmore Street, several insurance companies, two Roll-ses and a Yorkshire terrier called Sam. Jewish, he had been brought up in England, served with the American army, been imprisoned for a while in Germany and travelled on an American passport. He was a mystery man. Some said he was a spy. It is known that at one time he ran a gold-smuggling ring to the Far East, and later dabbled in arms deals; there are still endless rumours about him. One top detective from the Yard has taken a long interest in his career and says that 'he will almost certainly end with a bullet in his back'. What has saved him so far has been his canniness and the unlikeliness of his appearance. He stands 5 feet 7 inches tall and has a sad moustache, sparse hair and a faint stutter which gives his conversation a melancholy air. He never boasts, always appears defensive about his passion for good living, and says nothing of his flats in Brussels and Geneva and his big house on Campden Hill – nor of the many women in his life.

Cooper was always on the move and used his bank as

cover for his deals. He readily agreed to help the twins, and forged certificates for the stolen shares were soon concocted at the bank; as an extra service Cooper even offered to help the twins market them in Germany. He was quite sure it could be done and the proceedings be credited to London quite legitimately via the Hamburg branch of the Deutsche Bank. Within ten days the twins would have their money. All Cooper wanted in return was their help as allies. Charles Richardson, the twins' old fellow-prisoner from Shepton Mallet, was expanding his South London gang and starting to move into the West End. For some time he had fixed his eye on Cooper and his shady businesses and was becoming threatening. Cooper required protection; the twins were delighted to assist.

And so, through Cooper and their Mafia connections in America, the twins were launched upon the path of international adventure. Backed by their name, the traffic in stolen North American securities flourished, with Cooper soon supplanting Leslie Payne as organizer and go-between for the major deals; through Cooper, too, the twins began to meet a whole new clientele ready to profit by their services.

Centred on Brussels was Europe's most elaborate forged-currency syndicate. In northern Germany and Amsterdam there was the ring that had virtually cornered the international market in stolen jewellery. Peace-loving Zurich was the centre for international arms deals, Paris and the South of France for stolen major works of art, London and Geneva for gold-smuggling. Then there were the drug-runners and the spies. Each of these criminal trades had its acknowledged virtuosi and leaders, who formed a sort of international underground of crime. These were the men Cooper knew, and here was a rich field for the twins: international crime is different from national crime only in quantity. There are the same feuds and jealousies, and every specialist in crime is vulnerable to one super-specialist – the specialist in violence.

That autumn Frances showed her first signs of a break-down. A change would probably have cured her, but she had nowhere she could go. Sometimes she was with Reggie, imagining that everything could still work out, sometimes with her parents, saying the twins scared her.

Most days she still saw Reggie; when she did he tried to get her back. Sometimes she spent a day with him. In September they drove to Dartmoor to visit Ronnie's friend, the 'Mad Axe Man', Frank Mitchell. She remembered him as 'a huge man with the biggest hands I ever saw, yet he was gentle, like a child'. Reggie gave him a transistor radio; Mitchell had made Frances a present in the prison work-shop – a small wooden jewel-box lined with velvet.

On days like these it was easy to be happy. Back in London it was different. One night at Vallance Road she had a row with Reggie which brought Ronnie down in his pyjamas, bellowing at his brother to 'throw the fucking woman out for good.' Frances began to sob hysterically; her brother had to come and take her home. A few days later she was back with Reggie, but by now she was heavily on tranquillizers and pep-pills. She suffered headaches and severe depressions. Like Ronnie she began to fear the dark.

Then in October she decided there was no hope for her marriage and told her mother that she wanted it annulled. Her mother swears that she was still a virgin. That same month a Cypriot waitress called Anna Zambodini brought a paternity suit against Reggie. It was dismissed, but the publicity helped counteract the slur of the threatened annulment. A few weeks later Frances entered the clinic of the Harley Street psychiatrist who was treating Ronnie. She had been married just six months by now.

That autumn Ronnie started to compile his list again. Fame, money, foreign deals all had their uses, but he still felt threatened. The twins still had enemies. One was 'Mad' Frankie Fraser. It was a good nine years since this aggressive little man had taken sides with Billy Hill against the twins and gone to prison for his attack on Jack Spot. Now he was out, and Ronnie had heard rumours that he was friendly with another of the twins' old enemies – a fair-haired tearaway from Watney Street called Myers. There was resentment over a long-firm of his the twins had destroyed. Since meeting Fraser he had changed his name to Cornell and moved south of the river, where they had both joined forces with the Richardsons. By October Cornell, Fraser and both the Richardsons were down on Ronnie's list.

Even today there are criminals in London who puzzle over why the Krays and Richardsons ever had to clash: the criminal activities of the Richardsons seemed to begin at the opposite pole from those of the Krays. The twins were traditional cockney villains, dangerous men who soon became the most powerful criminals in London. Charlie and Eddie Richardson were different. They were not cockney villains, violent outsiders like the Krays. They were straightforward, middle-class businessmen. Charlie Richardson ran scrap-metal yards and long-firms south of the river, dabbled in government surplus, floated dubious companies. Eddie Richardson had a legitimate wholesale chemist's business bringing in at least £4,000 a year, Charlie had his office in Park Lane and his family house at Bromley. A year before the twins would have dismissed the Richardsons as straight men. But there is a natural tendency for large-scale fraud to need the threat of violence in the background. By 1964 the Richardsons had started to enjoy it. After their arrest it was the details of their gang brutality that caught the headlines – the mock courts in the Park Lane offices before the Richardsons, the pliers on the teeth and finger-nails and the electrode treatment for those who let them down.

This did not worry Ronnie very much. What did disturb

him was the threat of competition. He also heard that Cornell – himself one of the Richardson torturers – had called him 'that fat poof'. Reggie urged caution. Ronnie wanted blood and was soon finding reasons of his own to shed it. Fraser had taken over a chain of fruit machines the twins had owned. Cornell had moved in on the West End pornography business. Just before Christmas 1965 Ronnie and the Richardsons met late one night at the Astor Club off Berkeley Square. Both sides were armed. Insults were exchanged and at one point it looked as if shooting was just about to start.

A few weeks later the twins were summoned to a meeting with two important visitors from the American Mafia. They spent two days together, talking as equals, and reached an understanding. The Americans were anxious to increase their stake in London gambling. 'Junkets' – big organized gambling parties – would soon be flying in on a regular basis from California and New York. This meant big money, on which the Americans were anxious to take their cut. In readiness they were investing heavily in several new London gambling clubs and hotels. Millions of dollars were at stake; nothing must go wrong. Provided the twins were ready to guarantee the new clubs freedom from trouble they would have their percentage.

It was a nice nest-egg to look forward to, but not if the Richardsons began throwing their weight about.

From then on all that counted was war against the Richardsons. No further business was accepted, no risks were taken. The Firm was mobilized and the information service stepped up. Fresh arms were purchased; caches of arms and ammunition were established in different parts of London. Everybody in the Firm was issued with an automatic. Ronnie wanted something more impressive for himself and Reggie; through Alan Cooper he bought two brand new Browning machine-guns for £75 each. He also asked for Mills bombs and limpet mines; Cooper reported these were not available.

Ronnie enjoyed the Brownings, spending hours oiling them and studying the instruction manual. But weapons didn't make a war; he wanted allies, too, and in January held a meeting at Fort Vallance with the two other gangs who had most to lose from the rise of the Richardsons. From Clapham came two brothers who led a gang of thieves who had been closely involved in the Great Train Robbery and had clashed with the Richardsons. From North London came three more brothers whose gang had long operated by courtesy of the twins.

Ronnie was eloquent about the menace of the Richardsons; after everyone had drunk a lot he began talking of his old dream of a federation of gangs. They should form a defensive alliance, a firm treaty that if one gang were attacked the others would come to its aid.

'And if someone's killed?'

'It'd be up to the rest of us to do something about it.'

This seemed a good idea and they shook hands on it.

The war broke out that February after a shouting match in the Stork Club between Ronnie and Fraser; the twins left Cedra Court, the Colonel took command. The following few weeks were probably the happiest of his life. He was the guerrilla leader, armed to the teeth and ready for anything. Messages passed back and forth in code, meetings were summoned beneath forgotten bridges and in the backs of lorries, spies brought in a flow of tidings of the enemy. Obscure East End pubs became the Colonel's overnight headquarters. Raids were planned and ambushes prepared; Reggie was with him, as he always was in time of trouble, the worries about Frances now forgotten, the humdrum business of the Firm irrelevant.

For once the twins appeared to have an enemy worth fighting. One night a raiding-party shot up The Widow's Pub in Tapp Street from a car, five minutes after the twins had left. A few days later a car mounted the pavement in Vallance Road, knocking down a man who looked like Ronnie. The twins put on bullet-proof vests and started making preparations to use the machine-guns against the Richardsons. Fate robbed them of the pleasure.

An early morning fight broke out on 8 March 1966 between two rival gangs at Mr Smith's Club on the London–Eastbourne Road at Catford; a thirty-year-old gangster called Richard Hart was killed. For once the twins were uninvolved: this was a Richardson job. For some time they had been infiltrating this drab segment of South London suburb; the night Hart was shot, Eddie Richardson and Frankie Fraser had arrived at the club soon after midnight, armed and ready for a showdown with the local gang protecting the place.

It should have been a routine takeover, but surprisingly the local gang fought back, shooting it out over the blackjack tables. When the police arrived Hart was already dead, Fraser was badly wounded and Eddie Richardson was having his gunshot wounds treated at Lewisham Hospital. Most of the top Richardson gangsters were involved; the police had clear evidence against them and it was obvious the Richardsons were finished. In one night at the 'Battle of Mr Smith's Club' the only gang that had tried challenging the twins for control of London had stupidly destroyed itself.

The twins had had their war won for them. All their competitors had vanished and at this moment they could have made themselves the richest criminals in Britain. Instead Ronnie slipped a 9-mm Mauser automatic into his shoulder holster and asked Scotch Jack Dickson to drive him to The Blind Beggar.

It was a very casual death. Cornell was perched on a stool at the far end of the bar, drinking light ales with a couple of friends that night after Hart was killed. The pub was almost empty; it was 8.30 p.m. and the evening trade had barely started – a couple in the saloon bar near the door, an old man sipping Guinness in the public bar on the far side of the partition. The barmaid had just put a record on the juke-box to liven things up when Ronnie's arrival made this unnecessary. Ian Barrie was with him. Both had guns.

'Well, just look who's here,' said Cornell, and smiled. He had an unattractive smile. Instead of answering Barrie fired two warning shots into the ceiling to send the barmaid scurrying for safety in the cellar. Then Ronnie shot Cornell through the head and walked back to the street where his car was waiting. When he had gone, the barmaid went to the wounded man, but there was little she could do. By the time Cornell reached hospital he was dead. When the police arrived at The Blind Beggar nobody had seen a thing.

'I never like hurting anybody unless I feel it personally,' Ronnie had always said: when he shot George Cornell he was repaying him for several ancient insults as well as for calling him a 'fat poof' behind his back. But there was more to it than that. Ronnie believed his honour as a leader was involved, for Hart had been an ally. As one of the Firm put it, 'One of ours had gone so it was up to Ronnie to do one of theirs.'

It had to be Cornell: there was no one else left from the Richardsons' gang worth killing. Fraser was in hospital with a police guard by his bed. The Richardson brothers were in custody, along with everyone who had been at Mr Smith's. Cornell was the one important member of their gang who was not involved and so was the ideal victim. Thanks to his information service, Ronnie had known exactly where to find him; he had been trailing him for weeks.

Ronnie Kray's shooting of George Cornell was soon the worst-kept secret in the East End. Ronnie had done what he had always dreamed of: he had killed openly as a gangster should. As he lay hiding in a small room over a barber's in the Lea Bridge Road he lovingly recounted how it felt – the noise and the recoil of the gun, the look of blank surprise on Cornell's face, and how his head 'burst open' as the bullet entered. Ronnie felt no remorse, no fear, only exhilaration. Reggie was taking care of things.

Superintendent Butler, Scotland Yard's greatest detective, came down to Whitechapel to nail the murderer, but could not touch him. He knew who was guilty. The whole of Bethnal Green knew, but nobody would talk. Butler was putting all his hopes on the barmaid from The Blind Beggar, who must certainly have seen the killer if not the killing. He was too late: someone had spoken to her. When Butler put Ronnie into an identity parade at Commercial Street Police Station, the woman nervously insisted that her memory was weak.

So the great Butler of the Yard departed, leaving the Cornell killing as one of the few 'unsolved' murders of his career. He must have known that he was also leaving an entire area of London ruled by gang law.

THIRTEEN

Axe Man

In 1966 one of the potentially most dangerous prisoners in Britain was Frank Mitchell, the so-called 'Mad Axe Man'. Gaoled originally for robbery with violence, he had spent eighteen of his thirty-two years in detention. He was immensely strong, but prison and the punishment he had received for violence had numbed what scant intelligence he had. His body bore the scars of birchings for attacks on prison officers. He earned his nickname when he threatened an elderly couple with a felling axe while on the run from a hospital for the criminally insane, and was detained at Dartmoor during Her Majesty's pleasure, i.e. indefinitely.

By now he seemed to have accepted life in prison. Handled with understanding he was easy to control, and during the four years he had spent in Dartmoor, warders had come to like him. The prison governor, Mr Denis Malone, took a particular interest in him and always called him by his Christian name. He saw that it was useless to impose too strict a discipline on Mitchell – warders would get hurt and Mitchell was strong enough to take any amount of punishment. He would just end up more rebellious and brutalized than ever.

Instead of this the governor allowed Mitchell a loose rein. He was given the blue arm-band of a trusted prisoner and promised that if he behaved himself the governor would do everything he could to get him a release date from the Home Office. Mitchell seemed happy with the arrangement, and Dartmoor became something of a home for him. He spent hours in the gymnasium improving his extraordinary physique and during the day seems to have had more freedom than anyone in Dartmoor. Most days were spent on the moors in working parties guarded by a single warder, who often let big Mitchell wander away on his own. Mitchell liked this. He had a way with animals, taming the wild moorland ponies and riding them for miles. Wearing his shirt and denim trousers he was quite free to visit isolated Dartmoor pubs and often brought a bottle of Scotch back for the evening. He bought a budgerigar for his cell, and even had a mistress for a while, a village school-mistress he used to make love to in a deserted barn. Each night, when he was locked up in his cell, he did his press-ups and his weight-lifting and went to sleep dreaming of the release date the governor would get him.

Another reason for Frank Mitchell's peace of mind came from knowing he had friends outside and was not forgotten. It was ten years now since he first met Ronnie Kray in Wandsworth, but the Krays still kept in contact with him. They visited him and wrote quite regularly. The radio which Reggie brought him allowed him to listen in to the police and the prison authorities' short-wave conversations and he was well supplied for money. Kindness apart, Mitchell was a legend among long-serving prisoners, and the life he led in Dartmoor was a good advertisement for the twins' 'Away Society'. This was one reason why they had taken such care of him when he was charged with the attempted murder of another prisoner during his period at Wandsworth. Word was passed round the prison that Frank was a friend of the Krays and that anyone giving evidence against him did so at his peril. Nemone Lethbridge, the attractive female barrister who appeared for Ronnie in his car-stealing case in 1961, was briefed to defend him. And Ronnie even paid his West End tailor to make Frank a suit so that he would look his best at the trial. After Mitchell was acquitted, he always spoke of the twins as 'the two best friends a man could hope for'.

During these ten years there was one thing the twins never did – encourage Mitchell to escape. It would have been no problem for him to get away from Dartmoor, but they agreed that much his best hope was to rely on the governor's ability to get him a release. They also knew that if he escaped he could never stay at liberty alone; his size made him conspicuous, his simple-mindedness a liability.

Then suddenly they changed their minds. A few months after George Cornell was shot they told Mitchell they were going to get him out. Mitchell was thrilled. If the twins told him to escape it must be right. From that August on he thought of nothing else and began planning on his own account.

This strange decision of the twins has never been properly explained. In court the only explanation offered was that the twins required Mitchell on the Firm as a strong-arm man. This is absurd. They had all the strong arms they needed and Mitchell's would have been superfluous. But the twins' own account, that they were 'simply feeling sorry for Frank', is equally implausible. They had been feeling sorry for him for years. The truth is that the whole idea of helping Mitchell to escape began as a simple exercise in underworld public relations, a gesture of the sort the twins could not resist – especially that summer when it was clear that something needed to be done about their reputation.

For, contrary to Ronnie's arguments, the Cornell murder had backfired, scaring their friends more than their enemies. Business was suffering. Payne and Gore had both left town. Even the protection business seemed to be suffering. London's top gambling club, which the twins had 'minded' for three years, decided they were far too dangerous to have around and offered a £10,000 lump sum to end the arrangement. Something was needed to convince the underworld that the twins were more than trigger-happy murderers. The idea of using Mitchell for this purpose seems to have come from one of Ronnie's friends, 'Mad' Teddy Smith. Smith was an unusual gangster. The BBC had recently accepted a play he had written about a bank robbery and he was tending to see life in dramatic, televisual terms. He had been interested in Mitchell's story for some while and asked the twins to let him visit the Axe Man. He found him starting to get worried about his release date and formed the idea of helping him to win some public sympathy.

Smith put his plan to the twins. Mitchell should be helped to escape, then kept in hiding. While in hiding he could write letters to the press, pointing out the hardship and injustice of his case and promising to surrender if his sentence were reviewed. There was a new Labour Home Secretary and a current mood of sympathy for the underdog. Mitchell would be sure to get his case looked into, and most of the credit would belong to the twins.

The twins were easily convinced. This seemed the sort of coup they needed, something to restore their image as benevolent, responsible public figures. Ronnie began to think of several journalists and politicians he could put pressure on to back up the campaign, including the inevitable Tom Driberg. And Mitchell was informed that he would definitely be home for Christmas.

But this remained an awkward period for the twins; reactions to the Cornell murder were making life uncomfortable for both of them. Ronnie saw potential traitors all round him and wondered whom to shoot next. Reggie was drinking heavily. Most nights they slept at Vallance Road and one night Cornell's widow came and smashed the windows, screaming that the twins were bloody murderers. Violet was most upset that anyone could say such things about her boys.

In fact nobody was talking to the police, but the twins had grown so jittery that when they heard rumours of fresh police evidence about Cornell they fled the country.

They had had an escape route ready for some time and a private aircraft was waiting for them in a field near Bognor. This flew them to a landing-strip near Calais, where they were picked up by a car and driven to Paris as dawn was breaking. Tickets were waiting for them both at Orly under assumed names and they flew on without incident to Morocco.

Here they spent three untroubled weeks and for the first time since his marriage Reggie enjoyed himself. Billy Hill was there, a respected figure with his big white car, to show them round. They spent most of their time in Tangier, drinking and swimming and lazing on the beach; Ronnie enjoyed the Arab boys, Reggie invited out a blonde hostess from the Latin Quarter Club in London. During her fortnight with him he never once referred to Frances or the East End. Instead he spoke of settling in Tangier and buying a small club. The girl agreed to join him. Reggie was wondering how to break the news to Ronnie when the police saved him the embarrassment. The chief of the Moroccan police arrived in person at their hotel to inform them they were undesirable aliens. Two seats were booked for them on the next plane back to London – this time in their right names.

They returned expecting Butler to be waiting for them to charge them with the death of George Cornell. Instead the Yard had got no further with the murder and they walked through the airport free men. Their departure had naturally caused something of a panic in gangland. Their safe return meant they now had work to do, repairing the damage. Members of the Firm who had prudently made themselves scarce resurfaced and were greeted as if nothing had happened. Fresh warnings were put out against talking to the police about Cornell. Arrears of protection money were collected, fresh deals for marketing a new batch of stolen American securities arranged. When someone in the Firm asked Ronnie if they were still proceeding with the Mitchell escape he replied, 'Of course' – Frank was his friend.

That same week in October 1966 Frances Kray made her first attempt to kill herself, locking herself in the front room of her parents' house in Ormsby Street, putting a rug against the door and lying on a cushion by the gas fire with the taps turned on. Her father, who came home at midday, found her just alive. When she revived in Bethnal Green Hospital she was murmuring, 'Leave me in peace. Why can't you let me sleep?'

That night Reggie visited the hospital but was refused admission to his wife. Later he finished off a bottle and a half of gin and dropped off, muttering that he would have to kill his in-laws.

Mitchell was counting off the days to his escape and had made a mask from a piece of his girl-friend's black nylon nightdress in readiness. Various members of the Firm visited him to discuss the final plans. He would escape from a working party. Two of the Firm would pick him up in a car and drive him to London; 12 December was fixed as a provisional date, but at the crucial moment Ronnie involved himself in a curious case with a senior policeman.

According to the twins a police inspector had offered Ronnie the use of an East End pub with guaranteed police immunity for a regular £20 a week. The last thing the twins needed was fresh involvement with the police, but Ronnie was unable to resist a chance of scoring off the Law. He laid his preparations cunningly and hired a private detective to bug the pub and wire Ronnie up with a tie-pin microphone and shoulder-holster tape recorder. Prepared for anything, Ronnie invited the inspector for a discussion. A few days later Ronnie lodged a formal complaint against the police and tapes from the recorders found their way to the office of the Director of Public Prosecutions. For some weeks nothing happened; then Ronnie was informed that the inspector would be prosecuted. Ronnie was required as prime witness for the Crown. The trial would start on 28 November.

Ronnie insists that all he could do was disappear. It was a matter of principle. 'I'd do most things, but I'd never go in no witness-box for the Law to get someone put away – not even a copper.'

The squeeze was put on a Mayfair property man to find the twins a suitably discreet flat; within a few hours Ronnie had exactly what he needed – a five-room furnished flat in a quiet road in Finchley. The day before he was due in court he moved in and for the next eight months remained officially on the run.

Ronnie was quite sincere about refusing to appear in court, but he could hardly have found a worse moment to disappear. He went to ground completely and had soon turned his flat into a fortress. It was crammed with guns and he kept one of the machine-guns under the floorboards. The curtains were kept drawn and he never ventured out. Instead he got the Firm to bring in stocks of food and gin and bottled beer so he could stay hidden there for weeks on end. Codes were invented for the telephone and letters. He played Italian opera on the gramophone and had a fresh boy every night. During the day he would be busy working out who needed murdering.

As usual in the twins' crises, everything fell on Reggie – running the Firm, coping with Ronnie, worrying about Frances. On top of this 12 December was approaching. His brother Charlie said that he was mad to think of springing Mitchell at a time like this. Reggie agreed, but Ronnie wouldn't hear of letting Mitchell down. As usual Ronnie got his way. But nothing was properly planned now. Reggie was forced to improvise as best he could and he asked several members of the Firm if they had relations prepared to put up Mitchell for a week or two. Predictably, none had. Someone suggested a man called Lennie Dunn, who kept a bookstall in the East End.

Lennie had trouble – with his nerves, his business and his wife. He lived alone in a ground-floor flat in Barking and was sufficiently scared of the twins to do as he was told and keep his mouth shut. Reggie ordered him to expect a visitor.

Then came a further problem. Mad Teddy Smith and Albert Donaghue, another member of the Firm, had both agreed to collect Mitchell in a car; neither possessed a valid driving licence. Reggie had to borrow one so they could hire a car. Someone else produced clothes for an extremely large man. 12 December arrived.

Mitchell was wearing his black nylon mask as he came lumbering through the moorland mist towards the green Vauxhall parked on the Princetown road. Donaghue told him to change his clothes and take the mask off to avoid attracting attention. Nobody was interested in the car as it sped to London. It was to be another four hours before Mitchell was missed. By the time the police were checking the roads from the moors Mitchell was eating steak and chips in Lennie's flat in Barking and feeling faintly disappointed. He had expected something grander, a hero's welcome from the twins, a great party with champagne and girls and the congratulations of the underworld. Instead Smith had to explain as best he could that the twins were unable to see him that night and that Scotch Jack Dickson and Lennie Dunn would be taking care of him. Just for a few days he would be the most wanted man in Britain and must make no attempt to see anyone or contact his family. He must be patient, lie low, trust the twins.

Mitchell was reassured. The twins were his best friends and they were very smart. Now that they had freed him he had nothing to worry about. They gave him more to drink; he brightened up. When they turned on the television news at 10.00 P.M. and watched marine commandos combing the moors for him he laughed until the tears came.

'If they try coming for me now, I'll kill the lot of them.'

'You won't have to, Frank,' said Dickson. 'Now that the twins are looking after you, no one will ever find you.'

'But I'd kill anyone rather than go back to prison. Anyone at all. Even you.'

They gave Mitchell the back bedroom with the double bed; Dickson took the front bedroom; Lennie swallowed two sleeping pills and stretched out on the living-room sofa. At 3.00 Dickson was woken up by Mitchell, who was standing by his bed with a knife. He said he was restless and couldn't sleep. Dickson made him tea and they talked – about his family, about his friends and the animals on the moor, and about the twins. He hero-worshipped them, Ronnie especially. Ronnie had told him that when everything was sorted out they'd live together, just the two of them, in a beautiful rich house in the country. He could keep all his animals there. He loved animals, particularly little ones – birds, mice and kittens – anything he could be gentle with. Ronnie had promised him all the animals he wanted; Ronnie was an animal-lover too.

He waited all next morning for him, but no Ronnie – Reggie came instead. Rather than say that Ronnie too was in hiding, he told him he was away on business and would soon be coming. In the meantime Teddy Smith would help him write his letters to the press and the twins would see that he had Christmas with his family.

Mitchell was reassured by this. Soon he was suggesting one of his favourite games, a trial of strength. To humour him, Reggie took off his jacket, sat down at the kitchen table and gripped Mitchell's enormous hand with his own. Reggie was exceptionally strong in the arms and shoulders, but Mitchell smiled and pushed and slowly Reggie's arm went back until his knuckles touched the table. Mitchell was delighted.

'See what I used to do in Dartmoor,' he said, and picking up both Dickson and Lennie Dunn by their belts, lifted them, one in each hand, until their heads touched the ceiling.

'That's what I'd do with anyone who tried to catch me.'

That afternoon Mad Teddy and the Axe Man worked on the letters to the press and the Home Secretary. Mitchell had learned to write in prison but was slow and lacked the literary touch which, as a writer, Mad Teddy thought the letters should possess. After some false starts they agreed on a rough outline and, with Smith dictating, Mitchell laboriously penned his letter to the *Mirror* editor and to the Home Secretary, care of the editor of *The Times*.

> 'Sir, the reason for my absence from Dartmoor was to bring to the Notice of my unhappy plight. to be truthful, I am asking for a possible Date of release. from the age of 9 I have not been completely free, always under some act or other.
>
> Sir, I ask you, where is the fairness of this. I am not a murderer or a sex maniac, nor do I think I am a danger to the public. I think that I have been more than punished for the wrongs I have done.
>
> Yours sincerely,
>
> Frank Mitchell.'

While Mitchell waited patiently for Ronnie, Ronnie was having troubles of his own. His depressions had begun and he was spending most of the day behind drawn curtains, armed and watching the road for the police. One of the Firm had brought his favourite records of Churchill's wartime speeches; he played them endlessly and drank a lot.

Sometimes he ordered a full meeting of the Firm and talked about the future – further link-ups with the Mafia, control of a London-centred narcotics network, a Kray representative running the rackets in every major British city, an international strike force ready for villainy anywhere in the world. Ronnie was thinking big. At other times he was obsessed with private grievances and wanted someone hurt. A boxing manager had been impolite about a young boxer he fancied; a villain they occasionally employed called Jack McVitie was becoming unreliable; Payne was suspiciously silent. What was he up to?

Sometimes the strain of hiding seemed unbearable and even Churchill's wartime speeches were no help. All he could do was drink himself insensible or lie in bed taking more Stematol until the depression lifted.

Time passed slowly for both prisoners. While Ronnie had his nightmares in Finchley, Mitchell in the basement flat in Barking talked obsessively about him and the life they'd lead together. He would be Ronnie's right-hand man; they would become inseparable, the greatest criminals of the century. He would willingly die for Ronnie – that was the one way he would like to go. But when could he see him?

For more than a week Dickson and Lennie made excuses; then Mitchell seemed to understand that Ronnie would never come and stopped talking about him. Two men were always with him; Donaghue and the ex-boxer Billy Exley took turns with Dickson and Lennie. All they could do was make the time pass. For hours on end they played cards with Mitchell; he was no card-player but they always let him win to keep his spirits up. He ate hugely, cleaned his teeth a dozen times a day and constantly combed his hair, examining his appearance in the mirror. He was inordinately vain.

There was a day's excitement when *The Times* and the *Mirror* published his letters, both of them in full. The *Mirror* included an appeal from its editor for Mitchell to give himself up. Then nothing happened. Reggie called in next day, but he had no news, only fresh promises that Frank would see his family for Christmas. Mitchell became restless. This was worse than prison. A few nights later he threatened to go out and find himself a woman. He was beginning to groan in his sleep. Dickson told Reggie that if he didn't get a woman soon, there would be trouble.

They brought a girl for Mitchell in a taxi at 2 A.M. With Reggie was Tommy Cowley, a little gambler with pale eyes and short red hair who always seemed a cut above most members of the Firm. The girl was thirtyish; Cowley said they could count on her discretion. He and Reggie picked her up at Winston's Club in New Bond Street, where she was a hostess. In the taxi they had informed her of her duties. Reggie said that if she did as she was told she would have the gratitude of the East End. She replied that gratitude was all very well: she preferred cash. Reggie agreed with her.

She had a lot of blonde hair and a good figure. Her name was Lisa. She was expensive. When she entered Lennie's flat in a long black dress and heavy make-up Mitchell was all for having her at once. He appeared almost childish in his enthusiasm, but Lisa was no child; since Reggie had gone on to Vallance Road without paying the £100 she wanted, she told the Axe Man he would have to wait.

Mitchell could have forced her. Nobody would have stopped him. Most girls in her position would have done as they were told. But Lisa had her professional pride, and Mitchell wanted someone he could love, not rape. She kept her dignity and her black lace dress, and both of them sat in the kitchen, drinking tea, while Scotch Jack Dickson drove round to Vallance Road to collect her fee. Reggie grumbled but paid – a hundred used notes in a carrier bag; Dickson gave them to her, less twenty for expenses. Reggie had promised that if she kept Frank happy there would be more to come. And on this tender note Lisa and her Axe Man went to bed.

They stayed there for the next two days, curtains drawn, the glow of the electric fire providing the only light, and Mitchell sometimes leaping out of bed for fifty press-ups. Mitchell was an enthusiastic lover – 'His virility was greater than that of any man I have known,' the girl wrote later.

But even sex was no real answer to the twins' dilemma. It was soon obvious to everyone that he would not remain cooped up in the flat much longer. He was becoming moodier; only the girl could quieten him. On 20 December he gave Lennie £5 and asked him to buy enough drink for a small party as he was going to ask his family over before Christmas. The twins had promised he could see them.

Lennie and Scotch Jack Dickson had been guarding Mitchell for ten days now; both were afraid that he would break out soon. Rather than this they asked Lisa to try persuading him to give himself up. The first time she mentioned it he said that he would do whatever the twins thought best. Next day she spoke about it, but the idea sent Mitchell into a rage, shouting about the eighteen years he had spent inside and how he would kill anyone who tried to get him back. She tried calming him, but he went on shouting, and for a while the others thought he would make a dash for it.

'Give me your gun,' he yelled at Exley, who was too frightened to argue. The gun calmed Mitchell.

'I'll hang on to it,' he said. 'It's nice to know it's there in case I need it.'

Next day, 22 December, Mitchell woke late and appeared cheerful, knowing he had a gun. Later his mood began to change. By afternoon he was weeping, shouting and saying he would go out and shoot the first policeman he encountered. When he was quieter he told Dickson he wanted him to take a letter round to Reggie.

It took an hour to write; in it he said that unless the twins got him away at once he would get in touch with his parents. If anybody tried to stop him, he had a gun and would use it. Reggie was visibly annoyed at Mitchell's letter. 'Who does he think he is? He's got everything he wants, even a bloody woman, but he goes telling us what to do.' Then he asked Dickson more about Exley's gun and Mitchell's threats to leave. This clearly worried him.

'Jack. Go back to Mitchell and tell him he'll be all right.

Tell him not to do anything silly and he'll be out of the flat in forty-eight hours. I think it's time I had a word with Ron.'

The twins and several members of the Firm discussed what should be done with Mitchell that night at the flat in Finchley. Although Ronnie was cut off, he had been receiving regular reports on Mitchell. He even knew about the gun, and according to one story he had heard Mitchell was threatening to go round to Vallance Road and use it on the Kray parents.

Certainly the Colonel's attitude to his old friend had changed dramatically: suddenly he seemed to understand just what could happen if the police caught him. The twins and many of the Firm would be involved. Mitchell could destroy them.

That night as the twins discussed what should be done, Frank Mitchell was no longer a friend but a threat.

Next day a further complication: Frank Mitchell was in love.

'Wherever they're taking me to in the country, Lisa must come as well. We'll never be apart again.'

Later the girl whispered to Dickson, 'He can think I'm going but I'm not. Just tell the twins I'll keep my mouth shut and that's that.'

'OK, but don't say anything to Frank. If he thinks you don't love him, he'd really do his nut.'

When Reggie came, Mitchell asked him about the girl. Of course he could take her. It was a lovely place the twins had ready for them, with animals and servants. Lisa and Frank could both be there together.

Reggie gave Lennie Dunn money to buy Mitchell fresh clothes for the journey; his friends were calling for him the following evening. Mitchell was thrilled; to show how happy he was he put his arms round the piano and lifted it right off the floor. Everybody laughed. Reggie looked relieved, shook hands all round and promised to be down to visit Frank and Lisa for Christmas.

It must have seemed the most exciting Christmas Eve in Mitchell's life: for the first time in nearly twenty years he would be spending Christmas Day in freedom, and with the girl he loved.

Reggie rang during the morning saying that Donaghue would be calling around 8.30 P.M. and that Frank was to be packed and changed and ready to leave immediately.

Dickson asked what was planned for the girl.

'Don't worry about her. Albert will see to her.'

Mitchell and the girl got up around midday. She cooked them all a late Christmas Eve lunch. Afterwards everyone exchanged cards. In his Mitchell wrote, 'To Lisa, the only one I've ever loved', and she wrote back, 'Darling Frank, may this Christmas be the best you ever had'. They kissed, drank to the future and went to bed for the last time in the flat.

At 7.30 P.M. the telephone rang twice, then stopped, the sign that Reggie was on the line wanting to talk to Mitchell. Was he packed? The friends would soon be round.

Just before 8.30 Donaghue arrived. A big grey man with thinning hair, he was one of the enigmas of the Firm. He was a drinker and a fighter and an Irishman but he never talked much, never gave himself away. The year before, Reggie had shot him in the foot during an argument in a pub off Vallance Road. Since then they had made it up and 'Big Albert' was regarded as Reggie's man, but he still limped. Mitchell trusted him because he had helped him escape; Donaghue said Reggie's friends were outside with their van, the Axe Man laughed and asked where they were taking him.

'Kent, Frank. A farm in Kent.'

'That means we're driving through the tunnel under the river,' said Mitchell to the girl.

'You know your way round pretty well for a man who's

done the time you have, Frank,' said Donaghue. 'Got your things ready?'

Mitchell had nothing much to carry and was anxious to be off. He shook hands with Dickson, then with Lennie Dunn, promising that Ronnie would be sending him £500 after Christmas for all his trouble.

'Get your coat now,' he said to the girl. 'They're waiting for us.'

'I'm not coming yet, Frank.'

'That's right, Frank. Ronnie's orders. It's risky enough getting you there on your own. We don't want her involved, do we, if there's any trouble? Cowley will bring her down in his car. She'll be there as soon as you.'

There was no time to argue; Mitchell nodded and kissed the girl goodbye.

'See you at Ron's place, then. Don't be long.'

At a sign from Donaghue, Lennie turned the lights out. A few moments later Mitchell stepped through the back door. There, in the Barking Road at 8.30 P.M. on Christmas Eve 1966, the story of Frank Mitchell, the Mad Axe Man, officially ends. As far as the police know there was no farm in Kent; if there was they have no evidence to suggest that Mitchell ever turned up there alive.

All that is known is that ten minutes or so after seeing Mitchell off the premises, Donaghue returned and helped Scotch Jack Dickson and Lennie Dunn to clear the flat of all trace of him. The girl hung on to the prison comb and the Christmas card he gave her. Otherwise his few belongings went – the beret and mask he wore during his escape, a pair of shoes and a couple of paperbacks he had been reading. Every surface in the place was cleaned of fingerprints.

Then a car driven by another member of the Firm arrived for Donaghue and the girl, and they ended up together at a Christmas Eve party in Evering Road. Reggie was there and took the girl aside. She was to forget all she had seen and heard during the last five days. She had never heard of a man called Frank Mitchell. If she mentioned him to a living soul the twins would hear of it and in the end they'd deal with her, wherever she was.

'I'll forget all right, and the sooner the better.' She drank a lot, did her best to enjoy the party and spent the night in bed with Donaghue. After Christmas she was back at Winston's, demure as ever in the black lace dress. For her, as for everyone who came into Frank Mitchell's sad and violent life, he had ceased to exist. She kept the card that said she was the only woman he had ever loved, but those were the only words he ever wrote to her. None of his few friends nor his family ever heard from him again. Lennie Dunn never received his £500.

The months went by and the police continued their search. The twins had told the Firm to answer any inquiries about Mitchell by saying he had gone abroad. There were reports that he was seen in Melbourne, in Casablanca and the South of France. A postcard supposedly written by him was received from Tangier.

But more persistent were the underworld rumours that Frank Mitchell was dead.

If Frank Mitchell's grand escape did end in death, his remains were disposed of with some thoroughness. For two years later, when the Kray brothers and a South London gang leader called Frederick Foreman were accused at the Old Bailey of murdering him, the prosecution had to admit that they were alleging a murder without the evidence of a body.

The case was long and complicated. The Krays admitted responsibility for helping Mitchell to escape and for harbouring him; that was all. The absence of any trace of a corpse threw doubt on the prosecution, and Frederick Foreman and the Krays were finally acquitted. But it was during the evidence for the prosecution that the girl Lisa, Lennie Dunn and Albert Donaghue gave their own versions on oath of what happened during those ten minutes after Frank Mitchell left the flat and how the story of the Axe Man ended.

Lennie Dunn and the girl both said they remained in the darkened flat, and their evidence was essentially the same. Both claimed to have heard loud bangs from the street outside, two or three minutes after Mitchell left. Lennie Dunn took them for a car backfiring, but the girl was hysterical and screamed that they had shot him. Later when Reggie Kray told her to keep her mouth shut she did so because she 'knew the Krays and what they could do'.

But it was Donaghue's evidence that created the greatest stir in court. In the first hearing of Old Street Magistrates' Court he had been in the dock, along with Foreman and the Krays, accused of murdering Mitchell. But by the time the case reached the Old Bailey he had turned Queen's evidence. The murder charge against him had been dropped and he went into the witness-box to give his version of what happened between 8.30 and 8.45 P.M. that Christmas Eve.

According to him, the Krays were desperate to get Mitchell away from Barking before he landed them all in trouble, and Reggie Kray and Donaghue had a meeting with Foreman, an old friend of theirs, to arrange the move. Foreman had said he would lay on a van and a driver to take Mitchell down to the country. It would be waiting outside the flat at 8.30, and as Donaghue was one of the few people Mitchell trusted he was told to bring him out.

To start with, said Donaghue, everything went as expected. When he led Mitchell out of the flat a dark-painted Thames van was waiting, double-parked, twenty yards or so down the main road. There were three men inside, including Foreman. One of them opened the back door and Donaghue and Mitchell got in, Mitchell sitting on the wheel casing on the right-hand side of the van and Donaghue going to the front beside the driver.

Continuing his evidence, Donaghue described how the

doors slammed to, the van drew away, and Foreman and the man beside him drew their guns, Foreman a silenced automatic and the other man a revolver. Mitchell made a dive towards the driver, but before he could reach him he had been shot several times in the body and collapsed, groaning, with his knees doubled up beneath him. By now the van was travelling down Ladysmith Avenue, a turning off the main Barking Road, and three more shots were fired into Mitchell's chest in the area of the heart. For a moment, said Donaghue, he lay still. Then he lifted his head. Two final shots, claims Donaghue, were fired into his head and everything was over.

This was Albert Donaghue's story from the witness-box of the Old Bailey. He said that he telephoned the news to Reggie from the flat, telling him briefly, 'The geezer's gone', and according to another witness who was there, Reggie Kray wept when he heard the news.

As for the disposal of the body, Donaghue alleged that Foreman later told him they had to hold on to it for five days over Christmas, before taking it 'down to a man in the country' for disposal. He also described how Foreman told him that they took the body to pieces, that the heart was ripped open and three bullets found in it, and that he had a tiny brain – 'He cupped his hands to show me just how small it was.' Donaghue believed the body had been burned.

All this was strenuously denied by Foreman and by the Krays, and the judge ruled that under English law, Donaghue's evidence required independent corroboration before the jury could accept it, as Donaghue was himself criminally involved in Mitchell's escape. There was no corroboration. Frederick Foreman and the three Krays were found not guilty of the murder of Frank Mitchell, and to this day the Axe Man is still officially on the run, one of the few men in history to have made a successful getaway from Dartmoor.

FOURTEEN

The Murder Machine

The curtains were kept drawn now in the Finchley flat, the electric light stayed on throughout the day; Mitchell had disappeared but Ronnie remained a prisoner, locking himself away from the police. Like Mitchell he was armed and going mad from solitude; unlike him he had a powerful gang and a twin brother ready for any sacrifice to keep him happy. For Ronnie the war against the Richardsons continued, for he was certain there were men at large seeking revenge for George Cornell. He had to kill them first. They were all on his list and through his spies he still received regular reports upon their whereabouts. As he lay locked in his bedroom he planned exactly how to kill each one of them. This was exciting, his favourite activity, and it would keep him occupied for hours until his thoughts turned from other people's deaths to his own. Then the depression would begin and he would suddenly be terrified, powerless and trapped and horribly alone.

Life was a waking nightmare for him then. His violent life had turned against him. He was his own corpse. The bullet he had seen enter Cornell's head was entering his own. He dreamed that he was being disembowelled, slowly castrated, drowned in his own blood. Once he woke and slashed his wrists, but someone in the next room heard his groans and saved his life. During these attacks he generally lay drugged or drunk for days, with Reggie or his favourite boy watching until the terror left him. Members of the Firm calling at the flat would often hear him shrieking in his sleep. Once he woke in the early morning and was found by Reggie's bed with a gun, saying that he would have to shoot him.

Soon after this Reggie arranged for him to see his regular psychiatrist. So as to avoid involving the psychiatrist with the police, Reggie arranged to meet him in Trafalgar Square. When he showed up, a big car was already waiting by the kerb – the psychiatrist was hustled in. Ronnie was in the back with his collar up and wearing dark glasses. For the next hour as the car cruised through Hyde Park Ronnie described his symptoms and had fresh drugs prescribed. They helped, and at the start of February 1967 Ronnie changed hiding-places. Reggie had found him a room above an antique shop off the King's Road. There was a new boy, too, a Scandinavian with fair hair. Life became easier.

Throughout this crisis Reggie remained calm; those who knew him found his self-control almost unnatural. Helped by his brother Charlie, he seemed able to keep the routine business of the Firm ticking over – nothing adventurous, but the protection money was still regularly collected from the West End, various frauds continued, clubs continued to make money. Somehow the prestige of the Kray name was preserved.

He had grown thinner and the drink made his eyes bloodshot, his face blotchy in the mornings; these were the only signs of strain. Like Ronnie he possessed great stamina and he knew everything depended now on him alone. It was his love of Ronnie that kept him going; or if not love it was the necessity to protect him, an instinct that went back to childhood and proved stronger now than anything. Even when Frances made a fresh attempt to kill herself towards the end of February he managed to keep calm: Ronnie needed him most. Because he knew this and could understand Ronnie's sickness he could usually endure his drunken taunts, his sneers, the raucous boasts that he was the only man in the family. He made no reply, just as he made no reply to those who whispered that he was responsible for Frances, that he had got her on to drugs and that she had tried to kill herself from fear of the twins.

It was at night before the drink began to work that he would sometimes wonder how much longer he could go on. So many people knew too much – some would keep quiet from loyalty, others from fear. Others would always hate the twins. Sooner or later somebody would talk and everything would be over.

When spring came life seemed easier. Ronnie appeared to have survived his months in hiding. Nobody had talked; no one had been killed. The case against the police inspector was nearing its time limit; once it expired Ronnie would be free. He was already talking about his holiday and his new plans for the Firm. The police seemed to have forgotten the Cornell case; inquiries about Frank Mitchell had still to reach Lennie Dunn's flat in Barking and the girl in Winston's Club. The twins had luck if nothing else.

There even seemed a chance of a fresh start for Reggie with his wife now she was out of hospital. She was no longer with her parents but with her brother and his wife in a big block of flats called Wimbourne Court. Frances was listless, thinner than she used to be. The pert cockney bride had become a waif of nearly twenty-three, too tired to bother with her friends. The annulment proceedings had been held up during her time in hospital, so she was still officially Mrs Kray; when Reggie suggested a day out together she accepted. She found him changed, more like the man he had been when he first knew her. He said he realized his mistakes, still loved her, wanted her back. They could have a new flat, right away from Ronnie, a new life quite apart from the Firm. As a start they could have a holiday abroad, even a second honeymoon – Ibiza – at the end of June. Frances agreed. On 6 June 1967 they went to book their tickets.

Reggie believed in premonitions: that night he woke knowing that something was wrong with Frances. He couldn't sleep again and just before 6 A.M. drove round to Wimbourne Court to see her. He would have rung the bell but realized that everyone would still be sleeping so went away. An hour later Frankie Shea got up and went to his sister's room with a cup of tea; she seemed to be still asleep so he left the tea by her bed and went off to work.

Around lunchtime her father had just returned to Ormsby Street when his son came rushing in, shouting that Frances was dead. He had his Mini parked outside and they drove to the flat. Frank Shea did not believe she was really dead. Twice he had saved her from attempted suicide; somehow it must be possible again, and when he saw her on her bed she seemed as peaceful as if simply sleeping. He took her hands to wake her, 'but I could feel her arms already stiffening. It was her third go – this time there was nothing wc could do. She had been dead some hours. It was a terrible thing, but all that I could think was how those bastards had destroyed my daughter.'

Reggie arrived later. When Frank Shea had gone his son sent a messenger to Vallance Road asking for him. He came, knowing that something had happened to Frances; but like Frank Shea, it was not until he took her hands that he knew she was dead. And like him, he felt enormous hatred at her death.

'I blamed her parents. They didn't want her to be happy with me. They just kept on and on until she killed herself.'

That afternoon he drank himself insensible. That night he stayed beside her, kneeling on the floor, and all the time the bitterness grew worse until it swallowed up his grief.

The Sheas spent the night at Ormsby Street remembering Frances and the things she said before she died. The twins alone had been responsible for what had happened; they had defiled her and used her and would never let her go. Now she had escaped from them for good, 'but they as good as murdered her, the two of them'.

At the inquest the dead woman's husband gave evidence of identification; a Dr Julius Silverstone spoke of 'personality disturbances'; the post-mortem showed that she had died of a massive overdose of phenobarbitone taken in the night. The coroner recorded his verdict of 'suicide while the balance of mind was disturbed'.

Then the Krays took over the girl's funeral just as, two years before, they had made all arrangements for her marriage. Reggie returned to Father Hetherington to ask him to perform the ceremony; this time he agreed. The funeral turned out to be as impressive a display of public grief as the marriage had been of rejoicing. Ten solemn-looking limousines were hired for mourners. Each member of the Firm had sent a wreath, as had the friends and allies of the Krays throughout the underworld. Reggie sent three, including a six-foot heart of scarlet roses pierced with a white arrow of carnations. He spent £200 on her plot in Chingford Cemetery, large enough for him to be buried with her when his time came. The funeral became a sort of triumph for the Krays: Reggie was treating Frances as lavishly in death as in life.

The graveside scene might well have been a gangster's burial – the fresh-dug earth heavy with wreaths, a mass of sombre villains paying their respects, police among the mourners on the off-chance that Ronnie might appear.

'The bastards,' Reggie said, 'had no respect for human dignity.'

But Ronnie was too canny to be caught like this and merely sent a large wreath of carnations. The funeral was the one occasion where Reggie was alone. Weeping for all to see as Frances was lowered into the grave, he watched the first spadeful of earth thud on the coffin, threw in a fiver for the gravediggers and walked away.

In a letter afterwards he wrote:

'I relived all the good times we had had together. Milan, where we had gone to the Scala Theatre to watch Madame Butterfly, Barcelona and the bull-fights, the South of France, Rotterdam, Holland, drinking in the Blue Lagoon Club and many other places and good times. The first time we had met and I had fallen in love looking at my wife's beautiful brown eyes and long lashes. Now all this was gone but the memories will stay for me forever.'

Then he wrote a poem, which was printed in a gold-and-white memorial card together with a photograph of 'my dear wife Frances who passed away, 7th June 1967, aged 23 years'. It was called 'If':

If I Could climb upon a passing cloud
that would drift your way
I would not ask for a more beautiful day,
Perhaps I would pass a rainbow,
With Nature's Colours so beautifully aglow,
If you were there at the Journey's End,
I would know
It was the beginning and not the End.
Reg.'

But behind the public grief and the sentimentality, a battle had gone on between the families: the mourning had turned sour with hatred.

Reggie insisted that Frances was to be buried in her wedding dress; when she was safely underground her parents said that they had arranged with the undertaker to have a slip and pair of stockings put on her so that as little as possible of the hated dress touched her skin. They also claim to have switched her wedding ring at the last minute for a small ring she wore as a child. Then there was trouble over the name to be used at the burial and on the tombstone. The Sheas said they found a note from her asking to be buried in the name of Shea; despite this the funeral took place in the name of 'Frances Shea, *otherwise* Kray', and her elaborate Carrara marble headstone carries the name Frances Kray.

She left no will; as next-of-kin Reggie inherited her estate. More bitterness was caused when he arrived at Ormsby Street and took away his letters and the jewellery he had given her.

'After the funeral, it was like he had a breakdown. He became like Ronnie, drunken an' full of hate, an' all the strength went out of 'im.' This is how one of the Firm remembers him, and according to Tommy Cowley, who was often with him now, the death of Frances triggered a complete collapse. 'Over the years Reg had simply had too much to bear from Ronnie, and it had got so bad that when Reggie had this trouble over Frances on top of everything he couldn't take it. That's why he was so badly hurt. When we're hurt we look around for somebody to hate and he looked everywhere. He really wanted to take vengeance on himself, but he took it against a lot of others on the way.'

Reggie said, 'I drank more than ever, but started to visit my friend, Father Hetherington, pretty often; he always made me feel a lot better after a visit as he is the most understanding man I know.'

At other times the gin would make him dangerous. He would start by getting maudlin over Frances but the sentiment soon turned to bitterness; he would sit up drinking gin laced with strong black coffee to keep him awake, all the time mulling over everything he could blame upon the Sheas. Hatred can sharpen up the memory and he forgot nothing; soon the Sheas became responsible for what had happened, not just to Frances, but to him. He was convinced that they had destroyed his marriage. Everything could then be blamed on them. Nothing was his fault or Ronnie's. All his unhappiness, the breakdown of his life, had one root cause – the Sheas.

'I should have killed 'em. Would have saved a lot of bother.'

However drunk he got he never dared. Frances would have known and not forgiven him. A few days after the funeral he got as far as having Frankie Shea brought to the pub where he was drinking, but he had forgotten the uncanny resemblance between the two Shea children. He began weeping and sent him away. If he had to have revenge, he would need other victims than the Sheas.

The first was a friend called Frederick. His name came up quite casually during a drunken row between the twins: Ronnie said something to make him think that Frederick had not liked Frances. This was enough. Reggie swore that he would kill him and sat up all night nursing his hatred; by 6 A.M. the third bottle of Gordon's gin had produced a sullen fury. The hatred of the last few weeks could spend itself.

Two members of the Firm were sleeping in Reggie's flat; he woke them. One had an old green van; they drove in it to a pub in Stoke Newington where the landlord always kept a gun or two for the twins. Reggie collected a revolver. The green van drove on to the modern flat where Frederick lived with his wife and children. By now it was nearly 7 A.M. and people were passing on their way to work. Reggie rang the bell. Frederick's wife was seeing to the children and answered the door.

'Tell Frederick Reggie's here,' said the man from the green van.

Afterwards she realized she should have slammed the door in their faces, but the children were all round her; Reggie blundered past her and one of the men ripped the wires from the telephone. Reggie began shouting for her husband. He was washing and came to the head of the stairs.

'You never liked my wife, you bastard. Now you talk

about her behind my back. You shouldn't talk about her. Not about my Frances.'

Reggie was sobbing at him, pointing the gun up the stairs; there was a scuffle as one of the Firm tried to bring Frederick down. The children and the wife began to scream, Reggie was shouting. Frederick was hit on the head, and as he came tumbling down the stairs Reggie started shooting. All except one of the shots went wide; the one that did connect passed through Frederick's leg, and he lay groaning and bleeding at the foot of the stairs. Reggie seemed satisfied. The others helped him back into the van and drove away. Hunched in the front seat he kept muttering, 'The bastard was saying things about my wife, about my lovely Frances.'

Tears streamed down his cheeks.

'Drunken slag,' said Ronnie when he heard what his twin had done. 'Risking our necks like that. Here we are, making ourselves a living and getting straight and you risk everything shooting one of our friends, you drunken pig.'

Their brother Charlie stopped the trouble going any further. An old friend of Frederick's, he was somehow able to smooth things over, calling a discreet doctor in to tend the wound, explaining about Reggie and making sure the police were kept out.

'You couldn't kill a man if you tried,' said Ronnie during his next row with Reggie. 'You're too fucking soft. When I did my one, I made a job of it. Cornell couldn't walk around no more like Frederick.'

For Reggie much of life was like a dream. There were quite lucid periods when he was sober and puzzled at what was happening. Sometimes he felt horror at himself; these were the times when he would visit Father Hetherington and ask him to pray for him. More often everything was so unreal that all he wanted was escape – a long East African safari where he could harden up and learn to live with himself again, North Africa, the piece of land he and Frances had bought at Bantry Bay. He did his best to keep in trim with early morning runs around Victoria Park and weekends by the sea at Steeple Bay.

The dreams of her recurred; the guilt, the hatred began stirring. Frances was gone. He was alone except for Ronnie. Once he began to drink and feel the violence rise within him, he was at Ronnie's mercy. In July the case against the police inspector was finally dismissed. Ronnie emerged from hiding. The shootings began in earnest. Reggie was usually drunk, always mourning Frances.

One night he turned up at the Starlight Club in Highbury demanding £1,000 on the spot from a man called Fields. Fields said he had not got it; Reggie shot him through the leg and left one of the Firm to smash his face in.

'I would have shot the bastard through the head,' said Ronnie.

Reggie bumped into Buller Ward at the Regency Club. Relations with the old boxer had cooled since the night Ronnie branded Jonathan for beating up his son. Reggie punched him on the jaw.

'You'll have to do better than that, Reggie boy,' said Ward, riding the blow. As Reggie had no gun on him he knifed his face wide open.

'Better to have done him with a shooter,' his twin insisted.

A few nights later, at the Green Dragon Club, Ronnie showed him how it should be done. A former friend called George Dixon had said something that annoyed the twins and was careless enough to be at the bar when they walked in. Ronnie went up to him as he did once to George Cornell, drew an automatic and pulled the trigger. Nothing happened.

'Here,' said Ronnie, taking the bullet from the chamber and handing it to Dixon. 'It's just saved your life. Wear it on your watch-chain as a souvenir.'

With Ronnie on the scene again, the Firm's business became wilder: big-money projects dwindled, but the twins' name was still sufficient to guarantee a likely living. That summer they began a racket peddling purple hearts from an address in Soho; they had an old acquaintance who was manufacturing them by the million in an Essex farmhouse. They took over fruit machines throughout the West End. They also ventured into the pornography business, taking their cut from several illicit wholesalers and importers.

Besides these actual rackets Ronnie had his dreams. Africa still beckoned: he was excited by a complicated plan to take over a diamond-mine in the Congo. Later there was talk of the Firm's services being used to assassinate President Kaunda. Neither proposal seemed to come to anything; nor did another idea of Ronnie's, to master-mind a big chain of forged currency deals, with the plates made in New York by a virtuoso forger, notes mass-produced in Switzerland and Europe flooded with a sea of bogus currency.

Ronnie was offered money to assassinate the Fascist leader, Colin Jordan. A member of the Firm was sent to Switzerland to negotiate a link-up with one of the Messina brothers for a new vice syndicate in London. Two others went to Tangier to meet a representative of the family of the late Moise Tshombe; Ronnie had been told that they would pay half a million dollars for a viable plan to free the hijacked Congo leader from detention in Algiers. His plan included the use of helicopters, nerve gas and a strike-force from the Firm fighting their way into the Tshombe villa. Tshombe would make his getaway by hovercraft. For two days discussions went on at the Rif Hotel between the men from the Tshombes and the men from the Krays; but Ronnie's ideas appeared extreme, and after a great deal of talking and drinking one more potential customer finally went elsewhere.

It was an uneasy summer. A tall man with a Belfast accent had been reported in the East End talking to people about George Cornell. When Ronnie checked on him he found that his name was Mooney. He was a detective inspector from the Yard's Flying Squad.

More rumours came in then about a police spy on the Firm. Ronnie had never trusted anyone except Reggie and his mother. Now his suspiciousness began to spread through the Firm: nobody knew who might betray him. One member of the Firm had a fight with Scotch Jack Dickson and blinded him in one eye with a bottle. When Dickson came out of hospital Ronnie told him he should get revenge.

The comradeship within the Firm was not improved when two of its members disappeared after trouble with Ronnie. One was his driver, a talkative young man called Frost; there was a rumour that he had tried blackmailing Ronnie over a boy. Soon after, he was followed by Mad Teddy Smith. There had been a long weekend at Steeple Bay with Ronnie and some boys; there was an argument, a fight and Teddy was never seen again. The twins never spoke about him; nobody asked questions. To this day Frost and Teddy Smith remain on Scotland Yard's missing-persons list.

From then on the Firm became an isolated world of violence and mistrust, with each man for himself. The man who left the Firm received various threats and a dead rat in the post; on his birthday there was a funeral wreath outside his door. But despite the danger and the atmosphere, there remained definite attractions in the Firm. Money was one: the twins could still ensure that everyone in favour collected a minimum of £40 a week in personal protection money. Prestige was another: the twins were still the most feared gangsters in the country. Anyone working for them could do much as he liked in gangland, drink what he felt like for free, cadge money on the side, never go hungry for a woman.

For some of the Firm this was enough; they were quite ready to desert when the time arrived but not before. Some of the younger ones genuinely lived for the excitement and intrigue. There was the twins' own cousin, Ronnie Hart, a big, good-looking one-time sailor from the merchant navy. As he explained, his greatest aim in life was 'to be different from the ordinary person. Best of all I'd like to have been a mercenary in the Congo.' Being with the twins was easier. 'It's the adventure that I really go for. With them it's just like being a spy or something in the underground movement.' The secrets and intrigue had their own fascination; so did the air of danger and depravity round the Colonel. One of Hart's favourite duties was to take the twins' special guests for a drink at the saloon bar at The Blind Beggar. The place where George Cornell was shot was becoming one of the sights of the East End.

There were a lot like Hart who hung around the twins for the kicks and the adventure – and because Ronnie was a murderer; this had become his principal social asset. That autumn a pair of unemployed half-Greek brothers called Lambrianou tried to become accepted in the Firm. Ronnie said they must prove themselves first.

Ronnie never understood the ordinary person's ambivalence over murder. Most people seem fascinated by it but never dream of doing it; he dreamed of little else. For him the terrible taboo between the idea of murder and the reality did not exist. Life was far simpler without it. The nearest he came to giving an excuse for shooting George Cornell was to shrug his shoulders and say, 'Well, it needed to be done, didn't it? Can't see what all the fuss was about.'

It was because he couldn't see, that further tension built up in the Firm, as he began persuading others to kill. Hart was one of the first; Ronnie seemed to think that because his young cousin wanted adventure, he felt as he did. But when he sent him off to kill a man for him in Romford Market, Hart fired a shot in the air, dropped the gun and ran for it. It was worse with Reggie. Time after time their arguments came back to the point that Reggie must 'do his one'. But Reggie found that while he could shoot a man in the leg or cut him in the face or break his jaw, he drew the line at murder. This saddened Ronnie; 'I have to do the dirty work for everyone. Somebody else should have a go.'

That autumn Ronnie felt increasingly put upon. There were a lot of people needing to be killed – the list was lengthening. Payne was on it now that he had left them; so was Freddie Gore. The man in Romford Market had been included as a favour to a friend in Broadmoor, whose wife he had slept with. Besides him there were the potential traitors, the competitors, the 'liberty takers'. There was work for everyone, and Ronnie had the idea now of using murder as a test of loyalty. Since all the talk of traitors on the Firm, he remembered what he had learned about the Leopard Men when he was in Nigeria: the secret brotherhood of killers who had terrorized the countryside with ritual murders. With them murder was used as an initiation to the gang; later it formed a bond of loyalty between the murderers.

Ronnie became excited at the idea. Reggie would have to kill; as his twin brother, his other self, it was imperative, for he and Reggie always shared their secret life. Only when he had killed would they be properly united. But this would be just the beginning. In time the whole Firm could be 'blooded', all share in the strange brotherhood of killing, all become equally involved.

When Ronnie first used Jack 'the Hat' McVitie he had seemed ready for any villainy. He was a well-known East End character, as strong as a dray-horse, and he used to boast that nothing frightened him. He was an old-style fighting man. Only that spring a gang had tried to teach him a lesson by smashing up his hands with a crowbar but as soon as they were healed he was brawling again. In fact, though, Jack the Hat was nowhere near as tough as he appeared. He was a drunk. His nerves had gone; his courage came from the bottle or from enormous pep pills called 'black bombers'.

Much of the time he was a cheerful soul, erratic, generous and kind to children. He was vain enough to have earned his nickname from the hat he always wore to cover his baldness, and was proud of his success with women. He treated them in the old East End manner. He casually pushed one mistress he was annoyed with out of his car while travelling at speed and broke her back. This caused him some remorse, but in a day or two he found another girl to live with. Jack was like that.

That summer Ronnie had employed him in the purple-heart business; it appears he cheated Ronnie on the money but Reggie, who liked him, smoothed things over. In September Ronnie became convinced that Leslie Payne had made a deal with the Law and realized that he would be a dangerous witness for the Crown. That same week Ronnie had a drink with Jack the Hat; he gave him £100, a gun and Leslie Payne's address. He explained that the £100 was payment on account. There would be £400 more when Leslie Payne was dead.

When Reggie heard, he disliked the idea. He disliked most of Ronnie's ideas, but lacked the power to oppose him: he was deep in his own hell and past the point where he could do much against Ronnie. The only peace he knew now was the hour he spent each day by Frances's grave. He had had it planted with red roses and was convinced that something of her spirit lingered there to listen to him. Each day he talked to her and each day he returned to Ronnie. There was no one else with Frances gone. Ronnie was someone to lean on; when he had drunk enough Reggie took on his power; when he indulged his hatred and his violence they became one person. Sober, it was not so easy. There were still moments every day when he was sane and weary with a deep longing to have finished with it all.

Jack the Hat went off to kill Les Payne one September evening and bungled it, as Reggie had predicted. He promised he would try again, but Payne had become wary. The days went by; Les Payne was still alive; McVitie still had Ronnie's £100. Threats followed. Ronnie heard that Jack had made a scene at the Foremans' 211 Club in Balham. This was 'a diabolical liberty', as Foreman was an old friend of the twins. Once again Reggie smoothed things over. There was a meeting at The Regency. Jack, sober and repentant, told him about his nerves, his debts, his child who was ill. A soft touch as usual, Reggie lent him £50.

'You should've paid George Cornell as well,' stormed Ronnie when he heard, and sent fresh threats to McVitie about his money. McVitie, thinking Reggie had let him down, took several bombers, got himself drunk and staggered into The Regency, hat askew, waving a sawn-off shotgun. Next day someone made a point of telling Ronnie how Jack the Hat had threatened to shoot the twins.

The Carpenters' Arms is a small pub in a dingy street near Vallance Road. The twins bought it that autumn. During these months of crisis they had not been able to keep their clubs going. This was the last place of their own. But here in Bethnal Green where they had grown up they felt secure and knew that they could drink in safety. There was a narrow doorway to the street, a narrow bar; one could see everybody who was there.

On weekdays the Firm assembled here for orders; at weekends there was sometimes a party for the Firm and friends, with womenfolk invited and drinks were on the house. The last Saturday in October The Carpenters' was crowded.

Violet was there. She had left her house just round the corner for a new council flat in Braithwaite House in

Shoreditch, but she missed Vallance Road and loved a night out with the twins. She kept herself smart for them – a blonde rinse for her hair, a big gold pendant round her neck. Sometimes she laughed and said the worry of the twins helped to keep her young; she was immensely proud of them. Charlie's wife Dolly was there too. She loathed the twins and they returned the compliment, but on this family occasion she had her place, standing aloof from them and very cool.

These ladies' evenings were extremely formal: the women sipped their Babychams beneath expensive hair-dos and kept their places in the old East End manner, genteelly twittering among themselves. All the men would be uncomfortably smart – small, strangled knots to ties, stiff white collars, gleaming shoes. They took their style from the Colonel and with his mother present would be painfully restrained.

Reggie was an accomplished host. He was attentive to the women and drank little; the serious drinking would start later, after the pubs closed. There was a party at the house of a girl called Blonde Carol in Cazenove Road, Stoke Newington; the Firm was welcome.

Ronnie was the only person at The Carpenters' that night who seemed out of things; most people recognized the danger signs and left him carefully alone. When Reggie talked to him he found him brooding about McVitie. Since Reggie would not do anything, Ronnie was going to deal with him as he had dealt with George Cornell. McVitie would be at The Regency around eleven.

Several people in the bar that night remember how quickly Reggie changed. He started drinking heavily and at closing time drove off to The Regency.

The Regency – 'North London's Smartest Rendezvous' – was very different from the down-at-heel illicit gambling place the twins had had a share in seven years before but they had no connection with it now. Two brothers, John and Tony Barry, had stepped in, both of them smart young businessmen. John was the elder and the tougher – broad-shouldered, short, with an assured manner and a white Mercedes; his brother was skinnier and shyer, very much the junior partner. They worked well together, had installed the big upstairs bar, dance-floor, restaurant and the gaming-room in the basement. It was a lively place. Much of the Barrys' success came from the way they could keep order without asking questions: tact was their stock-in-trade.

This was how John Barry had managed to disarm McVitie when he was waving his shotgun and looking for the twins a few days earlier. Still greater tact over the years had saved The Regency from having to pay regular protection money to the twins, although they took the place for granted as their preserve. They and the Firm would often visit; when they were there the regulars would be a little careful how they spoke and who was standing near. Drinking men would tend to stand in groups, ready for trouble – the sort of trouble that occurred that night just before 11.00 when Reggie burst in with several of the Firm, looking for Jack the Hat.

It should have been a simple death. Reggie had heard so many times how Ronnie had murdered George Cornell, and endured so many taunts about the proper way to kill a man, that it seemed perfectly straightforward. Now he was drunk and violent he had no scruples about killing; he could not go on letting Ronnie down for ever. If he let Ronnie kill McVitie, how could he face himself afterwards? There was no possible alternative. He had his .32 automatic. When he saw Jack the Hat he would quite calmly shoot him through the head as Ronnie had shot Cornell. That was what Ronnie wanted; twins had a duty to each other.

But slowly it dawned on Reggie that McVitie was not in The Regency at all. He searched the gaming-room, the bar, the restaurant. Ronnie Hart was with him and a man called Bender; the Lambrianou brothers joined them. They went to the Barrys' office to ask where McVitie was. Tony Barry was there and asked why they wanted him. Reggie told him. Barry would have known better than to argue had it been Ronnie. With Reggie it was different. He begged Reggie to be sensible. He knew McVitie; the man was a fool, a drunken nobody. He wasn't worth the trouble that would come from murdering him.

Reggie made no attempt to answer. Instead he stood chewing his lower lip and scowling as he always did at moments of uncertainty. Then he handed Tony Barry the .32, asked him to mind it, and quietly invited the Lambrianous to the party at Blonde Carol's. Hart and Bender were to come too. The violence had gone from Reggie's face. Barry put the gun in the drawer of his desk, thinking another spot of bother had been tactfully averted. He failed to notice that the man called Bender had a long knife tucked in the waistband of his trousers.

Blonde Carol was the sort of woman Ronnie approved of: a thin, pale woman in her middle twenties, she did as she was told, never complained and kept her mouth shut. The truth was she was scared of him. She had two young children from a broken marriage and lived with them in a basement flat in Cazenove Road, Stoke Newington, together with a man who ran a spieler for the twins. Sometimes she had nightmares about Ronnie.

The night of her party he arrived just after 11.00 with several of the Firm and two young boys. He didn't speak or even look at her but stood there scowling in the hall as one of the men explained that Ronnie required her flat for a private party of his own. She knew better than object and told the guests who had already arrived that they were moving to another party across the road. Nobody complained: everyone knew Ronnie.

As Blonde Carol's guests were leaving, Reggie arrived

with Hart, Bender and the Lambrianous. There were two women with them – Hart's girl-friend, Vicki, and a young red-head called Carol Thompson. The red-head was a girl Reggie had met at Steeple Bay. As they came down the basement steps they all seemed ready for a good time but Blonde Carol heard Ronnie tell his brother that this was no place for women. The women were to go with her.

Ronnie was taking charge. Without bothering to ask, he knew Reggie had failed him yet again. If things were left to him he would end up buying Jack the Hat a drink and lending him another £50; Ronnie was not leaving anything to him in future. If Reggie wouldn't kill McVitie, he would have to do it personally.

When they were in the sitting-room Ronnie began to give his orders. Before Frances died Reggie would probably have stopped him, but now he lacked the power and had drunk too much. Ronnie was in command. While Reggie poured himself another drink young Hart was ordered back to The Regency for the gun left in the office. To incriminate the Barrys and make sure they kept quiet, Ronnie gave strict instructions that Tony Barry was to bring the .32 to Cazenove Road himself.

Then it was the Lambrianous' turn. They were good friends of Jack the Hat; he would trust them as he never would the twins. Now was their chance to prove themselves fit to join the Firm. They were to follow Hart to The Regency, find Jack the Hat, buy him a drink or two, then ask him round to Carol's party without mentioning the twins. Hart and the Lambrianous left. Reggie appeared to fall asleep. The two boys put a record on and started dancing together. Ronnie watched them.

It was a crude trap for an old villain like McVitie; Hart, Tony Barry, the Lambrianous could all have warned him. Even when they failed to, he should have smelled something a little odd about this sudden invitation, but he was probably too drunk.

Barry brought the gun and drove off looking scared before becoming even more involved. Young Ronnie Hart returned; Ronnie posted him as a lookout in an upstairs window facing the street. Just before midnight Hart saw a beaten-up Ford Zodiac draw up. Five men got out: the Lambrianous, two brothers by the name of Mills and finally a man in a hat – McVitie.

Hart gave the alarm.

McVitie burst in, ready for a party.

'Where's all the birds, all the booze?' he shouted.

Ronnie was waiting for him, watching from the sofa. Reggie was behind the door. As Jack the Hat barged past, Reggie tried to shoot him through the head, but the gun jammed. Outside big Chrissie Lambrianou, who had wanted to be a gangster, suddenly realized what he had done and was sitting weeping on the stairs.

McVitie must have thought he still had a chance when the gun jammed. When the same thing happened with George Dixon, Ronnie had let him off with a warning; if he decided he deserved a beating up, Jack could take it like a man. But he must soon have seen from Ronnie's face that he was not to be so lucky.

Ronnie was shouting at him, his eyes bulging with fury. The Mills brothers and the two boys ran from the room. Reggie had thrown away the gun and was grappling him from behind. McVitie, very sober now, tried to be reasonable, but he seemed to have no voice left and Ronnie was shouting incoherently, the others joining in.

Suddenly he managed to break free. In the far corner of the room there was a window with a wooden frame that looked on to the garden. McVitie made a dive for it, but he got stuck, only his head and shoulders free. The others pulled him back by the legs, then hauled him to his feet.

'Be a man, Jack,' Ronnie screamed at him.

'I'll be a man, but I don't want to die like one.'

Then Ronnie grabbed him, locking his arms behind him,

and Reggie was holding Bender's carving knife. The room fell silent.

'Kill him, Reg. Do him,' hissed his brother. 'Don't stop now.'

McVitie had lost his hat through the window. He stood there looking very bald and gaunt, his long face sweating.

'Why are you doing this to me, Reg?'

Instead of answering, Reggie pushed the knife into his face below the eye. The butchering followed as McVitie sank to his knees. According to Ronnie Hart, Reggie stabbed his stomach and his chest and finished by impaling him through the throat on to the floor. Reggie claims it was Hart who did the stabbing. Hart admits pushing a handkerchief into McVitie's mouth to stop the flow of blood. Hart says that Bender put his ear to McVitie's chest and then pronounced him dead.

It was approaching 1 A.M. McVitie's corpse lay in the centre of the room, the carpet round him soaked in blood. The party opposite would soon be over, Blonde Carol soon be coming home. Before she did the body must be dumped, the worst of the blood mopped up. Once this was done the twins could say there had simply been a fight and she was not to talk.

So the dismal rigmarole of cleaning up began. The body was humped into the bedroom where Carol's children were asleep. It was slung on their mother's bed and covered with her bedspread. The Lambrianous started scrubbing the carpet with hot water from the kitchen. When the worst of the mess in the living room was dealt with, McVitie's body was wrapped in an eiderdown, dragged up the stairs and placed in Bender's car. Ronnie ordered him to drive it away. Then somebody remembered McVitie's hat. It was his trademark and could easily identify him. When he dived at the window it fell outside. It was retrieved.

Blonde Carol had still not returned, but the twins were restless, particularly Ronnie. Now that the job was done he had to get away; the others could take care of things. As usual the twins were worried about getting clean again so that they could face their mother. For this they chose the house of one man they believed that they could trust. Harry Hopwood had been their parents' best man, an army deserter with their father, and had advised the twins on the best way to dodge their own military service. They ordered Hart to drive them to his house in Hackney, where they engaged in a sort of ritual cleansing. First they both bathed thoroughly, soaping themselves all over. Hart says he remembers having to help wash Reggie's hair as he had cut his hand on the carving knife. Shoes, suits and every stitch of clothing were left in a pile; later that day Hopwood arranged to have them burned. He also burned their paper money and scrubbed their watches, rings and cuff-links. Then Hart went off to fetch fresh clothes and Hopwood helped him throw the knife and gun into the Grand Union Canal by Queensbridge Road. At this spot, ten months later, the police dragged up a jammed .32 automatic.

Just after 2 A.M. Blonde Carol came back to her flat; as she came down the stairs Bender was coming up, his hands in a pair of her children's woollen socks, carrying her plastic washing-up bowl full of blood and water.

'Somebody's been hurt,' he said. He emptied the bowl into the lavatory. She knew better than ask questions: instead she followed him downstairs and helped him with the scrubbing. When he told her it was no good and that the carpet would have to be destroyed, she still said nothing, but watched as he cut the stained part out and tried to burn it in the garden. It was so damp by now that it would barely smoulder. Later that day two men arrived with a van and removed every scrap of carpet and the furniture. The following day Donaghue arrived to mend the broken window in the corner of the room and redecorate the flat. A new suite of furniture arrived. No one said anything; Blonde Carol asked no questions.

* * *

Once they had washed and changed their clothes, the twins felt compelled to get away completely. Ronnie could not allow the deed to be obscured with its sordid aftermath: it was the act of killing he enjoyed, in all its dreamlike clarity. Others could cope with the dull reality of murder. He would have been depressed by it. Instead he made McVitie's death the excuse for a short holiday. Hart drove them up to Cambridge, where they booked in for two days at The University Arms. Now that Jack the Hat was dead, Ronnie could enjoy it all. He was in high spirits and quite irresponsible, relishing the details of the killing, talking about the way he died and how he looked, the noise he made and how much blood there was. The amount seemed to surprise him.

Reggie was stunned by everything at first and the drink took some time to wear off. Afterwards Ronnie's good humour was contagious. Here in this solid university hotel it was difficult to credit the drunken horror of the previous night. He felt safe with Ronnie near him, relieved to know he hadn't let him down. Ronnie's approval meant a lot to him these days.

The holiday continued. After two days in Cambridge they drove on to Lavenham, one of the prettiest villages in Suffolk, staying at the principal hotel among the wealthy tourists and country-lovers who were enjoying the English autumn. The twins enjoyed it too. They had an old acquaintance who lived nearby; with their help he had done well for himself and was now playing the part of the rich country squire with a large house and an expensive car. The twins visited him, ate his food, rode his horses and rambled across his fields to get fit. Ronnie was living his great adventure; he borrowed the car and had himself driven by the chauffeur to look for a country property for himself. He put on evening dress and went to the local hunt ball. He was beginning to see himself among the local gentry. Reggie got drunk.

* * *

It was some time before the police got wind that Jack the Hat was dead. The woman he had lived with reported him missing the morning after the murder, but his erratic ways were known; the police were inclined to think he had gone missing for some reason of his own. When there was no news of him there was still little for the police to go on. Ronnie had successfully produced a wall of silence by terror. The East End is full of police informers. There were a lot of people who knew that something had gone on that night between The Carpenters' Arms, The Regency and the flat in Cazenove Road. Not a word reached the police. Despite her new living-room carpet, Blonde Carol tried to pretend that nothing had happened. The Lambrianous joined the Firm; and Jack the Hat joined Frost and Teddy Smith on the missing list at Scotland Yard.

The body never was recovered. A year later the twins were to be found guilty of his murder, but the police and prosecution had to admit that there was no trace of the mortal remains of Jack the Hat. The twins' cousin, Ronnie Hart, turned Queen's evidence and went free, and it was largely because of his evidence that the twins were both convicted, along with Bender and the Lambrianou brothers. It was also because of him that two more men were brought into the case and finally convicted for helping to dispose of Jack McVitie's body – the twins' brother, Charlie, and their old friend Frederick Foreman from South London.

According to Hart's story in court, the twins telephoned Charlie from Hopwood's house when they had bathed and changed their clothes. They were extremely worried. They had told Bender to dump the body somewhere in the East End; instead he had telephoned to say that he had driven over London Bridge and parked the car near a church with the body in the back, covered with the eiderdown. Hart claims that Charlie was furious at hearing that the twins had killed McVitie, but that as usual he finally agreed to do what he could to cover up for them, telephoned his old friend Foreman and drove over to Foreman's pub, along with Hart, to make arrangements for McVitie's body to be collected and disposed of.

Hart claimed to have heard Foreman saying later that when he got McVitie's body from the car it was covered in slime, but nobody explained what happened afterwards. There were suggestions that McVitie ended up concreted into the foundations of a City block, or was made into pig food on a Suffolk farm, buried in Epping Forest or fed to the furnaces of Bankside Power Station.

All this is hypothetical. Ronnie himself liked spreading false rumours through the Firm, and several of these ideas certainly originated with him. But there are two important facts which suggest that Jack McVitie had a different end from any of these. The first is that the twins were widely credited with having their own means of disposing of bodies; the second is the evidence that Bender was originally told to dump the body somewhere in the East End. Ronnie seems to have been unconcerned about getting rid of McVitie's body until Bender disobeyed his orders and drove it to the wrong place. This would suggest that the twins had the problem taken care of locally and in some simpler manner than the dramatic methods that have been suggested.

The most convincing theory, which was never aired in court, is that the twins had a hold over a local undertaker and made him perform an occasional professional service for them on the side. It is an undertaker's calling to get rid of bodies; it would not take too much ingenuity to arrange for an extra one to disappear. Certainly there are stories of cremations which the twins paid for privately. Another theory is that sometimes an additional body was slipped into an already occupied coffin before the lid was finally screwed down.

FIFTEEN

Nipper's Secret War

Ronnie Kray often said that if anyone arrested him it would be Nipper Read. He regularly asked his spies for news of 'the cunning little bastard', but Read's duties as a detective chief inspector had kept him right away from the twins since the McCowan case. For Ronnie this had been a great relief: there was something about Read that made him uneasy. The most satisfying minor victory of the McCowan business came when he upset Read's career by involving him in the publicity of The Hideaway Club party.

Read shared Ronnie's relief at this lack of contact. The twins never quite managed to destroy his reputation, but he counted the McCowan case the biggest failure of his twenty-two years as a policeman; in his own eyes he had taken a long time to redeem himself, although success had followed quickly once he was away from the twins. On the Great Train Robbery investigation he seemed to typify the new style 'technocrat' investigator, as opposed to Butler, the star detective of New Scotland Yard. Butler ('every schoolboy's idea of what a great detective should be,' as Read described him) relied on speed, experience, intuition. Read was an organizer, believing in teams of efficiently directed detectives performing prodigies of detailed work. Butler got the arrests; Read and his men produced much of the detailed evidence to make the case stand up in court.

He had another big success organizing teams of detectives to keep down West End crime among the extra crowds in London for the Football World Cup in 1966; but

Read still nourished one ambition – the Murder Squad. The following year he made it. At forty-three he was promoted detective superintendent, posted to the Yard and entitled to wear the maroon tie with the embroidered globe pierced with a stiletto – the badge of Scotland Yard's twelve top detectives.

Early in the autumn of 1967 he spent several weeks settling into the Yard and hoping for a copybook murder for his first big case. When the case came, the assistant commissioner, Peter Brodie, summoned him personally to explain that he wanted him to take over a top secret investigation. It had been started some months earlier by Superintendent Ferguson Walker. Walker was being promoted and Read was the only man available to take his place. The aim of the investigation was to catch the Krays.

Despite his lack of height – at 5 feet 7 inches he is supposed to have taken stretching exercises to get himself accepted by the police – Read would make an ideal detective for a television series. A sharp-eyed, compact man with dark hair and a quiet smile, he looks the part; he also sounds it. The faint Midlands brogue mixed with the policeman's diction gives the impression of crispness and the common touch. He seems a very human man.

But Nipper Read is essentially a loner. Since he joined the force at twenty-one to escape from a job in Player's Tobacco Factory, Nipper has made the police his world. He has no hobbies and, despite the ease of manner, few intimate friends beyond his family; a policeman never knows when friendships and outside interests could impinge on his duty, and Nipper acts as if policemen should not be quite like other men. He has a Scottish wife and a teenage daughter; both have long ago accepted that he is 'a copper first, a married man second, and that's that'.

Had he been a vindictive man, he might have been excited at the chance of getting even with the twins; but he had been a policeman far too long to believe in vendettas. They were a dangerous self-indulgence, a betrayal of his ideal of the cool police professional; and no revenge was worth getting mixed up with the Krays again. And so a very downcast Nipper Read drove his red Volkswagen back to his home in Barnet after his interview with Brodie. It seemed as if he could never shake free from the Krays. This should have been his moment of success. Brodie was talking about top-priority investigations to catch the twins, but Nipper knew from experience what an interminable business this could be. He knew how cunning they were, how difficult to catch. A failure was not the way he wanted to begin his new career with the Murder Squad.

Next day he started finding out how much was known about the twins: hardly enough to cheer him up. In 1964 they had been publicly denounced in the *Sunday Mirror* for what they were – the leading organizing gangsters in the country. Since then they had committed murder and tangled with several top detectives from the Yard. But thanks to the strange class structure of the Yard, none of this knowledge can have reached the levels where the decisions were made. There had been a curious lack of urgency about the police investigation of London's leading gangsters. Even the killing of Cornell had done little to change things. Reports on the twins were scrappy; there seemed little attempt by the police to keep up with them or even to assess them. It had needed a shake-up of the top men at the Yard and public outcry at gang warfare to persuade New Scotland Yard to notice them at all.

This had occurred earlier in 1967; Sir John Waldron had replaced Sir Joseph Simpson as commissioner, with Brodie as his second-in-command, and the Richardson trial was giving London gang life its first real publicity. This was when rumours started that it would be 'the Krays' turn next'. Ferguson Walker took charge of the small investigation that was starting, but the Yard possessed so little on the twins that he had to begin at the beginning. In the months since, he had uncovered certain details of their frauds and the connection between the twins and Cooper's private bank. Apart from this, his work confirmed what Read had learned about the twins three years before, and made it plain that they were now so strong that it would take a lot to shift them.

There was just one thing Nipper Read had not foreseen – the revived interest in the Krays among the senior members of the Yard. After the years of apathy they were prepared at last for almost anything to catch the twins. One man who demonstrated this was John du Rose, head of the Murder Squad. A shrewd, silent old detective, who earned the nickname 'One-day-Johnnie' from the speed with which he used to solve his murders, he helped Read plan the facilities he needed. The investigation of the Krays soon turned into a full-scale campaign, backed by the full resources of the Yard, with Nipper firmly in command. He wanted police teams ready to dig out evidence against the twins similar to the teams he used against the Great Train Robbers. There were few detectives who had worked with Walker; Detective Sergeants Hemingway and Lloyd-Jones had been checking on the twins for months. So Nipper's first request was for more men; soon he had fourteen working for him.

The next demand was for total secrecy, both from the Krays and from the Yard itself. During the trial of the Richardsons there had been disturbing rumours of a spy at Scotland Yard. The twins were known to have told potential witnesses that anything they said would always get back to them; so rather than take chances John du Rose arranged for Nipper's team to be an undercover operation run from outside Scotland Yard. On the far side of the river was Tintagel House, a modern block of government offices used by the department of the Receiver of Metropolitan Police. Nothing could appear more nondescript.

Once they had offices here Read and his men could disappear into the anonymity of the civil service.

Even within the Yard contact with Tintagel House was kept to a minimum – effectively to Brodie and du Rose. To damp down speculation over what was happening across the river, a rumour was put round that the personnel were busy on a number-one docket – a full-scale inquiry into police corruption. And Nipper got a cover story too: a full-scale murder of his own to solve. A girl had died in Dublin; Nipper's name and the inquiry went up on the Murder Squad detail board in Scotland Yard.

With all this Nipper still had one request: a strict time limit to his assignment. Du Rose agreed to a conditional three months, after which Nipper could move on to something else.

Nipper Read had been nicknamed for his speed and cunning when lightweight boxing champion of the police, and he was to show the same qualities against the Krays. His vitality was catching – also the sense of drama at the task which faced him. This was a dangerous, clever enemy he and his men were fighting. Secrecy was vital; all members of the team were to have revolver practice, all were to take elementary precautions to protect themselves and their families. Cars should not be left out in the open where they could be tampered with, routes home were to be varied every day, care taken against being followed.

Despite all these elaborate precautions the twins soon knew that Nipper Read was back. By mid-October they had learned about the new department in Tintagel House. At first they were a little flattered, then they began to take precautions of their own. One was the attempt to silence Leslie Payne. Ronnie believed that he was just about to talk to Read. Yet in November when McVitie died, despite all Nipper Read's vitality and the high-powered planning at the Yard, the police were still so far from the twins that no one at Tintagel House connected them with the murder.

The first the Yard heard was that Jack the Hat was missing. Later an informer said there was a rumour that two men with Greek-sounding names were involved. Cypriots were blamed.

Nipper believed that there was still one way to get the twins. The strategy was simple but required an immense amount of work. This was an attraction in itself: work appealed to him.

All previous police attempts to get them, his own included, had failed through trying to catch them over one big crime. The twins had proved that this would never work. The Law was weak; the twins were powerful enough to twist it any way they liked. They could employ the finest lawyers to defend them. They had intimidated witnesses and threatened jurors. They could always pay others to take the blame or give an alibi. They had their friends in the press and parliament to make the most of any slip by the police.

But there was just one point where Read knew the twins were vulnerable – their past. For more than twelve years now they had been extorting money, maliciously wounding and organizing large-scale crime. Each of their crimes had had its victims; if he could find them and get them to talk, the twins were finished.

Nipper wrote thirty names down in a small black notebook. He called it his 'delightful index'.

There was no more talk now about his three months' attachment to the case: for the first time he began envisaging himself as the man who caught the Krays. But for his plan to work he needed further help from Scotland Yard. Just before Christmas he and John du Rose had a long session with the top police lawyers. Read had a way with lawyers. Unlike most policemen he is at home in court, clear-cut, unsubservient, extremely sharp, and as he faced the lawyers he explained exactly what he needed. He was confident he could catch the Krays, but the evidence against them would have to come from criminals. These were the men the twins had worked with and the police must have discretion to overlook serious crimes as the price of talking.

No lawyer likes the idea of deals with criminals; Nipper insisted there was no alternative. As he explained, could he have found a set of bishops and top businessmen to testify against the Krays he would have done so, but since the twins did all their business with other criminals, these were the only witnesses available. If the lawyers disapproved, now was the time to say so. The Law would certainly be saved a messy case; the twins would just as certainly stay free.

There was a long discussion. Nipper Read is a forceful man in a debate and his case appeared unanswerable: this was the price the Law was being asked to pay for having left the Krays immune so long.

By the end of that long afternoon Nipper had obtained the pained assent of the lawyers, and was prepared to 'go down into the sewers after the twins'.

The twins soon guessed what Read was up to as word began to filter back about the people he was seeing. There was not much they missed. This was the sort of secret warfare they could understand; both had good memories for people they had hurt, and soon began to block the loopholes in their past. Several of the men they had shot or wounded were brought to their solicitors and told to swear affidavits exonerating the twins. A general warning was passed out through gangland in case anybody felt like talking to the police. Each member of the Firm was made responsible for keeping tabs on two or three potential witnesses.

A few days later Nipper found himself asking a man the twins had maimed and ruined why he would not help him put them safely away for good.

'I hate the sight of blood,' the man replied, 'particularly my own.'

Then when it seemed as if the twins were winning, one of their old mistakes caught up with them. Nipper got his first big stroke of luck.

There had been no need for Ronnie to send Jack the Hat to try to silence Leslie Payne – Payne was too shrewd a criminal to talk to the police. But Jack McVitie's vain attempt to kill him and his subsequent disappearance made Payne think twice about his safety and his family. Had the twins left him alone he would have done nothing to harm them. But once they had tried to kill him he had no future until they were safely locked away.

Payne is a cold fish, with his pale-blue eyes and careful manner. He had no way of knowing whether the twins would try again, but he was on his guard; he made doubly sure about the locks on his doors, kept all his curtains drawn and stayed out of sight. When Sergeant Hemingway approached him as part of Nipper's plan to check all contacts with the twins, he told them he was prepared to talk. He would give everything he knew; it would take quite a while.

Read was sceptical. He had enough on Payne to know that he was too big a name to give himself up for nothing. He agreed to meet him next night in a West End bar, but went convinced it was a trap. Payne was at ease, dressed in a lightweight dark-blue suit and foulard tie; Read had a gun and was covered by two police marksmen. Finally he was convinced that Payne meant every word he said and was prepared to talk.

The full interrogation lasted three intensive weeks. Payne shrugged aside the offers of police protection, so Read chose a quietly down-at-heel hotel in Marylebone, hoping that the Krays' eyes wouldn't reach that far. He arrived each morning punctually at 9.00; Payne would unhurriedly appear an hour later in a taxi. Then, with a police guard sitting in the next-door bedroom, the questioning would start. The guard made coffee, meals were sent in from the café round the corner. Nothing was omitted from the questioning; each morning Read read over what Payne had said the day before. Payne had a meticulous memory. Nipper checked places, names, dates and bank-account numbers against his statement. Payne would then sign and date it and the questioning continued.

It was nearly Christmas before it finished. Payne's statement ran to more than two hundred pages and detailed everything he knew about the twins: the early frauds and gang fights, the entry into Esmeralda's Barn, protection and the long-firm frauds, the share deals, rackets, woundings and connections with the Mafia. All the names Payne remembered were included, together with the figures, facts and places. It was a blueprint for a prosecution. All Nipper needed now was proof and witnesses.

As his war against the twins gained ground, Nipper's real talents showed. Like a good general he could see his one advantage over the twins and make the most of it. He had the initiative now and numbers on his side. He could no longer hope to keep the investigation secret, but he could keep the twins guessing by working fast. Speed and surprise might crack their wall of silence.

Over Christmas Tintagel House was mobilized. Twenty men were working on the case; Superintendent Donald Adams had taken charge of documentation with three policewomen as assistants, leaving Nipper and his detectives free for action. It was a very big, simultaneous investigation. The different crimes and victims named in Payne's statement had to be verified before the twins could get at them. There was no time for conferences or the sequence of routine inquiries. Each policeman operated separately, directly responsible to Nipper Read. As well as countless inquiries in London detectives had to go to Scotland, Canada, Belgium, Spain and the United States. Prisoners were interviewed. All the time Read's men knew they could easily be signing a potential witness's death warrant.

Although the twins had failed to silence Payne there were a lot of others still worth shooting.

They tried. Just before Christmas one of the Firm was sent to Scotland to deal with a potential witness rumoured to have talked to Read. Read heard. The twins' man was picked up with a gun in Glasgow. Naturally he admitted nothing. Not all the twins' attempts were so inept. Time after time detectives visited someone they believed would talk, only to find that somebody had been there first and he had changed his mind.

Despite these setbacks, Read began to get results. The whole department was now working round the clock; the pile of statements stood several feet high and was growing daily. The police knew more about the twins than they ever had, and were closer to destroying their whole organization than at any time since 1964. Only one difficulty remained. As a firm safeguard for his witnesses and an inducement to make them talk, Nipper devised a clause attached to all their statements which guaranteed that the evidence would not be used until the Krays were safely under lock and key. He still had to get them there.

Clad in their slacks and vests, smoking and drinking endless cups of hot, sweet tea, the twins would meet late every afternoon in their mother's flat to argue about their latest plans. They picked up the current rumours, made certain of what each member of the Firm was doing, heard the reports sent in by spies and allies.

Since Read took over the investigation it had become a personal affair. Ronnie was for killing him. Reggie was more reasonable. He knew about the clause in all the statements. He was also satisfied that none of the key witnesses in the Cornell, McVitie and Frank Mitchell cases dared talk. The Firm was keeping constant watch on all of them. Reggie was coming to his senses fast. The blonde who had stayed with him in Tangier was fond of him. 'He was so sad and such a lonely man. I never knew quite what he wanted – nor did he.' Once he stopped drinking he could be remarkably efficient. During this time he introduced fresh standing orders to the Firm: no risks or unknown propositions were to be accepted. Unnecessary violence would cease. Firearms and weapons were to be moved to safer hiding-places; no one would carry guns without an order from the twins. Telephones were for emergencies; conversations would be coded and kept short.

He understood the pressure there must be on Read to tie the case up quickly. This was to the twins' advantage: they could let everything tick over now indefinitely. All the Firm's energies could be used for keeping people 'loyal'. No one was permitted to forget that 'if we go, half London will go with us'.

So while Read and his men were rushing round the world and making do on four hours' sleep a night, the twins and their close followers could take life easy, with weekends in the country and most nights drinking. Their regular sources of income were so carefully tied up that money still came in with very little effort; not quite as much as in their wildest days, but still enough for most of what they wanted – and it was safe. The hard core of protection business stayed with them to the end. They had their bankers too, who were far more secure than ordinary banks.

'Banks are crooked as arseholes. Shop you to the law as soon as look at you. That's what they did with the Richardsons.'

Instead they had entrusted money to several of the rich men they had known, men who would always have enough to hide to make them vulnerable. Such men were useful in emergencies. Ronnie pulled one out of bed at 3 A.M. to write a cheque for several hundred pounds he needed. Another took care of the purchase of the house he chose in Suffolk.

'We've got no need to worry,' Ronnie said. 'Reg and me'll never go short of a bob or two.'

* * *

The Brooks at Bildeston, near Sudbury, was an unlikely place for his retirement; that was why Ronnie wanted it. This comfortable Victorian mansion set in a sleepy Suffolk village offered the perfect cover for the new life he was planning. The house was tile-hung and gabled, with long lawns, flower-beds, a paddock and a strip of woodland out beyond the billiard-room. The twins would come here for the weekend, bringing their favourite members of the Firm for company. While Nipper's men kept watch from the damp shrubberies Ronnie would play his latest part – the country squire. The police would see him as a burly man in tweeds, leaning on the white gate by the lodge, smoking a cigar or patting the donkey in the paddock. Sometimes he strolled down to the village for a drink, or wandered round his land swinging an ash-plant. He and the Firm began redecorating rooms; on Sundays everyone would eat a mammoth lunch cooked specially by Violet. Like a good cockney mother she would make the boys drink the 'greens water' the vegetables were cooked in. 'They needed all their vitamins these days.'

Nipper was getting worried now; he had to get results and the twins were being far too canny for his liking. Now that he had the broad foundations of his case he hoped to tempt them into making some mistake. Instead their cunning looked like saving them again. He couldn't know how brittle a façade their show of easy living was. The strain of the investigation was affecting them: behind the parties and the long weekends the twins were in the middle of another crisis.

Reggie, who had almost recovered from his bereavement, was all for caution. When he could bear to think about McVitie he was horrified, but the whole killing seemed so utterly unreal that he could usually avoid the memory of it. Most of the time he thought about survival and escape. He was in love again. It was the same old dream – only the girl was different. The idea of the understanding blonde was taking the place of Frances. Writing about her in a letter he said:

'I hope to settle in the country with Christine, get married and have a couple of children and leave the past behind me. Christine and I both like the country and I'm sure it's the best place for a fresh start. With her and some children and the country as our home, I know I will be happy. Meeting her has been a lucky break for me as she is a wonderful person. I intend to cut away from all my drinking companions in London. Recently I have had anonymous phone calls saying I'm going to be arrested soon, others saying I'm going to be shot or run down by a car.'

All Reggie wanted was to shut up shop, forget the past and vanish, but this hardly suited Ronnie. Reggie could not desert him now, when he needed him so much. This was the culmination of their lives. He had tried to make a man of him, but he was just a coward. How could he let Read frighten him? To show Reggie what he thought of the police he rang Harrods' pet department, knowing the Law had tapped the telephone. He asked for the most cunning snake they had. They sent a python round to Braithwaite House. He named it Read and sat for hours with it twined round his arm. He called it rude names and fed it live mice.

When the rows started over Reggie's girl or the need for caution Ronnie would scream that Reggie's fears were 'babyish'. Read was a snake and grown men weren't afraid of animals.

He would don his best suit, then stalk off through the streets of the East End under the noses of the police. Cautious no longer, he would be himself, scattering money, picking up his boys, wearing his heavy jewellery and dreaming of his grandest coup of all. He was still not quite sure what it would be, but he was burning with impatience. Time was short, the enemy was all around. He was an artist with his greatness to consider. Nothing he had done counted against what he could do if he put his mind to it.

Where Reggie thought of nothing but escape, Ronnie had everything worked out. Soon he would leave the East End for the house in Suffolk; it was to be a fortress and a pleasure house. To guard against his enemies he would have the house surrounded with an electrified fence. Mountings for searchlights and machine-guns were being fixed in the roof, steel shutters made for all the windows. There was to be a secret well, a hidden stock of food, a radio transmitter, an underground garage for his Rolls.

His parents were already living in the lodge on the estate, leaving the flat at Braithwaite House for him and Reggie when they wanted it. Within a few months a good-looking friend was coming out of prison; he would join Ronnie at the big house as servant and companion. They would have friends to stay, enjoy their boys, conduct their parties, live in style. But before that Ronnie had to fight his last big battle.

If Reggie had lost interest in his dreams, others could still appreciate them. Alan Bruce Cooper disappeared when Walker and his men swooped on his private bank; he seemed to have a knack of floating clear of trouble. Now he was back and Ronnie found in him the man he needed. Others saw Cooper as a stuttering American with thinning hair and wondered why he came to Whitechapel when he was clearly scared of Ronnie. He couldn't drink because he had an ulcer, so sat and smoked his long, thin Swiss cigars while Ronnie drank; he would talk, his sharp voice stuttering out details of international crimes, a twilight world of licensed killings, monumental deals, unmentionable men. This was what Ronnie longed to hear. Reggie was sceptical but Ronnie reminded him that the machine-guns Cooper sold them had certainly been genuine; so were his contacts with the Mafia, his various flats around the world and his big Rolls-Royce.

Sometimes, as if to prove that he was genuine, Cooper would bring photostats of Scotland Yard reports. These would invariably prove to be correct. At other times he would become the informed adviser, always impressing Ronnie with the need to think big. He kept insisting that Ronnie was on a par now with the top men in the Mafia and important Continental gangsters: he had the chance to be the man behind the scenes, building a syndicate of killers to work anywhere in Europe. Cooper could be the brains, Ronnie the power, living in the country like a gentleman, directing crimes that Scotland Yard would never hear of. As Cooper put it, Ronnie would soon be like the head of General Motors, president of a business corporation, working with international associates.

Reggie kept hearing rumours about Read. He dreamed of breaking free, but there was Ronnie: apart from all the ties that bound him to his twin, he knew that Ronnie on his own would certainly do something to involve them both. After McVitie's murder Reggie had to stay. All he could hope for was to hold on long enough for the investigation to blow over and for Read to be discredited again. He was a very anxious man, and sometimes questioned journalists and old friends from the past.

'What've you heard about the other side?' he'd ask. 'Is the Law cracking? What do people think about us? Do they believe we're as bad as the Richardsons?'

Ronnie had never cared about such things. He was becoming bored with Reggie's neat precautions. Cooper was giving him ideas. Reggie saw Cooper as a menace. How could they trust him? How could his brother know he wasn't working for the other side? For some while Ronnie sullenly refused to answer; he needed Cooper. Then to keep Reggie quiet he said he had a test for the American: murder.

* * *

A murder is the ultimate guarantee and test of criminal loyalty, since it remains the only crime no spy from the police can actually commit. In Cooper's case it had additional attractions. As well as testing him it would involve him, giving the twins a hold on him for the future: it would also offer Ronnie a chance to cross someone off his list at no risk to himself. Ronnie proposed the idea casually to Cooper early in January 1968. Cooper agreed.

The victim Ronnie chose was one whose death would place another gang firmly in his debt. He was a small-time London villain who some months earlier had started an underworld vendetta by firing a sawn-off shotgun into the groin of his young wife's lover. The wounded man was the brother of an important London gangster who was an ally of the twins. Already one man had been killed in error for revenge; Ronnie suggested that Cooper should get the right man.

Normally this would have been impossible: the man was hiding. But Ronnie knew that in two weeks he would appear in public, as a witness at the Old Bailey. Cooper seemed more than willing, treating the whole idea of killing him as a professional assignment; he said he had arranged a lot of murders in his time, but a killing at the Central Criminal Court was something of a challenge. He would employ one of his best men on the job; in the meantime he would work out the means of the perfect murder. Reggie was sceptical.

He began to change his mind a few days later when Cooper called at Braithwaite House to show them the weapon. This was no crude affair but a sophisticated means of killing a man in public with the minimum of risk. Cooper explained it as an old idea of his: the mechanism had been made to his design by one of the great specialists in the business.

Cooper produced a small attaché case covered in light-brown pigskin. He opened it. Inside was a hypodermic held by two steel clips. By the handle of the case there was a small brass ring. Cooper pulled it. The hypodermic slid forward so that the full length of the needle was projecting through a small hole at the corner of the case. He touched the needle; this released a spring within the case that worked the plunger. Cooper was very cool about it all. Reggie was intrigued and asked for a demonstration.

Cooper uncorked a bottle. Reggie sniffed. It smelled of almonds. Cooper said it was cyanide and filled the hypodermic. He set the spring, pulled the small ring by the handle and the twins saw the needle slide out from the corner of the case. He pushed it against the sofa and a thin jet squirted from the needle.

Cooper explained then how it could be used. 'Get close behind the man you want in a crowd. Pull the ring, jab the case against his leg, then make your getaway. He'll think that something's stung him; in five minutes he'll be dead. Symptoms will indicate a heart attack. Perfectly normal. Only a thorough autopsy would spot the pin-prick on the leg, and there would be no evidence of cyanide in the stomach.'

Plans for the perfect murder went ahead. Cooper brought the man who was to do the killing round to meet the twins. A tall, white-faced young man called Elvey, he seemed an unlikely murderer, but he was somehow in character with Cooper. He told the twins he had killed a lot of men. They spent some time together showing him photographs of the man he was to murder and having him taken to the Old Bailey.

But Elvey bungled it. He had his excuses, and explained that the man never appeared in the central lobby as the twins predicted. Cooper was angry but apologetic to the twins. He would immediately devise another means of murder.

A few days later he produced a high-powered hunting crossbow firing steel-tipped bolts lethal to fifty yards. Elvey had found out where the man was living; he would wait for him in his car, then shoot him silently in the street.

Again it was a plan that would appeal to Ronnie. He and Cooper spent a lot of time discussing it, but once again a last-minute hitch prevented Elvey making the kill. By now this hardly seemed to matter. Reggie was cynical, but Ronnie felt Cooper had established his credentials.

And then towards the end of January, with the police still waiting for the twins' next move, Cooper got his final hold on Ronnie. He seemed to take the place that Leslie Payne once held as father figure and adviser. Ronnie consulted him at any time of day or night: Cooper would always come, and always leave him happy. He seemed to understand him perfectly. Ronnie confided his ambitions to him. In return Cooper had the big ideas that Ronnie needed and seemed as thrilled as Ronnie by them all. They often talked about narcotics; Cooper had European contacts and clearly knew the market. This was the quickest, safest way for the twins to become millionaires. As a start Cooper suggested setting up a flat in Belgrave Square as a clearing-house for wealthy addicts and their pushers. Cooper got as far as renting the flat when Ronnie said he wasn't interested.

Other rackets they discussed were large-scale gold-smuggling, further currency deals, a takeover of an existing marijuana racket carried on through the diplomatic immunity of some Pakistani diplomats and the traffic in illegal Asian immigrants from Belgium. And each time it was Reggie's caution that prevented Ronnie from becoming involved.

Cooper was genuinely upset. Then he started talking of their oldest dream of all: the worldwide murder network operating with the Mafia and the European syndicates. The time had come, he said, for the twins to visit Paris and the States to arrange things personally.

In theory this was totally impossible. The United States rigidly excludes known criminals and the twins had Scotland Yard investigating them for almost every serious known crime, including murder. Yet Cooper solemnly suggested to the twins that they should fly to Paris, contact the leading gangsters in France, then travel to New York, where he would arrange more meetings with the top *Mafiosi* in America. Reggie thought he must be joking. When it was clear he was not, he said it was a trap. Ronnie replied that this was a risk worth taking; he trusted Cooper and could hardly wait to start the great new role he promised him. On 2 April Cooper and Ronnie Kray travelled to Paris on a scheduled flight and nobody stopped them.

As Reggie would not come, Ronnie brought an old friend, Dickie Morgan. Cooper had booked rooms in the Frontenac Hotel and seemed firmly in command. He took them out to dinner, talked of the possibilities of a European criminal common market – 'when you get trade between nations, crime follows' – and next morning introduced them to an impressive Frenchman with grey hair and a Brooklyn accent. This, Cooper said, was the man sent to meet them by the brothers who controlled crime in the city. He was a knowledgeable man. He talked of how he had killed various people in the States and had spent some years in San Quentin Prison before returning to France. Discussion followed on the sort of deals the Krays and the French gangs could fix together. The first need was for close liaison; Cooper said he was prepared to act as go-between. The Frenchman made it clear that several Continental gangs regarded England as an unexploited market: they thought the narcotics trade could easily be doubled overnight; expert criminals from Europe could fly in, commit a major theft and then fly back again; French gunmen could be used in England, goods stolen on the Continent disposed of there. They talked along these lines most of that day and visited the US consulate so that Ronnie Kray and Morgan could apply for visas. These were immediately granted – Cooper explained that the Paris consulate had no way of checking on the records of British citizens. Next morning all three flew from Orly to New York.

This was the life for Ronnie; this was better than cowering in Bethnal Green and worrying about Nipper Read.

Ronnie had always known that he was someone special, but it was still exciting to have this confirmed. Immigration gave him VIP treatment; there were no questions, no examination by the customs. Cooper explained that the Mafia had arranged things and their man was waiting. He was an old friend of the twins, a tiny Jewish Sicilian called Joe Kaufman. Ronnie had met him several times in London for business over gambling clubs and stolen bonds and Cooper said he had powerful connections with the Mafia.

As if to prove that Ronnie was the honoured guest of the Mafia, Kaufman then took over, driving them to town from the airport, booking them a suite at the Warwick Hotel and acting as their host. Kaufman is hospitable by nature. He has a pretty wife and knows a lot of people – gamblers, boxers, theatrical celebrities. With Ronnie he did all he could to make him happy, introducing him that night to several boxers, including Rocky Marciano, taking him to clubs where he could find a boy or two, and paying for the endless rounds of drinks. Cooper, on the other hand, seemed ill at ease. He spent a lot of time on the telephone. Morgan noticed that his stutter was worse. He kept reminding Ronnie that he had friends to contact.

Next day, when Ronnie started making his appointments, something had gone wrong. Angelo Bruno had mysteriously left town; so had the other leading *Mafiosi* Ronnie had met and entertained in London. Cooper suggested telephoning other friends long distance in Florida, and Las Vegas; George Raft would be glad to know Ronnie was in town. Ronnie might even make a trip to see him in Hollywood. When Cooper rang there was no reply.

It was Kaufman and not Cooper then who saved the day by driving Ronnie to Harlem and Brooklyn to meet some old-time criminals he knew. This was no top-line gathering of the Syndicate, but retired gunmen, former racketeers, old bootleggers. They were all characters willing to have a drink and ramble on about the old days and Ronnie got on well with all of them. One gave him details of how gang killings were organized by rival gangs and spent an afternoon offering technical advice about assassination; in return Ronnie gave him his star-shaped diamond ring. Later he met the bodyguard of one of the ward bosses of Harlem. Again they talked of killing; Ronnie gave the man his £800 white gold and diamond bracelet watch. Cooper seemed increasingly elusive but Ronnie was happy. He rang home to Reggie and his mother and that night went out again with Kaufman, drank, nightclubbed, saw Greenwich Village and a lot of 'interesting people'. At one club Kaufman asked him what he'd like. He answered, 'A brown boy about eighteen.' Cooper was the only one who didn't laugh; he was concerned that Ronnie wasn't seeing the men he'd come for.

The next few days were similar, with Ronnie in high spirits as they made the rounds of Brooklyn, Coney Island, Wall Street and Skid Row. He drank a lot, ate sparingly and met half the dead-beat criminals in New York City. New York appealed to him. He liked its size, its noise, its sense of possibility after the constraint of London. This was a holiday from Reggie and his worries, and from Scotland Yard. Kaufman was picking up the bills.

The only blot occurred when Morgan noticed they were being followed, always by the same two men looking suspiciously like plainclothes detectives. Ronnie was unconcerned, but on the night of 8 April they spotted them again waiting outside their nightclub in a dark-red Dodge. Morgan was certain they were tailing them all the way back to the Warwick, but Cooper said he couldn't see them; Kaufman thought them probably from the FBI.

Next day Cooper once more brought up the idea of flying

to Las Vegas. Ronnie announced that they were going home.

He came back to Bethnal Green in style, bounding with energy, laden with cigars, transistor radios, a big woolly dog for Violet, a stainless steel model of a knight in armour for Reggie. If his absence had proved anything, it was how much the Firm and his family relied on him for their existence. Ronnie was the centre of their lives. Rumours had started that he had cut and run for it; only three people in the Firm had known he was in New York. Tommy Cowley, one of the shrewdest members of the Firm, had decamped instantly for Majorca; most of the remainder started worrying about the future. Even Reggie had fleetingly thought of making his escape and asked Tom Mangold of the BBC, who was off to the Far East on an assignment, if there were any way of getting out to Vietnam as a volunteer.

The police had also been getting anxious over Ronnie's absence. Amazingly, for all the supervision of Tintagel House, none of them had known Ronnie had given them the slip and turned up in New York. Nipper did not discover this until some time later. So at first there was considerable concern that the prime suspect of their mammoth inquiry had disappeared. Just for a moment it had seemed as if this might be a new trick of the twins': everyone knew there could be no question of arresting one while the other was at liberty to scare their witnesses.

So Ronnie's return pleased everyone and as he went into action he had the edge on Reggie. He was the hero proving everybody's fears were groundless. Although he had not met the Mafia leaders, the trip had been a great adventure. His fantasy was coming true. He could do anything. While all the rest of them were cowering from Read and Scotland Yard he had been to America under the very noses of the police. This was the way a man should be – killing his enemies openly, taking money where he found it, drinking, enjoying sex, insulting the police just as his Aunt Rose did. A few days after his return he saw the film of Charlton Heston playing Gordon of Khartoum and came out of the cinema with tears still in his eyes.

'Gordon was a real man. He did what he had to do and he was bent like me. When I go I hope I face it just like Gordon did.'

There was no excuse for cowering pathetically until the police arrived to pick him up.

This meant an end of Reggie's siege tactics: after America, Ronnie was thinking big, and in place of caution, silence, avoidance of all risk, he was eager for a full offensive by the Firm. Now was the time to streamline crime as he had heard they did it in the States. Big crime should be big business.

On the return from New York Cooper had flown on to the Continent for business of his own, but when he came back he agreed with Ronnie – reorganize the Firm on strict American lines, kick out the useless hangers-on, get working with a nucleus of tough professionals. There were whole areas of humdrum life waiting to be exploited on the American pattern – unions, taxis, building sites, the docks. What with their reputation and their knowledge the twins could treble their income in six months.

This could keep Reggie occupied; the idea of tying up the docks appealed to him. He made discreet inquiries among a number of top businessmen and politicians to see whether the docks' management could use a properly organized force of strong-arm men in the next labour dispute. Drawing a blank, he tried the unions – also without success. Finally he persuaded some rich businessmen to start a moneylending business in the docks; the twins would back it with a loan repayment service of their own.

All this kept Reggie busy; Ronnie needed something more dramatic. Cooper kept telling him the time had come to show the world the Krays ruled London. He knew exactly how to work on Ronnie now. Maybe, he said, those *Mafiosi* in New York had picked up rumours that the Krays were slipping, that the police would soon be catching up with them. This might have been the reason why none of them had been over-anxious to meet him.

Ronnie was furious. In New York, it hadn't mattered who had entertained him. He had enjoyed meeting the men he did. But he could see that Cooper could be right. The only language the Americans understood was power: a few efficient killings would restore their faith in the Krays better than any arguments.

As a beginning Cooper suggested Ronnie should do the Americans a favour. A well-known Las Vegas gambler and club-owner had been challenging the Mafia. The man lived part of each year in Kenya and was staying at the moment at the London Hilton. If the Krays quietly eliminated him it would be excellent publicity throughout the States and would also place the Mafia in Ronnie's debt. Ronnie agreed and promptly made his plans. The man took an early morning constitutional in Hyde Park, so Ronnie arranged to have him shot by a marksman from a passing car. But this was a wary man and an unwilling victim, who seemed to know how to avoid presenting himself as a target: after several failures, Ronnie saw that if he wanted a dramatic killing to impress the underworld he must look elsewhere. Somebody suggested Caruana.

George Caruana was Maltese and a West End club-owner – a big, good-looking man. Recently there had been talk of trouble between him and another club-owner. Now came a rumour of an offer of £1,000 for anyone who killed him.

It seemed an economic proposition for the Firm. Ronnie had no strong feelings about Caruana, but a quick £1,000 was always useful and it was necessary to get his message over to the Mafia. As Cooper kept reminding him, the question of which London gang was to look after the big gambling junkets from the States was still not settled.

Ever since Ronnie had read his earliest books about Chicago gangsters he had dreamed of blowing someone up inside a car. In Sicily and the States it is a well-proved Mafia mode of death, but London gangsters had been slow to use it. George Caruana drove a bright-red Mini. This could give Ronnie his big chance to show that the Krays believed in progress.

There is no great problem in wiring a detonator and a parcel of explosive into the circuit of a car, but Ronnie had never been good with his hands, nor were there any real technicians on the Firm. Once more he had to turn to Cooper, and once more Cooper brought in the strange young man, Paul Elvey. Apart from all his other skills, Elvey was a qualified electrical engineer.

Eight months had passed since Nipper Read had taken charge of the inquiry against the twins, eight months in which his men had most methodically built up a dossier on their history and then ground to an almost total halt. There was a mass of detailed statements against them filed in Tintagel House, but until the twins were safely locked away none could be used. Also the great investigation, for all its thoroughness, seemed to have missed the biggest crimes: there was no evidence linking the twins with Cornell's or McVitie's murders; there was no hint of what happened to Jack Frost, Mad Teddy Smith or the Axe Man; no link had been established between the twins and the Clapham leader, Frederic Foreman, later to be charged with murdering Frank Mitchell and disposing of McVitie's body.

Hopeful as ever, the police were waiting for the twins to make their big mistake. Nipper was adamant that nothing must be done to scare them now or put them on their guard; the police were kept away from them, and the twins saw no sign that the whole of Scotland Yard was waiting to arrest them. As a result it seemed that they were living in a sort of limbo-land: they had their freedom but there was a shadow enemy who had to be imagined listening on every telephone, watching from doorways, never leaving them alone.

Reggie was rational enough but Ronnie made this limbo world his own, an airless, haunted place devoid of ordinary feeling: killing was normal, cunning and violence the only ways of striking at the unseen threat of an unseen enemy. As the twins stood in the bar of a pub in Bethnal Green with Cooper and Elvey, planning another killing, all Ronnie's fantasies seemed to have turned into reality. Reggie was opposed to the idea of killing Caruana but unable to stand up to his brother. Cooper could have been the stuttering echo of Ronnie's madness; Elvey was nothing but a bespectacled technician.

Ronnie had photographs of Caruana, a quiet-looking man with a plump face; next day he would arrange for someone on the Firm to take Elvey to see him in the flesh. Then the talk turned to the question of explosives. Ronnie explained that there was gelignite available: Cooper was not impressed. Gelignite was tricky stuff to use; dynamite was safer. He had a source in Scotland; Elvey could easily fly up to fetch it.

And so the plans for blowing up George Caruana in his Mini went ahead.

The next day Elvey, waiting in his raincoat outside the Dominion Cinema in Tottenham Court Road, was picked up by a former boxer from the Firm and driven through Soho. The former boxer showed him where the Mini was always parked; a little farther on a man was standing in the doorway of a club – George Caruana. They slowed down to let Elvey see the face he was to destroy with dynamite.

Two days later Elvey took the morning flight from Heathrow up to Glasgow, collected four sticks of dynamite from an address in the centre of the city and caught a taxi back to the airport. As he was boarding the London plane the police arrested him. Later that evening Nipper Read interrogated him.

SIXTEEN

Arrest

The strange stalemate was over: the twins had made the blunder Nipper had been waiting for. Elvey confessed to everything, not just the plans for the Caruana murder but the suitcase murder and the crossbow killing. Nipper had known nothing about these murder plans and until he searched Elvey's house was inclined to treat him as something of a crank; but he found the crossbow, the suitcase with the hypodermic and the cyanide. Elvey named Cooper as the brains behind it all, so Cooper was brought in for questioning.

It was a stormy interview, with Nipper threatening to charge him straight away with three attempted murders and Cooper replying coolly that he could prove that for the last two years he had been working with the Yard.

Cooper's story was as follows; he admitted that his first contacts with the twins had been criminal, during the days when he was marketing stolen Canadian bonds for them through his European Exchange Bank; but soon after this, agents of the United States Treasury Department discovered proof of his activities as a gold-smuggler and offered him the choice of facing charges or working for them. He chose to work for them as spy and *agent provocateur*. He was controlled from Paris by an undercover agent attached to the United States embassy; this man controlled the Treasury Department's work in Europe. His chief concern was combating the narcotics trade to the United States.

The Krays' connections with the American Mafia

appeared important in America, and the Treasury Department was disturbed. Cooper had already been minimally involved since the stolen shares originated from a Mafia subsidiary in New York. He agreed to keep in touch with the twins and keep the Paris embassy informed of fresh developments: meetings between the twins and Bruno and other leading *Mafiosi* visiting London were all reported back to Paris; so were the Krays' involvements with the Mafia over their London gambling interests.

According to his story, Cooper's American employers had allowed him considerable latitude in handling the Krays and he went to great lengths now to win their confidence. He said his Paris contact knew that he – a US agent now – supplied the twins with the two Browning machine-guns and paid for them from US government funds. He also claimed he had done his best to make sure that the other weapons he supplied were faulty: the .32 automatic which jammed when Reggie tried to shoot McVitie was one of his; so was the gun which failed to shoot George Dixon.

He said that at the start the US Treasury Department had informed the Yard of his presence with the Krays. Du Rose, he said, knew all about him. He also said that no one at the Yard had trusted him and Nipper had been told nothing of the plot. As a result he had found himself in the unenviable position of 'the man on the tightrope', balancing between two homicidal gangsters who would kill him if they found out what he was and a police force who would do nothing for him. And all the time, the Americans in Paris wanted action.

At first he tried 'setting up' the twins, involving them in some big crooked deal so that he could betray them to the police. Several times he seemed to have persuaded Ronnie, only to have Reggie stopping things from going any further. Then came the trip to Paris and New York, over which Cooper and the US Treasury Department took a lot of trouble. Cooper had flown several times to

Washington to fix the details. The man in Paris arranged the visas and an actor friend of Cooper's played the part of the killer from San Quentin to perfection. Cooper was hoping that once they reached New York he could offer the FBI a grand slam of compromising link-ups with the top syndicate bosses of America – 'We were counting on Ronnie meeting Meyer Lansky, the Las Vegas people, Angelo Bruno and the Gallo Brothers. But Ronnie was so hot that none of them would risk seeing him.'

As for the three murder plans, Cooper insisted that all of them had been essential to retain the twins' confidence. All had to be sufficiently feasible for Ronnie to think of Cooper as a fellow murderer. This was the basis of their friendship; it would have been fatal had he doubted him. The cyanide needed to be genuine, the crossbow capable of killing. Elvey, too, needed to be convinced that the murders were in earnest. Cooper could never risk taking an accomplice into his confidence, so he chose Elvey because he knew he was hard up but incapable of killing anyone. Elvey was such a bungler that anything he did was bound to fail.

Cooper had known the risks he was taking but his American employers still held the threat of possible imprisonment against him should he back out now. When he was with the twins he was entirely alone. 'The Americans couldn't help me, the Yard didn't trust me, and I knew that once I slipped up with the twins, I'd soon be propping up a bridge.'

Read was furious; here was he working for eight months on a major investigation of the two most dangerous men in Britain only to discover that this so-called American agent had been quietly planning sophisticated killings totally without his knowledge. Backed by American government money, Cooper had supplied them arms and machine-guns, taken Ronnie to New York and encouraged them in countless crimes.

The truth of Cooper's story will always be something of a mystery. He claims that someone in the Yard supplied him information to pass on to the twins; the Yard denies this. One police view of him is that he was a lone operator who had the nerve to play off the Krays, the American government and Scotland Yard against each other for his private interests. What is quite indisputable is that he was employed by the US Treasury Department and that the killings and the crimes he helped set up for the twins could certainly have taken place with anyone but Elvey as the killer. It is also indisputable that part of Scotland Yard knew who he was. Cooper claims: 'From the very start I was working for John du Rose.'

Quite how much that shrewd old man knew about Alan Cooper is another of the mysteries of the case. When asked, he smiled enigmatically.

Cooper is more specific. 'Du Rose is straight and hard and a hundred per cent. He was the man who really caught the Krays.' But even so, Cooper admits he could not tell du Rose everything. Du Rose knew in advance about the New York trip; he knew the Paris agent personally and understood that Cooper was trying to implicate the twins. Beyond this Cooper had been on his own; he felt he could not risk telling even du Rose about the murder set-ups because of the danger of security leaks.

John du Rose, it seems, had tolerated Cooper's presence, and not trusted him. Nipper had not been encouraged to get near him; Cooper had been a spy. A keen fisherman, John du Rose had known when to fish with several hooks.

For all his resentment and undisguised dislike of Cooper, Nipper could not ignore him now, for Cooper had in fact succeeded. By leading Ronnie Kray to Caruana and helping him set up a murder, he had produced that final break in the twins' defences everybody wanted.

Cooper maintained it had been a blunder to arrest Elvey; but for this one mistake he could have delivered the twins red-handed to the Yard for attempted murder. Now they were warned; Ronnie's great mood of daring which Cooper had carefully built up was rapidly dispelled; Reggie was back in charge and pulling up the drawbridge; there would be no more mistakes as the Firm looked to its defences.

Cooper offered to go back to Bethnal Green and try to implicate the twins again; he was convinced he still possessed sufficient hold on Ronnie to make this possible. Nipper refused to let him go; now he had Cooper he was holding on to him. So while the twins were anxiously sending out their spies for news, Cooper, the ex-gold-smuggler, sat doing nothing in a small hotel in Kent. He had his wife, his Yorkshire terrier, a police guard on the door and a stock of Swiss cigars. Despite all this he was soon bored and frustrated; relations with Read deteriorated. Neither felt the need to be polite; Cooper believed Scotland Yard was 'bone-headed, incompetent, inflexible'; Nipper made it plain that Cooper was under his orders, that he didn't trust him and was making sure from now on that he worked for him alone.

But Nipper knew that even now Cooper remained his best hope of catching the twins; for Cooper was still in touch with them. Every morning he had been ringing them from the hotel and telling them he wasn't well and was having a short holiday in the country with his wife. Nipper had listened in to all these conversations. There was no mistaking the twins' eagerness to see Alan Cooper now as soon as possible.

This was what Nipper banked on when he made his final plans to trap the twins. Cooper was told to exaggerate his illness when next he spoke to them, saying his stomach ulcer was causing him real pain. At the same time Nipper booked a pair of adjoining rooms in a nursing home in Harley Street. Cooper was brought up to the Burford Bridge Hotel below Box Hill. From here he rang the twins again saying that in the night his ulcer had burst. Ronnie was sympathetic and said he would like to come and see him. Cooper said that when he was a little better that would be wonderful. Next day he rang from the nursing home in London.

Nipper prepared the trap convincingly. Cooper was in bed in pyjamas, surrounded with flowers, medicine bottles, temperature charts. Nipper and his deputy, Frank Cater, were in the room next door recording everything from a microphone by Cooper's bed. Nurses and doctors were all taken in, but this time when Cooper rang the Krays, Ronnie was cagey and replied he might be able to come round. Cooper was set to do his best to incriminate him when he came, but late that afternoon it was not Ronnie but Reggie's friend Tommy Cowley who arrived. Cooper tried drawing him out about the twins but Cowley was too sharp. He went back and told the twins that Cooper's nursing home smelt of the police. From then on the line from Cooper to the twins went dead.

The one success Nipper could claim for all his trouble was with little Joe Kaufman. While in New York Cooper had made arrangements with him about another parcel of stolen securities from New York. Cooper was hoping he would bring them with him when he arrived in London. When Cooper spoke to him at the Mayfair Hotel he learned that they were being posted. When Kaufman came to the nursing home, the police in the next-door room to Cooper recorded the conversation.

By May it looked as if the twins had got away again. Every conceivable way of catching them seemed to have misfired. They were alerted now. Cooper could no longer get near them and the real crisis was not for the twins but for the police. Nipper's investigation was now in its ninth month, and seemed to have yielded all it could. The hope the twins would make some fatal error if the police were patient seemed no longer feasible.

The twins were quietly confident and seemed to understand that they had been luckier than they had any right to expect. Reggie felt safer with Cooper off the scene; Ronnie had a new blond boy and was turning his attention to home-making – homicide could wait. The house at Bildeston was pretty in the spring. Reggie was confident that nobody would talk; furthermore he had been hearing rumours of a despondent Nipper Read. Maybe they were true. The twins spent the first weekend of May at Bildeston with several of the Firm. Violet as usual cooked them lunch; the sun shone, Reggie felt that now that Ronnie had his country house life could settle down. Ronnie's great friend 'Duke' Osborne would soon be out of gaol; Reggie might yet marry blonde Christine, live in the country and have children.

It was du Rose who called the conference on the twins. He knew that something must be done about them now if they were ever to be caught; as a policeman he also knew that a point arrives in all police investigations when one must cut one's losses. There had been blunders, but despite them all, the law still had some firm advantages. Nipper's plan for using Cooper at the nursing home had not worked, but Cooper on his own could still provide crucial evidence. There was the evidence of Elvey; there were the suitcase and the crossbow, and Payne could give the facts about the long-firm frauds. Maybe the case was flimsy as it stood, but these were serious charges, certainly strong enough to ensure that the twins would be remanded without bail when charged. This would immediately unlock the safety clause from Nipper's mass of statements; his undercover witnesses could make their statements openly and add their evidence to the charges against the twins. From then on everything would depend on how much more the police could rapidly uncover.

Superintendent Harry Mooney felt that once the twins were safely behind bars he could persuade the barmaid of The Blind Beggar to give enough evidence to convict

Ronnie of murdering George Cornell. Apart from this the police still had little to connect the twins with any of their major crimes.

It was an uncomfortable gamble Nipper had to take. The twins had shown their cleverness in the past at dodging firmer evidence than this. If they did again Scotland Yard, as one detective put it, 'might just as well put up the shutters and go home for good'.

On the night of 8 May 1968 none of the police from Tintagel House went home. John du Rose and Read had been there since early afternoon. With them were the other senior officers on the case – Superintendent Donald Adams who had supervised the paperwork, Superintendent Harry Mooney, who performed much of the investigation, and Read's assistant, Chief Inspector Frank Cater. Soon after dark, fresh police began arriving from the regions: more than sixty of them, all with their cars and two-way radios, none of them knowing why they'd come. Strict security was enforced. Once they had parked their cars they were conducted to the big main office with the view of the river; they were served sandwiches and coffee, and then locked in. No private telephone calls were allowed; they were warned they would not be getting any sleep that night.

Soon after midnight the main conference began: John du Rose announced that the three Kray brothers and their gang were to be arrested at dawn. Some might be violent and the police must be prepared. The success or failure of the operation would depend on making sure that everyone on the police list was rounded up at once. In all there were twenty-six names to be accounted for.

Nipper spoke next, standing on a filing cabinet; he was crisp and lucid, very different in his young man's way from the old-style Yard man, John du Rose. He was in his element as the perfect staff officer allocating duties and outlining the whole complex operation. Twenty-four separate addresses across London had to be raided simultaneously. Since early morning the Krays had been under constant observation. At that moment they were in a nightclub in the West End. When they went home central control would be informed. Provided nothing unexpected happened all the arrests were to be synchronized for 6.00 A.M. No member of the Firm must be allowed to warn another. Once arrested they would be brought immediately to West End Central Police Station.

Nipper had had index cards prepared with photographs of all the wanted men, along with their addresses and particulars. These were distributed among the raiding-party. Somebody asked who would be going for the twins. That, explained Nipper Read, was a privilege he was reserving for himself.

The twins were entertaining Kaufman. They started drinking at The Old Horns pub off Bethnal Green Road at 9.00 P.M. It was a gala night. Ronnie was anxious to show Kaufman the two sides of London, the beery *bonhomie* of the East End and the bright lights of Mayfair. Kaufman was happy to be back in London, but both twins appeared preoccupied. There had been rumours of fresh trouble from the police. Reggie suspected Cooper of betrayal since his Soho office was still heavily guarded by police. Reggie's girl was on holiday in Spain; rumour had it that the affair was over.

At closing time, as they all left their private bar at The Old Horns, none of the Firm noticed the courting couple in the back of the car parked opposite; a detective and a policewoman from Tintagel House hard at work keeping the twins under observation. But at the Astor Club Reggie was jumpier than usual: when a photographer insisted on taking flashlight photographs of him and his guests he became aggressive. Ronnie calmed him down. Ronnie was happy. It was 5 A.M. before Tintagel House had its report that the twins and the Firm had just left and were on their way home.

Nipper was armed when they smashed in the door at Braithwaite House two hours later and rushed in for the twins. It was not necessary. Both were fast asleep, Reggie with a girl from Walthamstow, Ronnie with his latest fair-haired boy. Read had the handcuffs on the twins before they had really woken up. His was the first car back to West End Central.

SEVENTEEN

Retribution

When Nipper Read hauled the twins from their beds on 9 May 1968 their power was by no means over and the police were taking a considerable gamble. Thanks, largely, to Alan Cooper there was sufficient evidence about the crossbow and the murder suitcase to keep the twins and all the Firm in prison on remand, and make sure they came to trial before a magistrate. That was all. The police possessed no proof of murder yet; much of the existing evidence connecting them with the bond deals and frauds was complex and obscure, while Cooper on his own was a distinctly shaky witness for a major trial. Nobody needed to tell Nipper Read what this meant. On the existing evidence, the twins might get five years apiece if the police were lucky; and if they weren't, there was nothing to prevent them repeating their performance at the McCowan trial and once again emerging from the court scot-free. Recognizing this, the police began the last and crucial stage of their investigation.

They had the few weeks before the preliminary hearings to clinch their case and persuade their major witnesses to talk. They knew exactly who they were, but had to be able to assure them that this time the twins were finished. Otherwise, as one old cockney put it, 'if people talk to the police and the twins get off again, they'll have to send the plague carts into Bethnal Green and shout, "Bring out your dead!"'

With so much at stake the police meant business. A top

Scotland Yard detective talked of 'driving the Krays and all they stand for into the ground'. To do this the Yard was finally prepared to use its full resources, and the investigation had the highest backing. Through contacts in the underworld, warnings were sent out that the police would tolerate no nonsense on the Krays' behalf from other criminals. Witnesses were offered round-the-clock protection. The police were set to crack the Kray twins' 'wall of silence' and challenge time-honoured myths of East End villainy – the idea that East Enders never 'grassed', that there would be a terrible revenge on those that did, and that the police were a common enemy.

Their task was not going to be easy, and at this stage the twins appeared confident and in high spirits. Since their arrest they were both in Brixton Gaol, but even here there was a lot they could do. As they were still technically innocent they had more privileges than other prisoners. They wore their own clothes, and could have alcohol and cigarettes and food brought in from outside. This helped to keep up their morale and, more important still, they both were allowed as many visitors and letters as they wanted.

As a result the two of them maintained something of a court in Brixton. They were celebrities as well as prisoners. The warders treated them with definite respect, and the twins managed to make it seem that they were still the centre of a rich and influential world. Most days Violet would organize cold chicken dinners and a glass of wine for them and for each member of the Firm. Actors and pop singers wrote to them, boxers and film producers came to visit them, and all the time the twins seemed calm and unconcerned about the future. Although the key members of the Firm were nearly all in prison too, there were enough old friends visiting Brixton to ensure that their messages were circulated round the East End. Soon the twins' confident demeanour seemed to be having its effect.

'The law may think they're clever,' said one old lag who visited them, 'but those twins can still run bloody circles round 'em. You'll see. The twins have got so many strings to pull, so many important people they can ruin, that in the end you'll find that Scotland Yard won't dare go on with it. The twins have had their plans in readiness for years. In three months they'll be back amongst us. And they'll remember who their friends were, mark my words.'

There seemed a chance that he was right. Why else should the twins appear so cheerful at a time like this? For most of May people in Bethnal Green who knew them seemed to be waiting to see which way things would go.

There were naturally a lot of rumours – most of them in favour of the twins. From Brixton they were hard at work directing what they called their 'propaganda war' against the enemy. But soon there were clearer indications that the Krays were losing their last battle. For some time one of their strongest cards had been the presence of two of the most powerful members of the Firm at liberty. Their young cousin, Ronnie Hart and Scotch Ian Barrie, who was with Ronnie when Cornell was murdered, had both escaped the 6 A.M. arrests on 9 May. Both were considered dangerous, and the knowledge that they were free must have scared many of Nipper Read's potential witnesses. There was a strong rumour that the twins had specially arranged for them to avoid arrest to guard their interests. They were reported to be armed and in secret touch with Brixton.

Hart was the first to go – the police found him hiding miserably with his girl-friend in a caravan. He confessed everything without a struggle. Then a few days later Barrie was spotted in the East End. He was drunk, broke and lost without the twins. Like Hart he put up no resistance. With these last members of the Firm in gaol, the idea of the twins' 'reprisal force' was quietly forgotten. People began to doubt the existence of the 'emergency plans' the twins had always claimed to have prepared for their arrest.

Criminals are realists. During these first few weeks after the twins' arrest, the con men, club-owners, racketeers who for years had provided their regular income had prudently been honouring old arrangements. Now they were forgetting them. So were the wealthy businessmen with whom the twins had 'banked' their money for emergencies like this. The vast amounts of money that the twins had taken had been squandered. Nothing was in reserve. The house in Suffolk was made ready to be sold, and then came the ultimate indignity – the twins applied for legal aid for their defence.

When the trial opened on 6 July it began before the Metropolitan Chief Magistrate at Old Street, Mr Frank Milton. Legally the purpose of this preliminary hearing was to discover if there was a case for the twins to answer at a superior court. But both the twins and the police were set to make these hearings something of a demonstration from the start. For the police this took the form of a massed show of force reminiscent of the precautions the Italian *carabinieri* mount for an important Mafia trial in Palermo. The court was in a state of siege, with police everywhere. Witnesses were closely guarded and produced in court from secret hideouts. The twins and their supporters were whisked straight from prison in a high-speed convoy, guarded by outriders and an élite task-force of police. It was a compliment of a sort to the legend of their power. The police were treating them like a hostile force still capable of challenging the State.

In response to this the twins decided they would waive the traditional ban on reporting from these preliminary hearings. It was a gesture. 'We want the world to see the diabolical liberties the law's been taking,' Reggie said. They also wanted their publicity. Once the case started it would soon be clear that they did not have much else. The 'driving of the Krays into the ground' had started. Nipper Read had gone to town, and the twins soon knew it.

Set-faced, unsmiling in the front row of the dock, they found themselves up against something they had never faced before – denunciations from their former friends who had 'gone over to the enemy'. One of the first was a man called Billy Exley, one-time lightweight boxer, thief and bodyguard of Ronnie's. His abrupt appearance in court was carefully stage-managed and most dramatic. The twins had no idea that he had turned against them. As far as they knew Exley had stayed absolutely loyal. Before he appeared in the dock the prosecution had announced that the next witness was suffering from an acute heart condition. A chair was placed in the witness-box, along with a microphone. Then in shuffled Exley, looking deathly pale. The twins watched, stony-faced, and in the hush that filled the court Exley began his evidence on how he used to run their long-firm frauds.

But his appearance meant considerably more than what he said about the frauds. He seemed to speak with difficulty. The court was warned he might drop dead any moment, so that his words seemed like the voice of conscience from the tomb. It was impressive that a man like Exley felt an obligation to recant before he died and name his former friends as evil men. What must have shocked the twins was the thought of all their other secrets he could reveal to the Law. Exley knew the truth about Cornell. Exley was the man who stayed on guard at Vallance Road armed with a shotgun on the night of the murder. Exley had helped to guard Frank Mitchell. If the police had him on their side, they must already know far more than had seemed possible when the case opened.

But the police had more than Exley, and in the days that followed it was clear that the Krays' wall of silence had collapsed. Forgotten victims, former accomplices trooped through the witness-box. The underworld was talking. From this point on the twins knew there were no secrets they could count on keeping. Most dangerous of all for them was the surprise appearance of the frightened barmaid from The Blind Beggar. Previously she had failed to identify Ronnie on the identity parade held after Cornell's murder. Since then Superintendent Harry Mooney had won her confidence and managed to convince her that she had nothing to fear from telling what she saw on the night of the killing. Now in the witness-box she claimed that the twins had scared her into silence, but in fact she had clearly recognized Ronnie and Ian Barrie as the men who fired the shots.

This was the true turning-point in the trial. Until now the twins still had a slender chance that the key witnesses might hold back. Now it was clear that the police had all the evidence required to destroy them. The only questions now were how much more the police investigations would reveal, and whether the twins could spring any surprises in their defence.

Their trial at the Old Bailey started in the New Year of 1969 and was to prove the longest, most expensive criminal trial to date in British history. By now the situation was quite different from the first days of the twins' arrest. The police had done their work – the case against them was complete. The twins had changed too during the eight months they had spent in Brixton on remand. The optimistic messages had ceased and both seemed quietly resigned to a long spell in prison. They were already turning their attention to their return to freedom some time in middle age, and for both of them the idea of crime was over. Reggie's dream still meant marrying Christine and starting a family somewhere in the country. Ronnie for once appeared more practical: 'I'll have grey hair by then, but grey's distinguished on a man. There'll be a spot of money still around and I'll find myself a nice boy and sail off round the world with him. There's still a lot I want to see and do with my life.'

In the meantime there was the trial to think about, and the twins seemed far more convinced with their lasting reputation than with mere details of defence. Since they believed the outcome more or less decided, they would concentrate on the impression they would leave posterity.

This was the moment when they sealed their myth. What they wanted was to be remembered as the greatest undefeated heavyweights of crime.

The attitude of the police towards the trial was not dissimilar, and like the twins they also wanted it to be something of a demonstration – in their case of the power of the Law, a full-scale warning for all future violent gangsters.

This explains much of what happened during the long weeks ahead in Number One Court. The first case to be heard consisted of a double murder – the Cornell and the McVitie killings were taken together. Reggie was accused as an accessory to the Cornell crime for knowingly helping Ronnie after his escape. And although Reggie was accused of killing McVitie with his brother's help, there was a group of other alleged accessories with them in the dock – Bender and the Lambrianou brothers, young Tony Barry, who was charged with bringing round the gun from The Regency, the twins' brother Charlie Kray and his friend Frederick Foreman, both of them charged with getting rid of Jack McVitie's body.

But from the moment the accused filed into the cage-like dock of the Old Bailey their greatest worry must have been the two men who were no longer with them – Scotch Jack Dickson, who had driven Ronnie to The Blind Beggar, and the twins' cousin, Ronnie Hart. Nipper Read had done his work efficiently – Dickson and Hart had both 'gone over to the other side' and turned Queen's evidence. Both were to be major witnesses for the police.

It was a long, long trial with little subtlety. The judge was Mr Melford Stevenson, a brisk old gentleman with a reputation as something of a 'hard' judge; from the beginning he was concise, concerned with facts. The prosecuting counsel, Mr Kenneth Jones, QC, was a plump, sonorous Welshman, 'somewhat afflicted', as he put it, 'with a want of height'. Like both the judge and the police, his main concern appeared to be with facts, although he was not above a certain lumbering theatricality to drive home the full horror of the evidence.

'Gentlemen of the jury, think for a moment of the horrifying effrontery, the terrifying effrontery of this deed. Two men can walk into a public house on any evening and there in cold blood kill another human being. You may well ask, who within striking distance would be safe? Who would come before the court and have the courage to say who the killers were? Cornell's companions took to their heels, but I will bring before you the barmaid, and she will tell you that she recognizes the killer of George Cornell.'

The greater the horror and the melodrama, the more it suited Ronnie. Shooting Cornell had been the greatest moment of his life – he felt that he was justified, and here it was being publicly acknowledged. This was almost fame enough.

All the defence could do was attack witnesses – Ronnie enjoyed this, too, for these were all people that he hated: they had betrayed him.

'So, Mr Hart, you admit that you have given all this evidence to save your own skin?'

'Not to save my skin, but because I thought it right.'

'But, just the same, because you thought it right, you have saved yourself from sitting in the dock beside the men you are accusing? Answer me please, Mr Hart.'

This sort of sniping could go on for ever; at times it seemed as if it would. When all the trials ended, twenty-eight criminals had been allowed to save themselves by giving evidence against the twins. Often it was hard to know which was the more nauseating – the crime or the unction of the man denouncing it. All these turncoats in the witness-box spoke vehemently against the twins – they had to justify themselves and had a bigger stake than anyone in seeing that their former friends were put away for good.

What Nipper Read had told the lawyers at New Scotland

Yard more than a year before was proving quite correct. The twins, it seemed, could be condemned only with the help of other criminals' evidence. Such criminals could be shown up for what they were, but their combined evidence could not be totally discredited.

The defence was led by John Platts-Mills, QC, for Ronnie: Paul Wrightson, QC, appeared for Reggie. Much of their time and energy in court was spent attacking witnesses and impugning the methods of the police – without conspicuous success. This trial was shedding little lustre on the Law, but Nipper and his men appeared to have worked scrupulously 'in their sewers'; it was a dirty business, but the essential facts could not be challenged.

Beyond this there seemed no particular plan of defence, only this endless war of somnolent attrition, with the twins at the centre of it, becoming less credible with every day that passed.

Ronnie made one unforgettable appearance in the witness-box as the case neared its end. People who knew him understood that this was the moment he had been waiting for and there was speculation over what would happen. If the twins really had some secret up their sleeves, now was the time to use it. Now was the time to mention all those public figures he had threatened to expose. It was also the point where he might have tried to put his own case forward, to enlist some public sympathy.

None of this was what he wanted. It would have seemed petty to give trouble to the many celebrities he could have named as his friends or to stir up scandals now. It would have been easy, but this wasn't how he wished to be remembered. Nor did he want the straight world's sympathy – still less its understanding. He was a criminal and he would act like one.

He was immaculately dressed – the usual dark-blue suit, white shirt and tightly knotted tie. He also wore his gold-rimmed spectacles. These made him look particularly sinister. His face showed no emotion as he began answering his counsel's questions. His voice was expressionless and flat and he seemed short of breath. But soon he began to dominate the court. He denied everything alleged against him. He and Cornell were friends. He never even entered The Blind Beggar on the night of 8 March 1966. After the mass of prosecution evidence there was a calm effrontery about anyone who could lie on such a scale. And it was not done meekly or apologetically, but with an undiminished hatred for all who stood against him. This hatred seemed a sort of pride. After the indignities of his defeat, the betrayals of his followers, he was admitting nothing and regretting nothing. If people said he was a murderer, let them prove it.

Under cross-examination by the prosecution he became still more confident. This was presumably what the prosecution wanted, for his attitude confirmed everything the court had heard against him. He was crude, sneering, violent, but at the same time he was trying to present the public self that he aspired to: arrogant and unconcerned, denying everything, friend of the famous – ('If I wasn't here, I'd probably be drinking with Judy Garland now') – benefactor of the poor and victim of the police.

What made the trial so strange was that the public image of the twins was all that anybody saw or mentioned. There were a few occasions when just a glimmer of their real selves broke through, usually in anger when they lost control: Ronnie beside himself with rage, calling the prosecuting counsel 'you fat slob' because the police had confiscated his grandparents' pension books; Reggie yelling that the police were 'scum' for daring to intrude at Frances's funeral. This was all. There was no real talk of motive, no interest in the minds behind the cardboard monsters who killed Cornell and Jack McVitie. Neither side so much as mentioned the one key fact that ruled their lives – that they were twins.

* * *

The Kray trial might have been not just the longest, but the most fascinating murder trial in history. That it was not was really the twins' own decision. They wanted privacy and got it; they were the ones who stopped the one defence that could conceivably have shaken the prosecution's case, a defence based upon the nature and responsibility of twins.

The fact that there had never been a case like this argued in law before need not have mattered. There had never been a pair of criminal twins like the Krays before, and only in recent years has the relationship between identical twins been understood. It seems indisputable that Reggie Kray could have built a powerful defence along the lines of diminished responsibility, had he chosen to. But this would have meant betraying Ronnie and denouncing him as his evil genius. It would also have meant the end of Ronnie's world, the destruction of the twins and of the violent dream that had sustained them both since childhood.

Gratefully the court was spared the task of settling responsibility for crimes committed when one disordered mind can dominate two separate bodies. Whatever may have been the truth, the twins were judged as separate and responsible individuals. This was what everybody wanted, themselves included. And it was as separate and responsible murderers that they were sentenced to life imprisonment, 'which I would recommend should not be less than thirty years', by Mr Justice Melford Stevenson on 8 March 1969.

The twins were thirty-four. Their active life was over.

Provided the judge's recommendation was respected they would be sixty-four before they emerged into the outside world again. After the McVitie-Cornell verdict there were still countless other charges waiting to be heard against them. Most important was the murder of Frank Mitchell, but this time there was held to be insufficient evidence, and although Reggie Kray pleaded guilty to helping Mitchell to escape both twins were found not guilty of the murder. This was enough – the remaining charges were kept 'on the file' and the twins consigned to live their lives until the onset of old age in maximum security.

Du Rose retired, Cooper disappeared, their chief betrayer Ronnie Hart attempted to commit suicide, and Nipper Read, after promotion to Commander, went back at forty-six to Nottingham as Deputy Chief Constable.

The twins were parted for three years. Reggie seemed happy enough alone, started weight-lifting and forgot the past. Ronnie began painting – always the same picture of a country landscape with a distant cottage and a tree. When he felt miserable he would paint a black sun in the sky. Only one thing really worried him – he wanted Reggie back. Violet campaigned for this with all her usual energy; early in 1972 the twins were reunited in the maximum security wing of Parkhurst Gaol.

Ronnie had everything he needed. Reggie could look after him. They were completely self-sufficient and kept their distance from the other murderers who made up their stationary world.

But it would be wrong to allow the Kray twins to be forgotten. Their trial was concerned with cutting them down to size and left a picture of them both as blundering murderers duly defeated by the police. In fact they were more dangerous than this. More disturbing than the gruesome revelations from the witness-box was something that the prosecution and the court tended to overlook – the actual scale of their success. The Kray twins are important not as cheap murderers, but as professionals of violence, and it is their career and not their downfall that is significant.

The odds against their rise appear to have been enormous. They lacked finesse and had no education and no knowledge of the world. They were emotionally unstable, and most criminologists would probably dismiss them as anachronisms – the last of the old-style cockney villains acting out half-baked fantasies of Al Capone's Chicago. Yet despite this they came close to building a true empire of crime in Britain – and did it with extraordinary ease.

It is this ease that is disturbing. Any society that lets two cockney villains get away with what the Kray twins did must be quite frighteningly vulnerable and, if nothing else, their rise to power shows just how fragile the whole skin of order is in Britain. All they really did was bring the threat of violence into areas that had previously been relatively free from it – the fringes of big business, society and politics, the world of the suburban clubs and of the new legalized West End gambling. They had no startling techniques, and violence apart their one unerring instinct was for corruption. They could smell out the vulnerable as a pig smells truffles, and the corrupt became their victims. The violent will always feed on the corrupt, and it was not surprising that the twins found greater possibilities in society at large than in the poverty of Bethnal Green.

The use the Kray twins made of these new possibilities is something of an object lesson in what violence can achieve in Britain. They used it to create an area of freedom from the law. In different quarters it was the twins' name, not the law's, that kept the peace. People knew that they had more to lose from the twins' enmity than they would ever gain from the law's protection. The twins' power was a challenge to the authority of the State and for a long time it appeared as if the State were powerless against them. For they seemed to have stumbled on the formula for an independent, self-perpetuating criminal power in Britain.

Part of their secret was size, for with crime as with business, the profits increase with the scale of the operation. The twins were adroit users of bribery, blackmail and connections and could afford good lawyers and advisers and pay well for information. They manipulated the establishment, and used politicians, even to the extent of having questions asked on their behalf in Parliament. More important, they could always stay behind the scenes, organizing other men to do their bidding and ensuring that they themselves were never compromised. One of the lessons of the twins' career is the ease with which they built themselves a position of immunity. Paradoxically, the fact they were so widely known as organizing gangsters proved an advantage. It added to their reputation, made people fear them more and even brought them a status as celebrities. Journalists and public figures could be used, certain policemen had their price, trials could be fixed and prisons infiltrated.

The potentiality of power like this was vast. Protection rackets formed the largest single source of income, but on top of them the twins easily controlled a network of associated crime, part of which they initiated and from all of which they took their toll. They were already well into large-scale fraud, crooked share deals, organized intimidation and blackmail, and were thinking of extending to drugs, deals with foreign criminal networks and prostitution. Their contacts with the American Mafia in London showed what could be done. Control was easy to enforce through delegated violence. Profits would have been enormous and they would have found no difficulty investing overseas and building up legitimate businesses abroad. With power like this the twins could easily have become invulnerable.

That they did not was due entirely to their personal deficiencies. What limited them was not the law but their incompetence and instability. As criminals their major defect was lack of seriousness. They proved incapable of exploiting the power they created and in the end became self-indulgent and erratic, soon bored and often surprisingly timid.

Society was lucky; the twins destroyed themselves. Another time we may not be so fortunate.

Postscript

The careers of most criminals, however ingenious, cruel or outrageous, take the form of climax followed by anti-climax – the climax being their crimes up to their arrest and trial, and the anticlimax everything that follows, as they are sentenced, imprisoned and almost invariably forgotten.

Take any year, then try remembering a criminal who hit the headlines in a major trial, and say what has become of him. It's usually impossible, with just one exception – the Kray twins.

Today they are in their early sixties, 'old men' as Ronnie used to call any male over the age of forty, and have served twenty-five years of their 'recommended' thirty-year sentence. Ronnie remains in Broadmoor maximum security psychiatric hospital, where he was sent on being certified insane sixteen years ago. It is a tribute to the Broadmoor doctors that he doesn't look it – Broadmoor's regime appears to suit him. He is thinner than he used to be, but often wears the dark-blue suit and the solid gold wristlet watch that were once his trademarks and still make him the best-dressed man in Broadmoor. On heavy medication, he seems untroubled by the fact that he is unlikely to be released for many years to come – if ever.

Reg, on the other hand, with less than five years of his sentence still to run, is busily preparing for his life of freedom. He exercises vigorously, writes poetry, is a born-again Christian and is hoping for parole before his time is up.

But although they are now apart and living very different lives, one thing distinguishes the twins from the forgotten faces all around them: the fact that as convicted murderers they are now national celebrities.

When the Prime Minister requires a synonym for violent criminals he cites 'the Kray twins'. When Ronnie stages a bogus heart attack it is mentioned by the BBC in their morning bulletins. And when either of them marries or divorces – as they do with dreadful regularity – the details of the lovely bride are recounted in the tabloid press with the seriousness reserved for the mistresses of erring politicians.

Even before the film *The Krays* was made about them, there was a flood of books and articles recounting yet again the saga of the doings – and mis-doings – of the Krays. Never ones to miss a trick, the twins actually employed a real-life 'celebrity', none other than Southern Television's newscaster Fred Dineage, to ghost their 'memoirs'. With so much flattering attention, it was as if their life in crime had simply been a preparation for their great media careers.

There is something relatively new about the idea of convicted murderers enjoying this sort of active reputation. In the days of the death penalty the fame of convicted murderers was, by necessity, posthumous. Men like Dr Crippen, Haig of acid bath fame, and ex-special constable Christie, the serial killer of Notting Hill, never lived to see themselves depicted in the movies – let alone make deals with editors and film producers for the rights to their personal stories. It is a sombre thought that twenty years earlier the twins would have shared their fate, and that neither would have been able to pursue, let alone enjoy, this late flowering of their extraordinary careers.

It is unlikely that when the death penalty was abolished anyone foresaw that the authorized story of the murder could one day become a source of profit to the murderer. Yet with the Krays the details of their crimes have become big business. With books and films and non-stop journalism now produced about them, large amounts of money are involved. Fugitive Films invested £3 million in making *The Krays*, and the twins, however modestly and indirectly, naturally received their share. With a sequel to *The Krays* already in production, it is clear that the twins, despite their lack of liberty, have created a growth industry with a steadily increasing rate of profit.

In its way it is a remarkable achievement. From prison they have actually made murder pay – even if the money has to be held by outside nominees they hope that they can trust (a serious problem since the death in 1984 of the only person they could totally rely on, their mother Violet).

They have their fan club, and a pressure group campaigns for Reggie's early release. They have their literary agent, their publishers, and for a period Reggie engaged a public relations man to boost his image and get him favourable media coverage. While ageing cockney actresses insist that they were 'really lovely boys at heart', a rich pop star is currently anxious to invest a large amount of money in the sequel to *The Krays*, which is billed to be even more violent and bloody – and more profitable – than its predecessor.

Unless paroled beforehand, Reg will be released in 1999, five years off his seventieth birthday. But his thirty years in prison won't have been completely wasted. Having kept in trim he'll be in excellent physical condition, and unlike most ex-criminals who find themselves forgotten when they come out of prison, the reporters and the TV cameras will be there to greet him. Providing someone hasn't run away with it, a tidy nest-egg will also be awaiting him – as will his faithful agent bearing contracts with the British media.

'When murderers become celebrities,' wrote Salman Rushdie, 'something has gone seriously wrong.' But what? And why did it happen with the Krays?

* * *

Part of the answer is that the twins were determined that it should, long before they were arrested.

The pursuit of fame is actually extremely rare among criminals, and successful criminals, almost by definition, tend to be modest, self-effacing human beings. All a good burglar, conman, forger or swindler asks of life are the pleasures of obscurity and the modest joys of happy anonymity.

Not so the twins, however. Fame really was the spur that drove them on from puberty until practically the day they were arrested. Even as teenage tearaways in Bethnal Green, what distinguished them from the other adolescent criminals round about them was always their desperate desire to be noticed.

In the teenage slashings, woundings, beatings-up with which they livened up the street life of the old East End, what mattered more than blood and broken noses was the effect of every scuffle on their all-important reputation.

By the time they had made themselves virtuoso gangland fighters, they were intensely jealous of their prestige, which they tended and projected like precocious pop stars. In her quiet way their mother Violet would have made a perfect pop star's mother. Extremely presentable and nice, she was endlessly concerned about their health, the state of their underwear, the dreadful hours they kept and how her boys' career was currently progressing.

One of the prized possessions at their house in Vallance Road was their cuttings book (no pun intended), the bible-like album neatly kept up to date by Violet of the boys' press-notices – first as boxers, then as criminals. The two activities were in a sense co-terminous. Both brought respect and showed the world that, unlike all their humdrum neighbours, the Krays were 'somebodys'. The point of life, as Ronnie never tired of saying, was 'to be a somebody', and not let any other bastard take 'a liberty'.

As long as the twins were somebodys, Violet could go on being proud of them; which meant that, since they were both good sons, they could be proud and happy with themselves. And once they had started up their clubs, like The Double R and Esmeralda's Barn in Knightsbridge, they could begin to mingle with the 'straight' celebrities whose lives they envied – hence their passionate pursuit of that curious medley of old boxers, show-business personalities and members of the House of Lords, which increasingly occupied their time and energies in the early sixties.

How Ronnie loved a lord! While Reg preferred being photographed with film stars like George Raft and Judy Garland, Ron's proudest moments came when dining in the House of Lords with some silly nobleman, as he did on a number of occasions.

But as I trust this book makes clear, the celebrity status of the twins was only part of the story. They were also very clever and sophisticated criminals who became something which was relatively rare until their appearance on the scene – home-grown British organizing gangsters. As such they were remarkably successful. Having moved 'up West' from Bethnal Green in the early sixties, five years later they were 'protecting' much of the West End gambling in conjunction with the US Mafia. They planned. They made alliances with lesser criminals. And they steadily increased the fear – or, as they liked to call it, 'the respect' – in which they were held by other villains. They had something which was curiously rare among professional criminals – genuine imagination, great ambition and a natural instinct for corruption.

Stupid they emphatically were not, and anyone who thinks they were should study the way they exploited the aftermath of the Boothby scandal to extract maximum advantage for themselves. It was thanks to this that they achieved what every professional criminal dreams of, effective immunity from the attentions of the Yard, as well as of the mighty British press and the politicians at Westminster. It was as if collectively the British establishment, having been made fools of by the Krays over Robert

Boothby, had decided they were far too hazardous to tangle with.

For the three years following the Boothby case, the Krays appeared to be succeeding in building up an international crime cartel based in London. Once they were trusted allies of the US Mafia, 'protecting' their investments in central London gambling, these connections brought them further business in the international marketing of stolen bonds. They became busily involved with fraudulent big business, blackmail and property frauds. They bribed senior policemen. They were contemplating contract killings, money-laundering and arms dealing.

Thanks to their virtual immunity from the press and the police, the twins could act largely unhindered. Reggie was particularly smart at knowing how to work behind the scenes in the grey area between licit and illicit business activities, and at using the Krays' growing reputation for maximum effect.

Their model was essentially the US Mafia, with its universal power to corrupt, to deal and to enforce. They also copied them in the way they made their links with politicians and show-business personalities. The business was still growing six months before they were arrested.

Had they avoided this and been able to consolidate their organization, the Krays could certainly have controlled much of the narcotics business and the financial rackets which were just beginning in the early seventies. They could have become immensely rich. They might have made themselves impregnable.

Instead, as this book describes, Ronnie's fantasy life took over and his private dreams of violence became self-fulfilling. Bored with business, which his twin did so much better, he still hankered after the old East End-style violence, which he had loved and grown up with – but which by now was purest self-indulgence.

Like his hero, Gordon of Khartoum, he longed for action,

and once he decided he would shoot the utterly unimportant gangster, George Cornell, it was as if the film of Ronnie's life had started. Cornell had insulted him. Cornell was scum. 'I had to kill him. It was as simple as that,' says Ronnie, and the murders started.

What was so scarey about them was their unreality, the victims being killed like extras in a gangster movie – which is essentially was what was happening. Action was needed, and the hero had 'to do the business'. Gangster movies need at least a few dead gangsters and a lot of blood. As if with the plot of *The Krays* firmly in his mind, Ronnie set about providing them.

He went on acting out this mental movie to the day he was arrested. One of the last memories I have of him when he was free is at the house he'd bought for his 'retirement' at Bildeston in Suffolk. It was a comfortable, unassuming country house with white walls and a grey slate roof, and he was already planning how his friend Duke Osborne would join him there when released from prison.

That day he was happier than I'd ever seen him, painting the shelves in what was to be the 'library' and talking about the film and who would play the part of himself.

He was quite happy to be portrayed as homosexual. 'It's nothin' to be ashamed of. But I don't want to be made to seem a cissy – 'cos I ain't one' – which was true. He wasn't.

Nor did he seem remotely troubled by the problem of the police who were closing in and waiting for the moment to arrest him.

Reg was more realistic. A few nights before he was arrested he asked me if I thought he could go to fight in Vietnam for the Americans.

'You're too old,' I said. (He was thirty-four.)

He nodded.

'It's too late, anyhow,' he answered. 'And someone has to keep an eye on Ron.'

* * *

During these last few years in which the twins have made their comeback as criminal celebrities, they have also succeeded in creating certain myths about themselves, some of which require correcting.

The first of these is that during their years of power, they were not so much criminals and gangsters as a sort of East End Benevolent Society, pledged to protecting orphans, single mothers and old ladies.

This was in fact a fairly common theme one heard about the twins before they were arrested, and much of it was put around either by the Krays themselves or by their followers. There was one old gangster who used to hang around the twins; he enjoyed telling anyone who cared to listen that they weren't dangerous at all, but kind and good and caring.

'Benefactors,' he used to say, 'that's what those two boys are. They're not criminals at all. They're public bloody benefactors. One day, mark my words, there'll be a statue erected to them both in Bethnal Green.'

Possibly there will be. But the point about the twins' 'benevolence' is that, like all good gangsters, they were generous with 'their own', and great free spenders. The booze flowed freely in their presence, and for the 'aways' (their friends in prison), they would ensure that their families were paid for and protected. But I never heard of them doing any favours for their victims' families or for ordinary people.

The second claim one hears is that the Krays 'kept London clear of crime'. To the extent that few other criminals dared to raise their heads above the parapet when the twins were around, this was true. But as their 'power' involved recurrent gang wars, with knifings, shootings and killings – not to mention bribing the police – it is hard to take them all that seriously as a force of law and order.

The most misleading myth of all is the one that the increasingly violent films about them will perpetuate as they portray the twins simply as sadistic killers in ever more violent situations.

It was bad enough watching pretty boys like Martin and Gary Kemp indulging in designer violence in *The Krays*. But there will undoubtedly be worse to come, with the film-makers now convinced that the box office appeal of the Kray twins is exclusively confined to blood and violence.

They may be right. The pornography of violence may yet make everybody's fortunes – the twins' included. But if it does, it will mean that the real lesson of the Krays has been forgotten.

When I wrote this book I tried to show that the most important thing about the twins was not violence for its own sake, but the use they made of it. They were clever criminals who did many more important things than simply murder people. Their true significance was as organizing criminals, and the real lessons that they left were not what they did to Cornell and McVitie, but the vulnerability they revealed in a society that permitted them to build an empire such as theirs. They were not just bloodstained monsters, any more than they were old-style cockney villains with hearts of gold.

They were something much more dangerous.

JP, 1995

Index

Adams, Superintendent Donald, 272, 298
Allen (boxer), 207
Amsterdam, 213
Artichoke (pub): 110
Astor Club, 216, 300

Bailey, David, 207
Baker (murderer) 29–30
Barrie, Ian, 173, 219, 304, 307
Barry brothers (John and Tony): 256–8, 308
'Battle of Frith Street', 95
'Bear of Tottenham', *see* Brown
Bender, 258–61, 262, 264–5, 308
Berg, Ted 'Kid', 42, 183
Berry, Checker, 114, 146–7, 158
Bethnal Green (twins' home): 20, 28–9, 32–3, 34–5, 36 *et passim*; eleventh commandment of, 38, 302
Bethnal Green Hospital, 226
Billy (twins' cousin): 35
Birmingham, clubs in, 185
Black, Bernard, 194
Blind Beggar (pub), 218–19, 252, 298, 306, 311
Blonde Carol, 256, 258–9, 261–2
Blythe, Billie, 95, 97
Boothby, Lord 13, 194–9, 202–3, 321–2
Boston Strangler, 129
Boy's Town, 85, 121
Braithwaite House, flat at, 255–6, 278, 281, 301
Britannia (pub): 110–11
Brixton Gaol, 202, 303
Broadmoor, 317
Brodie, Peter, 267–8, 270
Brooks, The (house in Suffolk): 277, 279, 298, 305, 323
Brown, Tommy 'Bear of Tottenham', 119
Browning Club, 41
Bruno, Angelo, 208–9, 285, 293
Brussels, forged currency syndicate, 213
Burton, Sybil, 119
Butler, Superintendent, 220, 225, 226

Cambridge Rooms, 186, 188
Camp Hill Prison, 121–5
Canada, bank robberies in, 208–9, 212, 292
Capone, Al, 129, 183, 314
Carpenters' Arms (pub), 255–6, 264
Carston Trading Company, 182, 184, 187
Caruana, George, 289–92
Cater, Frank, 297, 299
Cazenove Road, Blonde Carol's flat at, 256, 258–62
Cedra Court, Walthamstow, 173, 190–1, 200, 210–11, 217
Chapman, Annie, 30
'Charlie' of Watney Street gang, 109–10

Christie (murderer): 318
Christine, Reggie's blonde girl-friend, 225, 275–6, 278, 298, 300, 307
Churchill, Winston (*later* Sir Winston): 194, 231
Clark, Charlie, 197
Colchester military prison, 57
Collins, Jackie, 119
Comer, Jack 'Spot', 58, 93–9, 100–1, 215
Congo treasure hunt idea, 172
Connolly, 'Big Pat', 119, 173, 185
Cooper, Alan Bruce, 216, 269, 279–98, 300, 302, 313
Cornell, George, 215–16, 218–20, 240, 242, 248–50, 268, 275, 290, 299, 306–7; McVitie-Cornell trial, 308–13
Cornell, Mrs (widow of George): 224
Cowley, Tommy, 232, 246, 287, 297
Crime as Destiny, 16
Crippen (murderer): 318
Crowder, Petre, 202

Daily Express, 170, 199
Daily Mirror, 196, 230–1
Daneford Street School, 36
Daniels, Billy, 186
Dartmoor, 214, 221–3, 230
de Faye, Stefan, 156–60
Dickson, 'Scotch Jack', 173, 218, 228–36, 251, 308
Dineage, Fred, 318
Dixon, George, 249, 260, 293
Dodson, Sir Gerald, 112
Dominion Refrigeration, 184–5
Donaghue, Albert, 228, 235–9, 262
Double R (club): 117–20, 130, 132, 136, 139, 144, 146, 151, 153, 321
Downes, Terry, 183
Dracula (film): 134
Driberg, Tom, 183–4, 190–1, 197–8, 224
Dunn, Lennie, 227–38, 242
du Rose, John, 269–71, 293, 295, 298–9, 313

Eagle (pub): 20
East End: underworld, 19–21, 31–3, 36–7; way of life, 19–21, 29; changing pattern of life, 101–2
East London Advertiser, 64, 178
Effingham, Lord, 168, 178
El Morocco (club): 203–4
Elvey, Paul, 280–3, 290–2, 294, 298
Enugu (Nigeria), Ronald Kray's proposed scheme in, 186–8
Epsom Races, 93, 95–7
Esmeralda's Barn, 155, 157–65, 168, 170, 172, 176, 185, 189, 274, 321
European centres of crime, 213
Evans, William, 36, 38
Evering Road, Christmas party at, 236–7
Exley, Billy, 197, 231, 233, 306

Fields, of the Starlight Club, 249
Finchley, Ronald in hiding there, 227, 234, 240
Firm, the, 103–12, 189, 203; becomes Ronnie's private army, 153; mobilization against Richardson brothers, 216; suspicions within, 251–2; arrest of, 300–1
Fisher, PC, 56, 64
Foreman, Frederick, 237–9, 264, 290, 308
Foremans' 211 Club, 255
Foster, Father, 207
Fraser, 'Mad' Frankie, 95, 97, 98, 103, 215–17
Frederick (friend of the twins): 247–8
Frost, Jack, 251, 264, 290

Gallo brothers, 294
Galton, Sir Francis, 15
Gambling, 145–6, *see also* Esmeralda's Barn, Gaming Act *and* Junkets
Gaming Act, 157, 159
Gardiner, Gerald (*later* Lord Gardiner): 194, 199, 203
Garland, Judy, 211, 311, 321
Geneva gold smuggling, 213
Germany, crime in northern, 213
Gerrard, Det. Chief Superintendent Frederick, 193–4, 200–1
Gielgud, Sir John, 179
Goodman, Arnold (*later* Lord Goodman): 194–5, 198–9
Goodsell (boxer): 45
Gordon of Khartoum, twins' respect for, 69, 288
Gore, Freddie, 182, 185, 209, 223
Grant, Cy, 157
Grave Maurice (pub): 192
Green Dragon Club, 249
Griffith-Jones, Judge, 202

Hare, Councillor, 178, 183
Harry Jewboy, 324
Hart, Richard, 218
Hart, Ronnie (twins' cousin): 252, 258–62, 304; turns Queen's evidence, 264–5, 308; attempts suicide, 313
Harvey (boy victim): 43–5
Hayes, Timmy, 32
Hemingway, Det. Sergeant, 269, 273
Heston, Charlton, 288
Hetherington, Father, 35, 43, 46, 207, 244, 246, 248
Hideaway Club, 202, 266
Hill, Billy, 11, 58, 62, 93–9, 101, 136, 144–6, 148, 210, 215, 225
Hinds, Alfred, 139
Hirondelle (club): 172
Hopwood, Harry, 38, 70–1, 262, 264
Hospital Tavern (pub): 149–50
Hotel Organization Ltd, 157, 159
Howe Barracks, Canterbury, 65–71
Hoxton, 19

International Publishing Corporation, 196
Italian gangs, 94, 96, 99–100, 144, 148–9

Jack the Ripper, 30, 129
'jargoons', 92
Joe (boxer friend of the twins): *see* 'Tramlines'
Jonathan (friend of the twins): 189, 249
Jones, Billie, 109
Jones, Kenneth, QC, 308–9
Jordan, Colin, 250
'Junkets', 216

Kaufman, Joe, 285–6, 297, 300
Kaunda, President, 250
Kenny, Sonny, 16, 18
Kent, Duke of, 157
Kentucky (club): 178, 190
King, Cecil H., 199
King's Road, Ronald in hiding near, 241
Kraepelin, 128
Kray, Alf (twins' uncle): 185
Kray, Charles (twins' father): 16–18, 34, 37; as a family man, 30; as a fugitive and deserter, 30–1, 38, 52; attitude to twins' boxing, 41–2; avoids twins, 46
Kray, Charles David (twins' brother): 8–9, 18, 22, 73, 136, 142, 149, 227, 241; welterweight boxer, 41, 46; shares Reggie's success,

Kray, Charles David – *cont'd.* 119–20, 144; and gambling, 144–7, 168; suggests Ronnie goes on a cruise, 146; and McVitie's body, 264–5, 308

Kray, Dolly (Charles David's wife): 119, 207–8, 256

Kray, 'Mad' Jimmy (twins' grandfather): 16–17

Kray, Frances (Reggie's wife): *see* Shea

Kray, Reginald (*see also* Kray twins): character, 9, 26, 37; physical appearance, 9, 79, 142–3; in Purfleet army punishment cells, 57; business acumen, 81–2, 88–92, 171, 179; dominated by Ronald, 86–7; 'tweedle' and 'jargoon' confidence tricks, 92; attitude to women, 101–2, 119; and Ronald's shooting of docker, 106–7; supplies Ronald with tobacco in Wandsworth Gaol, 114–15; business activities alone, 116–19, 144–5; opens the Double R, 116–19; and Ronald's escape from Long Grove, 130–2; cares for Ronald in hiding, 132–41; reacts to Ronald's violence, 148–50; sentenced to Wandsworth Gaol, 153; appeal fails, 160; and Frances Shea, 167–8, 171–2, 175, 179; release from prison 169; acquitted on charge of housebreaking, 169; expands business activities, 171, 173–5; and Ronald's sadism, 188–90; marries Frances, 206–8; takes flat in Cedra Court, 210; Frances leaves him, 211–12, 214; new girl, 225, 277–8, 298, 300; Frances attempts suicide, 241–2; cares for Ronald, 240–1; pressures on him, 241; plans fresh start with Frances, 242; Frances' suicide, 242–3; poem for Frances, 245; remorse, 246–7, 254; attacks Frederick, 247–8; knifes Ward Buller, 249; shoots Fields, 249; McVitie's murder, 256–63; dreams of breaking free, 277–9, 280; fails to plead diminished responsibility, 312; pleads guilty to helping Mitchell escape, 313; preparing for freedom, 317, 319

Kray, Ronald (*see also* Kray twins): character, 9–12; physical appearance, 9, 79, 142–3; his boa constrictor, 12; obsession with firearms and knives, 44, 81, 97, 216–17; feigns madness, 66–7, 68; nicknamed 'the Colonel', 81, 85–7, 100 *et passim*; fantasies of, 54, 80, 287–8; at Wellington Guards Barracks, 57; Lawrence of Arabia his hero, 69, 80; fondness for the bizarre, 77; vision of himself as a gangster, 77–8, 85–6, 149, 164; 'little wars' of, 80–1; information service, 80–1, 176–7; homosexuality, 80, 85, 87, 102, 135, 146, 164–6 *et passim*; attitude to women, 85, 101–2; reads *Boy's Town*, 85, 121; has private barber, 86; afraid of the dark, 86, 214; and Italian gang, 96; first shots fired in pub, 100; and the 'politics of crime', 103, 175–6; consults clairvoyante, 104, 172–3; shoots docker, 104–8; and attack on Terence Martin, 110–12; in Wandsworth Gaol, 113–16, 120–1; moved to Camp Hill prison, 121–4; madness of, 122–5, 126–30, 136–43, 166, 183, 230–1, 240–1; moved to psychiatric wing of Winchester Gaol, 124; certified insane, 125; at Long Grove Hospital, 126–32; escape, 130–2; in hiding in Suffolk, 132–5, 137–9; visits to London, 135–6, 137; sees psychiatrist under false name, 137; returns to London, 140–1; given up to the police, 141; returns to prison, 142; back at Vallance Road, 142–3; admitted to St Clement's Hospital, 142; changed appearance of, 142–3; after prison and hospital, 146–9; takes up reins again, 147–52; ideas for capitalizing on violence, 149–52; meets Peter Rachman, 154–5; and Leslie Payne, 158–60; and Esmeralda's Barn, 160–4; activities during Reggie's prison term, 160–7; moves into Chelsea flat, 164–5; falls in love, 165; and Frances Shea, 168, 208, 210–11; acquitted on charge of loitering with intent, 169–70; leaves Reggie and the West End, 172, 173; plans Congo treasure hunt, 172; plans English Murder Incorporated, 172; plans crack regiment of London tearaways, 172; religious mood, 172; moves into Cedra Court, 173; new East End army, 173; reads *Mein Kampf*, 176; resources of, 176–7; dominates London, 176–9; flies to meet Gorbals gang, 185; African schemes, 186–8, 250; knifes Joe (boxer friend), 188; brands Jonathan (friend of twins), 189; masochism and sadism of, 190–1, 252; enjoys meeting celebrities, 191; and Lord Boothby case, 13, 193–200, 202–3, 321–2; shoots George Cornell, 215–16, 218–20; lodges formal complaint against police, 226; refuses to give evidence and goes into hiding, 227, 229, 230–1, 240; sees psychiatrist, 241; and George Dixon, 249; takes up reins again, 249–50; suspicious of the Firm, 251; attitude to murder, 252–3; plans murder of Leslie Payne, 253–5; goes to Hunt Ball, 263; and Nipper Read, 266; buys The Brooks at Bildeston, 277, 279, 298; flies to Paris with Cooper, 284–5; flies on to New York, 285–7; returns to Bethnal Green, 287–8; plans murder of Las Vegas gambler, 289; plans murder of Caruana, 289–91; arrested, 301; conduct at trial, 310–11; starts to paint, 313; Broadmoor, 317; fantasy life, 322–4

Kray twins, *jointly* (*see also* Kray, Reginald *and* Kray, Ronald): 8–13; background of, 16–18; birth of, 18, 19; babyhood, 22, 24; telepathic, 24, 60; contract measles and diphtheria, 24–5; separated, 25; childhood, 25–31, 33–41; rivalry between, 26–8; childhood fights, 27,

Kray twins – *cont'd.*
35–7; during Second World War, 30, 33–5; schooldays, 35–6; childhood contacts with police, 37–8; and with their Aunt Rose, 38–9; interest in boxing, 40–3; Harvey case, 43–5; first gun, 44; become professional boxers, 45–6; called up, 48; prove troublesome to army authorities, 49–57, 66–72; desert, 49; demonstrate advantages of twinship, 50–1; confined to guardroom, 51–2, 107; and Dickie Morgan, 52–9; escape from army again, 52; make first money out of crime, 54; take up smoking and drinking, 54; take Morgan to Tottenham Royal Ballroom, 54–5; returned to army detention cells, 56; at Colchester military detention barracks, 57; escape again, 57–8; concept of 'the good life', 57; attracted to the West End, 58–61; strange aura of, 60, 78; and Tommy Smithson, 61–2; take room in Finsbury Park, 63; spend few weeks in Peckham, 63; captured again, 63; further escape and assault of PC Fisher, 64; in Wormwood Scrubs, 64–5; at Howe Barracks, Canterbury, 65–6; hooliganism while in detention, 67–70; escape from Howe Barracks, 70–2; recapture, 72; court martial, 73; at Shepton Mallet military prison, 73–4; and the Regal Billiard Hall, 75–83 *et passim*; power as fighters, 76, 79–81; gang warfare, 78–9; stage courts-martial in billiard hall, 81; criminal friends of, 82; and Poplar dockers, 83–4; money earned from protection racket, 88–9; confidence trickery, 89–92; Billy Hill and Jack Spot, 93–9; concern for the 'aways', 102–3; beginning of the 'bigtime', 103; tension between, 108, 147–8, 172, 248; and the Watney Street gang, 109–11, 149–50; and Billy Hill, 144–6; foothold in illicit gambling, 144–5; back at Vallance Road, 146, 147–8; and Daniel Shay, 152–3; and Esmeralda's Barn, 155, 157–65, 167 *et passim*; rackets with Leslie Payne, 158–60, 180–2; 'scum on earth' case, 169; plans to murder them, 177; philanthropy of, 178–9, 186, 324; 'long-firms', 181–2; as boxing promoters, 184; relations with politicians, 183–4; plan to expand on the American pattern, 185, 287–8; expand outside London, 185; take over Cambridge Rooms, 187; and McCowan case, 201–3; discredit police, 204; business booms for, 208; dealings with international crime, 208–9, 212–14; and the American Mafia, 174–5, 209, 213, 216, 283–5, 287–9 *et passim*; dealings with Alan Cooper, 212–13; and the Richardson brothers, 215–18; and Frank Mitchell, 221–24, 226–37; fly to Morocco, 225; drug peddling and pornography, 250; and Jack McVitie,

253–62; in Cambridge and Suffolk after McVitie murder, 263; their one point of vulnerability, 271; and Nipper Read's investigations, 268–77; at The Brooks, 277, 279, 298, 305, 323; and Cooper, 279–87, 288; plan to tie up the docks, 288; plan murder of George Caruana, 289–92; arrest of, 301; in Brixton Gaol, 303–4; apply for legal aid, 305; at preliminary hearing, 305–7; trial of, 307–11; importance of, 313–15; limitations of, 314–15; notoriety, 318–22; 'credibility' of, 324–5
Kray, Violet, *née* Lee (twins' mother): 12, 18–19, 21–2, 85, 113, 124, 147–8, 155, 255–6, 277, 287, 298, 303, 313, 320; and twins' childhood, 24–8, 30, 33–4, 39; and twins' boxing, 42; relationship as twins grow up, 46–7; influence against dishonesty, 53; looks after Ronnie, 142; and Solway Cross, 186; moves to Shoreditch, 255–6
Krays, The (film), 318–19, 325

Lambrianou brothers, 252, 258–9, 264
Lange, Dr, study of criminal twins, 15–16
Lansky, Meyer, 294
Latin Quarter Club, 154, 225
Lawrence of Arabia, twins' admiration for, 69, 80
Lea Bridge Road, 219
Lee, Helen (twins' grandmother): 21–2, 29
Lee, Jimmy 'Southpaw Cannonball' (twins' grandfather): 21–3, 29, 34, 76, 206; coaches twins in boxing, 42
Lee, John (twins' uncle): 21–2, 29
Lee, May (twins' aunt): 21, 29, 150
Lee, Rose (twins' aunt): 21, 29, 34, 39–40, 44, 47, 124–5, 288
'Lee Street', 21, 28; *see also* Vallance Road
Leicester, club in, 185
Leopard Men (of Nigeria): 253
Lethbridge, Nemone, 169, 222
Levecq, Roy 'Chopper', 183
Lewis, Ted 'Kid', 29, 183, 207
Lewisham Hospital, 218
Lisa, from Winston's Club, 232–8
Liston, Sonny, 186
Littlewood, Joan, 179, 183
Lloyd-Jones, Det. Sergeant, 269
London, centre for gold smuggling, 213
Long, Bernie, 45
'long-firm' frauds, 180–2
Long Grove Hospital, 126–32, 142
Lucas, Norman, 198

McCowan, Hew Cargill, 201–5, 302
McGovern, Tommy, 46
McVitie, Jack 'the Hat, 9, 231, 270–1, 273, 275, 277, 280, 290, 293; murder of, 253–65; McVitie-Cornell trial, 307–12, 325
Mafia, North American, 7, 175, 208–9, 213, 216, 230, 284–5, 287, 289, 292–3, 315, 321–2; French, 175
Maidstone Gaol, 141
Malone, Denis, 221
Malone, Herbert, KC, 44–5
Maltese gangs, 76, 94
Mangold, Tom, 287

Marciano, Rocky, 285
Martin (murderer): 29
Martin, Terry, 111–12, 118
Mein Kampf, 176
Melvin (boxer): 62
Mendoza (prizefighter): 41
Messina brothers, 250
'Midgets Club', 41
Mills brothers, 260
Milton, Frank, 305
Mitchell, Frank (the 'Mad Axe Man'): 53, 121, 130–1, 242, 275, 290, 306; in Dartmoor, 214, 221–2; twins plan escape of, 223, 225–6; in hiding, 228–36; probable fate of, 237–9; trial re, 312
Mooney, Superintendent, 250–1, 298, 306
Morgan, Dickie, 52–6, 58–9, 142, 154; family, 53; influence on twins, 53–4; at Howe Barracks, 66–70; at Shepton Mallett, 73; in Wandsworth Gaol, 114; in France and America, 284–6
Morgan, Mrs (Dickie's mother): 53
Mr Smith's Club, battle of, 218
Mulla, Tony, 62
Mullins, Dodger, 32, 36
Murphy, Spud, 29
Myers (of Watney Street), *see* Cornell

Nashes (Islington gang leaders): 103
Newman, Wassle, 32, 36
Nigeria, proposed scheme in, 186–8

Of Mice and Men, 121
Old Horns (pub): 300
Osborne, Georgie ('Duke'), 130–1, 298, 323
Osbourne, Buster, 40
Ozzie (thief acquaintance of the twins): 90–2

Paddington, 150
Parkhurst Gaol, 313
Payne, Leslie, 156–62, 164, 171, 213, 223, 231, 283; and Esmeralda's Barn, 158–60; business ventures with the twins, 180–5; and African schemes, 187–8; and stolen Canadian securities, 209; the twins attempt to silence, 254–5, 270, 273; interrogated by police, 273–5, 298
Payne, Reginald, 194, 199
Piccadilly Circus, hotel near, centre for criminals in early '50s, 59
Platts-Mills, John, QC, 310
Plumley, 'Red-face' Tommy, 106–8, 112
Podro, Murray, 153
Poplar dockers, fight with the twins, 83–4
Profitable Bar Management, 156
purple hearts, 250

Rachman, Peter, 154–5, 160
Raft, George, 211, 285, 321
Ramsey, Bobby, 62–3, 109–11, 183
Read, Inspector Leonard 'Nipper': boa constrictor named after him, 12; early dealings with the twins, 191–2, 200–1; and McCowan case, 201–5, 266; returns to Kray case, 267–80, 285, 292–301; interrogates Payne, 273–4; interrogates Cooper, 292–7; arrests twins, 299–301; case against twins, 302–5, 308–13
Regal Billiard Hall, 75–92, 103, 113, 149
Regency Club, Stoke Newington, 167, 249, 255, 256–7, 259, 264, 308

Richardson brothers, Charlie and Eddie, 185, 213, 215–18, 276
Ritz Hotel, 8
Rolfe, Bob, 31, 37
Royal Ballroom, Tottenham, 54–5
Royal Bank of Canada, 208, 212
Royal Fusiliers, 48–52, 56–7, 65–70, 72–3
Rushdie, Salman, 319

Sabini, 'Derby', 33, 93
St Clement's Hospital, 142
St James's Church, Bethnal Green, 35, 207
St Stephen's Hospital, 188
schizophrenia, 127–9
Shay, Daniel, 152–3, 202
Shea, Elsie (Frances' mother): 208
Shea, Frances (Reggie's wife): 167–8, 170–2, 175, 179; marriage, 206–8, 210–12, 214; leaves Reggie, 209; shows signs of breakdown, 214; enters clinic, 214, 242; attempts suicide, 226, 241–2; death, 243–7, 311
Shea, Frank (Frances' father): 167, 171, 208, 243
Shea, Frankie (Frances' brother): 167, 171, 208, 243, 247
Shepton Mallet, prison at, 73–4
Shinwell, Ernest, 186–7
Shinwell, Lord, 187
Silvers, Police Sergeant, 63
Silverstone, Dr Julius, 244
Simpson, Sir Joseph, 193, 200, 268
Smirke, Charlie, 179
Smith, 'Mad' Teddy, 202–3, 211, 224, 228–30, 251, 264
Smith, Ritchie and Rita, 135
Smithson, Tommy, 61
Society Club, 165–6
Sokolok, Abe, 17
Solway Cross, racehorse, 186
Sparrers Can't Sing, 177
'spielers', 145, 151, 174
Spinetti, Victor, 179
Spinks, Jimmy, 32, 36
Spinks, Terry, 179, 207
'Spot', Jack, *see* Comer
Starlight Club, 249
Stern magazine, 194
Stevenson, Mr Melford, 308, 312
Stork Club, 217
Stragglers (West End club): 109, 116
Suffolk: twins evacuated to, 33–4; Ronnie in hiding near Sudbury, 133–40; The Brooks, Bildeston, 277, 279, 298, 305
Sunday Mirror, 193–201, 268
Sykes, Bill, 31

Teddy, Ronald's companion in Suffolk, 133–4, 137–9
Thompson, Carol, 259
Times, The, 196, 199, 230–1
Tintagel House, 269–70, 274, 287, 290, 299–300
Tottenham gang, 55
'Tramlines' Joe, 188–9
Tshombe, Moise, 250
Turif International, 187
'tweedles', 92
twins, Lange's study of, 15–16

United States: criminals of, 185; Ronald Kray in, 283–7; *see also* Mafia, North American
United States Treasury Department, 293–5
University Arms, Cambridge, 263
Upton Park Mob, 93

Vallance Road, No. 178: 18, 21, 28–30, 34, 37, 142; 'Deserters' Corner', 24, 29; 'Fort Vallance', 86, 97, 99, 113, 153, 217
Vicki (Ronnie Hart's girl-friend): 259
'Villains' of the East End, 31–3

Waldron, Sir John, 268
Walker, Billy, 179
Walker, Superintendent Ferguson, 268–9, 279
Wandsworth Gaol, 113–15, 121–2, 142, 153, 160, 167, 222
Ward, Buller, 249
Warner, Slasher, 40
Warren, Alf, 98
Watney Street gang, 32, 109–12, 149–50, 215
Watts, Queenie, 119, 178
Wellington Way Club, 120, 151
West End: twins attracted to, 58–60; control of crime in, 58, 99–100; gambling in, 145, 162, 174
White's Club, St James's, 197
'Whizz Mob' of Hoxton, 20
Widow's Pub, 217
Wilde, Jimmy, 29
Wilson, Harold, 194, 198
Wimbourne Court, 242–3
Winchester Gaol, 124–5
Windsor, Barbara, 119, 177, 179
Winston's Club, 232, 237, 242
Wrightson, Paul, QC, 202, 310

Zambodini, Anna, 214
Zürich, 213